DIRECTORY OF DESIGNERS 1991

The Design Council

ABOUT THE DIRECTORY

The **Directory of Designers 1991** includes details of over 530 design consultancies throughout the UK, the USA and Europe. Each consultancy has professionally qualified staff and provides an independent design service. Consultancies are listed in the **Directory of Designers 1991** only if they, or their principals or senior staff, are members of approved professional associations.

Those consultants which, in addition, have applied for and have qualified as members of the Design Council's Designer Selection Service are identified thus: DESIGN COUNCIL REGISTERED Registration with the Designer Selection Service is evidence that the consultants have submitted full details of their practice and portfolios of recent work.

The entries contain consultancies' basic details and include a company profile. They are listed alphabetically within one or more of the main design disciplines.

The directory includes three indexes: a Location index which lists consultancies according to the geographical area in which they are based (overseas consultancies are listed according to country); an International Expertise index which lists consultancies according to the countries in which they are active overseas; and a Consultancies A to Z index which lists the consultancies in alphabetical order.

All three indexes have cross-references to both the page(s) and the design discipline(s) under which each consultancy appears. The design disciplines are abbreviated as follows: Product Design, PRO; Engineering Design, ENG; Human Factors & Ergonomics, HUM; Materials Specialists, MAT; Graphics & Packaging GRA; Interiors & Retail, INT; Exhibition Design, EXH; Fashion & Textiles, FAS; Environmental Design, ENV.

CONTENTS

Entries

Stress
Structural
Testing/NDT
Thermodynamics

Transducer
Transmission
Tribology
Value Engineering

Vehicles
Vibration/Sound
Zygology

The **Directory of Designers 1991** is intended as an immediate and basic guide to design consultancy services. The Design Council's Designer Selection Service can provide much more specific guidance on selecting appropriate designers for particular projects.

DIRECTORY OF DESIGNERS 1991

Published in the United Kingdom by

The Design Council
28 Haymarket
London SW1Y 4SU
Tel: 071-839 8000
Fax: 071-925 2130
Telex: 8812963

Publishing Manager: Chris Lees

Designer: Tony Anderson

Printed in the United Kingdom by

The Bath Press
Lower Bristol Road
Bath BA2 3BL
Tel: (0225) 428101
Fax: (0225) 312418

The **Directory of Designers 1991**
was compiled by the Design Council on
Apple Macintosh using an Omnis 5
database and typeset using QuarkXPress
with output on Linotronic 300.

© The Design Council 1991

ISBN 0 85072 295 0
ISSN 0959 1710

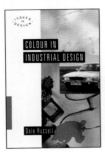

DESIGN COUNCIL REGIONAL OFFICES

The Design Council
28 Haymarket
London SW1Y 4SU

Tel: 071-839 8000
Fax: 071-925 2130
Telex: 8812963

The Design Council Scotland
Ca' d'Oro Building
45 Gordon Street
Glasgow G1 3LZ

Tel: 041-221 6121
Fax: 041-221 8799

Y Cyngor Cynllunio
The Design Council Wales
QED Centre
Main Avenue
Treforest Estate
Treforest CF37 5YR

Tel: (0443) 841888
Fax: (0443) 841407

The Design Council Northern Ireland
Windsor House
9-15 Bedford Street
Belfast BT2 7EG

Tel: (0232) 238452
Fax: (0232) 240683

The Design Council Midlands
Norwich Union House
31 Waterloo Road
Wolverhampton WV1 4BP

Tel: (0902) 773631
Fax: (0902) 26753

The Design Council North
46 The Calls
Leeds LS2 7EY

Tel: (0532) 449020
Fax: (0532) 446202

FOREWORD

Transformation by design

Markets today are open to world competition. For products and services to survive and prosper in the 1990s they need to be world class; they need a competitive edge. For Britain, I believe that this edge should be design and innovation.

We must endeavour to think about form and function and to incorporate new thinking in our development programmes. This is usually best achieved when client and designer develop a concept from the beginning, working as a single team. Companies must be prepared to open their doors to designers in order to look at how and why procedures and limitations exist; designers must be ready to probe, to question and to debate new concepts.

Working with designers is demanding, and calls for an open approach and a willingness to bring design to the boardroom. But from the experience of my own company, I know that a design, innovation and quality-led approach can really generate products that are world class and lead to excellent returns. The Studio range, for example – designed by a London based consultancy – is one of our major successes; it won a BBC Design Award in 1987 and now represents over half of Ideal Standard's output. The success of Studio and its strong market position are attributable to the design of all the items in the range.

Many companies, once their product or service is right, forget to apply the same care to their sales literature, packaging and instruction manuals, thus defeating the object of their original investment. To be truly world class, design skill and input must also be applied in these areas.

To those companies which have yet to bring design into their business: I urge you most strongly to find the design talent suited to helping you – choosing the right team from this book can make a major contribution to your success.

If you are in one of the industries nominated by the Design Council for extensive design support, as announced in February 1991, then embrace this help. It could transform your company into a truly design-led organization, ready for the challenges of 1992 and beyond.

Finally, I believe that you will find working with design experts both challenging and stimulating and, with care and a considered approach, you will give your company the competitive edge.

Roger Cooper
Sales and Marketing Director
Ideal Standard Ltd

Above and right: Kango chose Product First to design their 1400 electro-pneumatic drill, replacing the conventional metals with plastics

Far right: Neotronics' Exotox 60 gas detector, with exterior design by Colin Cheetham Design Partnership

USING A DESIGN CONSULTANT

The design consultants in this directory offer a wide range of skills and knowledge gained from the experience of working for clients in many fields. Their aim is to work in full co-operation with their clients. To achieve this they must be aware of their client's exact requirements, how they operate and how the end product will be used. The 'design brief' is the key to this process and good communications between client and consultant are essential to managing the project. No two companies manage the design process in the same way, though the British Standard for Design Management, BS5750, provides an excellent working structure.

When Kango decided to improve its electro-pneumatic hammer drills it hired a design consultant, and Neotronics followed a similar course when developing a brand new atmosphere monitor. Design consultants have different skills and different ways of working, so it is important to find the right consultant for your company's project.

Kango and Neotronics describe here how they built up a successful working relationship with their chosen design consultant, thereby achieving their design and, ultimately, business targets.

Kango
Kango produced the first electro-pneumatic drill in 1964 but had not redesigned its products since 1974. The range was successful, even in the face of increasing competition from Bosch, AEG and Hitachi, and the company had been satisfied that customers were happy. However, in 1986 the new technical director, Vic Lilly, changed company policy.

'To be truthful, our biggest threat had been ourselves,' he says. 'We frittered away our resources tinkering with old products, just tarting them up. It was a terrible problem and our image suffered.' Kango found that people were confused about their products, so the first step was to bring in a design consultant to create a new corporate identity. That done, Kango needed new products. Vic Lilly cast around for a suitable design consultancy, to stimulate and work with the company's 28-strong in-house design team.

'Working on our corporate identity had given us the flavour of outside consultants,' he says. 'We realized the value of objectivity that a consultant could bring and that it could help revitalize our product range. I wanted a consultancy that needed us and

would show commitment. And I wanted to know who was actually going to be doing the work so that I could be happy that the personal chemistry would be good.'

Product First was chosen as the right consultancy: 'I liked the presentation given by Product First and we had a good rapport with them.'

Kango briefed the selected design consultancy and asked for quotes. Kango re-engineered the inside of the 1400 electro-pneumatic drill and asked Product First to design the exterior. The consultancy identified shortcomings in the old product range, such as handles increasing with size in line with tool size which ignored the fact that hands don't get bigger according to tool size. It also demonstrated that the previous angle of the handle forced pressure in the opposite direction to that intended.

Unconventional material

A more major change was the switch from aluminium to plastics for the basic material of the concrete-breaking drill. This flew in the face of the traditional belief that users of a macho tool required it to have a shiny metal casing, but it did contribute to making manufacturing easier.

Throughout the development period Vic Lilly and his team kept in close contact with the design consultants. 'We started with initial sketches and then discussed detailed proposals,' he says. 'We had weekly meetings and the phone and the fax featured fairly heavily thoughout so that we were in daily contact. We used the consultants to look at our designs for tooling to make sure that our requirements were not going to affect their designs for the look of the drill. At times, contact with the consultants was so intense that it was almost as if they were part of Kango.'

The 1400 hammer drill was launched in 1989 and has lived up to the high expectations, surprising competitors and selling well. It also won a 1991 Design Council Award. Product First was retained to work on the redesign of Kango's second major new product, a smaller, 35mm drilling hammer. It has as many parts in common with the 1400 as possible and displays a distinct family resemblance. The first thousand have been built and are currently undergoing field trials.

Neotronics

Neotronics had been designing gas detectors for 12 years when the company had an idea for a new product, a personal atmosphere monitor which came to be called the Exotox 60. 'Most of the products in this market are square boxes,' says Mick Joyce, the manager of Neotronics' drawing office and responsible for design. 'We believed that the new product should break out from that format. Our drawing office was already fully committed and to some extent we had become a little stagnant in our attitude to the design of the exterior of the product, so we chose to bring in an outside consultant.'

More than half of the company's sales come from abroad, with 50 per cent of the group turnover originating in the United States where Neotronics has captured 10 per cent of the entire market for gas detectors. The company knew that a new product could consolidate its high export success if it was well designed, and it entered into discussions with the Design Council to find a good consultancy. It was during these discussions that it learned of funded consultancies, where the DTI helps foot the bill for a short period of consulting.

'This tied in nicely with what we had in mind, though we would have gone ahead with the programme even if funding had not been available,' says Mick Joyce. 'The Design Council gave us names of local consultancies and we vetted a few before choosing the Colin Cheetham Design Partnership. We had a good rapport with them and I could see that they were experienced in the kind of project we had in mind. It was important that they had a good appreciation of engineering and that they were interested not only in aesthetics. They were keen to utilize their engineering experience to design an attractive package which could actually be made.

'Other consultants we talked to presented us, potentially, with more problems. They had concepts which were fine to look at but difficult to engineer.'

Neotronics presented the Colin Cheetham Design Partnership with some sketchy ideas of what it wanted to achieve and they held long discussions about how the Exotox 60 would eventually be used, how it was to be mounted and what accessories would be available. 'They came up with schemes, then block diagrams and then pictures. By then we were really getting down to the nitty gritty and it was necessary to have the first block model made in foam so that we could get the feel of the product, to make sure the size was right,' says Mick Joyce.

Parallel development

While the consultants were working on the exterior, Neotronics was still developing the software and electronics to go inside the Exotox 60. It was a programme of parallel development to bring the machine to market as quickly as possible. Arising out of this were some fundamental changes to the electronics late in the project which necessitated some redesign of the exterior. In the end, four different foam models were built of the detector during the 18-month design period.

Mick Joyce controlled the costs of using a design consultant by implementing an agreed method of inspecting progress at predetermined stages. 'We paid at the end of each stage of work and considered whether we were getting where we wanted to go,' he says. 'This had been agreed early in our discussions, when we were still getting funding from the DTI and when the Design Council was helping us. It was a simple and effective management process.'

Neotronics believes that by working with a design consultant the Exotox 60 has been made an excellent product. 'It stands out from our other range of detectors and, beyond that, it has made our in-house team of designers more aware of what can be achieved. Perhaps we should have used the consultants even more than we did because our graphics and labelling might have been improved. Nevertheless, it has been well received, it has gained approval for use underground in the UK and we can now sell it in earnest.'

Most recently, the Exotox 60 has been used to demonstrate what sophisticated safety equipment is needed by sewer workers, in an attempt to discourage children from entering sewers in imitation of Teenage Mutant Ninja Turtles.

Kango and Neotronics identified the opportunities presented by their own marketplaces and took the initiative. The design process was just one part of their strategy but it was integrated with the whole development programme. Design is not an isolated part of a successful business – it is an essential element.

Top: The 1990 'Design for Export' exhibition at the London Design Centre

Above: Xenos (Neen Pain Management Systems), a nerve stimulator for use in relieving chronic pain, received a 1991 British Design Award

Right: The Nomix Compact (Nomix Manufacturing Co), a lightweight sprayer of ready-mixed herbicides, was a 1991 British Design Award winner

THE DESIGN COUNCIL

The Design Council was set up in 1944 under a remit from Churchill's wartime government. Its objectives were restated in the Council's 1976 Royal Charter as 'the advancement of British industry by the improvement of the design of its products'.

The Design Council has achieved success in helping to elevate an awareness of design in the public and in government. It has worked continuously to persuade management of manufacturing industry and commerce of the implications of improved design on market performance.

With limited financial resources, the Design Council can only succeed in its aims by working closely with other areas of strategic influence. These include government, particularly the Department of Trade and Industry, other industrial, engineering, management and design institutions, and education and training.

Design Council Activities

Good design is essential to the market success of manufactured goods. As the nation's manufacturing performance slips into deepening crisis, the Design Council must ensure its activities are appropriate to the challenges.

For industry and commerce, design is an integral process that results in goods and services which are produced efficiently and in terms of function, aesthetics and cost, are highly competitive in the markets for which they are intended. A particular market can only be defended, expanded or attacked through the strategic development of new products which are better designed than those of its competitors.

The Design Council has a number of interrelated objectives: to help British industry and commerce understand better the nature of good design and the positive effect it has on market performance; to assist in achieving good design and its effective management; to promote a climate in which engineering and industrial designers have better career prospects in British industry; and to ensure that education and training in design is effective and responsive to the present and future needs of industry.

Over the last two years the Design Council has concentrated on its two central objectives: to help British manufacturing companies develop better products through the total design process; and to support and improve education and training in design. In doing so, the Design Council has devolved many responsibilities to its six regional organizations, including a London based office to serve the south of England.

Services to Industry and Commerce

One of the Design Council's primary tasks is to identify and target areas of manufacturing industry that have sufficient potential to make a real impact on home and overseas markets. For historical and structural reasons it is too late to turn round many areas of British industry. But there are always new opportunities that do suit Britain's current and future circumstances. So the Design Council is focusing its efforts on those areas where it can have the most influence.

Direct services are provided mainly for small- to medium-sized companies with limited resources of their own. Larger companies benefit indirectly through Design Council help for their smaller suppliers, and through educational and campaigning activities. A dialogue is also maintained with larger companies for the general dissemination of new ideas and technologies.

Sector Strategies

The Design Council's task is to convince UK industry that investment in design, and good design management, are crucial to long term profitability. By targeting its resources, the Design Council is able to fulfil this remit more efficiently. A more favoured approach will provide an opportunity for the Council to deepen its expertise, acquiring detailed knowledge of the target sectors.

The first sector strategies to be launched will address the furniture industry and the clothing and textiles industry. Later initiatives will concern the medical equipment, machine tools and ceramics and glass industries.

The campaigns will involve exhibitions, seminars and supporting literature.

Company Advice

The Design Council's direct services for individual companies are spearheaded by regional teams of Design Advisers who visit companies to help diagnose and solve design-related problems. They are able to recommend approved design specialists selected from the Council's Designer Selection Service database (see page xix).

These services also include assistance on design management, training, design protection and special projects. Advice and information is provided on specialist issues such as innovation, technology and materials.

Management Training

The Design Council is increasingly active in training to ensure managers are up to date in the use of design and its effect on business. It provides tailored in-house training on design relevant to a particular company, and is extending its range of seminars on specialist design topics. The 'Design To Win' programme of nationwide seminars is particularly important to this area. This is part of the DTI's wider 'Managing into the 90's' initiative and is supported by a special handbook, video, travelling exhibition and series of related booklets.

Design Initiative

The Council's own direct services complement the Design Initiative (part of the Enterprise Initiative), which is run by the Design Council on behalf of the DTI under a management contract. The scheme provides subsidized design consultancy for problem solving, new product design and product improvement.

Materials Information Service

The Materials Information Service is a major source of information on new materials and processing methods. In particular it aims to highlight the extensive British network of materials expertise and to encourage industrialists, designers and engineers to grasp the many opportunities offered by developments in this field.

The service also provides information on courses, forthcoming conferences and distance learning techniques on materials, as well as details of books, journals and videos available on materials subjects.

Awards

The country's premier design awards are the Design Council's British Design Awards, which attract a large entry each year from companies and designers. The Awards cover consumer, contract and engineering goods, medical and motor products, and computer software.

The scheme has been broadened to include British designers working for overseas clients, as well as British designers working overseas themselves.

Bookshop

The Design Council's Bookshop is an unrivalled resource for education, industry and the design profession. It carries a comprehensive stock of design-related books, magazines and journals from all over the world. The bookshop is situated in the London Design Centre and can be contacted at the address on page xvii.

Publishing

The Council publishes around 60 books and directories covering all aspects of design, from the educational and academic to the professional. Titles range from *Street Style* (Catherine McDermott) and *Did Britain Make It?* (Penny Sparke), to *Design Protection* (Dan Johnston). Recent publications include the **Issues in Design** series, consisting of *Green Design* (Paul Burall), *Packaging Design* (Howard Milton) and *Colour in Industrial Design* (Dale Russell), amongst others.

It also publishes two monthly business magazines, DESIGN and ENGINEERING, which have a wide audience in the industrial, design and commercial worlds. In terms of both circulation and readership these two are leaders in their fields.

As part of its educational publishing programme, the Design Council produces three termly magazines for education – THE BIG PAPER for primary schools, DESIGNING for secondary schools and D for industrial design students. These provide a rich variety of material for teachers as well as students and promote the broader cross-curricular view of design education.

The Design Council has developed a wide range of teaching and learning aids in the form of books (including the **Signs of Design** series), videos (such as the **Design Activities** series), slides and mixed media packs for all levels of education, as well as design education reports.

To subscribe to DESIGN or ENGINEERING please contact:

Subscription Department
Computer Action
Central House
27 Park Street
Croydon CR0 1YD

For sales enquiries on any other Design Council publications please contact the Sales Department at the address on page xvii.

Services to Education

Education and training are of immense importance in ensuring not only that industry and commerce have the right sort of design skills at their disposal, but also that all involved in our economic life understand the nature of design.

To meet the challenge, the Design Council has developed an extensive programme of education activities and services. The Design Council's education objectives are:

● that all pupils between the ages of 5 and 16 can learn how to practise design within a variety of contexts in the school curriculum

● that satisfactory courses of appropriate rigour exist for students between the ages of 16 and 19 who wish to study design

● that higher education courses in design reflect the requirements of industry

● that higher education courses and research in engineering contain a significant and appropriate design element.

The Design Council pursues these objectives both through close liaison with other organizations, such as the Department of Education and Science, the National Curriculum Council, the National Council for Vocational Qualifications, or the various engineering professional institutions, and through working with schools, local education authorities, colleges and universities (either directly or through conferences), seminars and training courses. It is particularly concerned to establish links between design education and design practice in industry.

Above: Packaging Design by Howard Milton; part of the Issues in Design series published by the Design Council

Right: Chair designed by Anne-Marie Kerr (Buckinghamshire College of Higher Education) during a YDI placement at Green Brothers (Geebro) Ltd

Young Designers Centre

The Young Designers Centre at the London Design Centre is the first national centre of its kind for anyone with an interest in design education – from students and teachers to managers and industrialists.

The Young Designers Centre provides a permanent exhibition area with changing displays of design work from primary and secondary schools, and by students from polytechnics, universities and colleges, as well as work by recent design graduates. It also runs a series of thematic exhibitions on specific issues in design education, including the Design Council's own educational competitions and award schemes and topics of current interest in design education. Many of these exhibitions also tour outside London.

The Young Designers Centre also includes an information service to help visitors and telephone enquirers with information on all aspects of design education, including video slide packs, posters and books, as well as a free slide loan service.

To find out more contact the Information Officer in the Young Designers Centre at the address below.

Campaigns

The Design Council is developing its campaigning role with the aim of changing attitudes and improving understanding of the fundamental aspects of design.

Exhibitions play an important part in stimulating interest and raising standards by promoting excellent design achievements. They are also becoming increasingly

Below: Leicester Polytechnic 1st-year project: children's shoes designed by Catherine Robinson, Samantha Streak, Sarah Edwards, Jackie Leggett and Louise Smalley

important as a means of attracting attention to issues where change is needed. Design Council campaigns are often supported by an opening exhibition which is usually mounted first at the Design Council's premises in London; many exhibitions then travel round the regions.

Design-related campaign themes now being developed by the Design Council include the need to produce more manufactured goods in Britain, the need for better design management, the environmental quality of factories, the reward and status of designers, the need for long-term planning and financing of industrial development, education and training, research and development, and the use of design management techniques in the service sector.

A recent example of a full-scale Design Council campaign is 'Design To Win'. Its objective is to improve the techniques of design management, mainly in small- to medium-sized companies.

Information about the work of the Design Council is available from the Press and Publicity Department, which is responsible for publishing supporting literature for the many campaigns, exhibitions and awards run by the Council, and for media relations and briefings. You can contact this and other Design Council departments at:

The Design Council
28 Haymarket
London SW1Y 4SU

Tel: 071-839 8000
Fax: 071-925 2130

DESIGN COUNCIL REGISTRATION

The 'Quality Mark' for design consultancies

Everyone concerned with the design business is aware of the surge of interest in quality marks and standards as the 1992 Single European Market approaches.

The need for the design consultancy profession to meet the quality standards expected by its clients grows at an ever increasing rate. Manufacturing companies, having experienced the value of their suppliers' certification to BS5750, see it as a natural extension to demand that their suppliers of services are similarly certified.

Meeting quality management standards is only part of a design consultancy's objectives; other requirements linked to professional capability are its principal *raison d'être*. Quality management and design capability are at the heart of successful design consultancy; they are the attributes which form the basis of Design Council Registration, the 'Quality Mark' for design consultancies. In this context 'Quality Mark' is seen as a term embracing both quality management and design capability.

Design Council Registration is accorded to consultants who meet established quality management standards through interviews, portfolio assessment and evaluations of project management procedures.

Design capability is determined by vetting professional qualifications, training and experience; in this regard 'track record' is a major consideration, determined in part from numerous references.

Increasingly the trend will be towards acceptance of a consultancy's certification to the British Standard for Design Management, BS5750, as meeting the quality management standards of Design Council Registration.

The Design Council is in the process of drafting an interpretation of ISO9000 (the international equivalent of BS5750) as it is clearly desirable that only one interpretation for design consultancies is used by all accredited certification bodies. It will incorporate guidance on BS7000 - 'Guide to Managing Product Design'. This interpretation will be reviewed by the Association of Certification Bodies (ACB), prior to review by the National Accreditation Council for Certification Bodies (NACCB), the government sponsored organization that approves applicants to become certification bodies.

These activities will further enhance Design Council Registration as the 'Quality Mark' for design consultancies, both nationally and internationally.

DESIGNER SELECTION SERVICE

The consultancy recommendation service

Many of the design practices included in the **Directory of Designers 1991** are registered with the Design Council. Registration provides design consultancies with an independent verification that their work meets high standards of design ability and quality management.

The **Directory of Designers** can only provide brief details on each of the registered consultancies included. More detailed up-to-date information is maintained by the Designer Selection Service to allow in-depth evaluation of consultants' skills and ability to undertake specific tasks.

Companies requiring the skills of a designer are faced with the difficult, time consuming and costly task of selecting the most appropriate consultant.

It is easy to make the wrong choice, so for a fee of £80 plus VAT the Designer Selection Service can help by providing details of the three most suitable design practices to undertake a specific project. Recommendations are made from the register of approved design consultancies to back up and supplement the information published in the directory.

A brochure or further information is available to companies from:

Designer Selection Service
The Design Council
28 Haymarket
London SW1Y 4SU

Tel: 071-839 8000
Fax: 071-925 2130

Designer Selection Service
The Design Council Scotland
Ca' d'Oro Building
45 Gordon Street
Glasgow G1 3LZ

Tel: 041-221 6121
Fax: 041-221 8799

THE CHARTERED SOCIETY OF DESIGNERS

The Chartered Society of Designers is the representative professional association for designers, working to promote and protect the interests of the profession, as well as raising standards of competence, professional conduct and integrity.

The current membership stands at over 8,000 designers practising in graphic, interior, product, fashion and textile design, design management and education. The Society represents the views and interests of not only its members but all professional designers on other advisory bodies such as the Design Council and the Royal Society for the encouragement of Arts, Manufactures and Commerce, the International design organizations, IFI, ICSID and ICOGRADA, and designers working in government departments.

The affixes MCSD and FCSD (Member and Fellow of the Chartered Society of Designers) are professional qualifications awarded, on application, only when a designer's work and business practices are considered of sufficiently high quality by the Membership Committee of the CSD.

To establish a workable pattern of conduct for the benefit of members and their clients, the Society publishes a Code of Conduct that is binding on all members. A Conduct Sub-Committee exists to question any members thought to be acting in a manner contrary to the Code. As a result of their report on any matter a member may be reprimanded, suspended or expelled.

The Society makes a significant contribution to the establishment of high standards throughout design education, working closely with the Council for National Academic Awards (CNAA) which validates BA and MA design courses and the Business and Technician Education Council (BTEC) which validates many vocational design courses.

A number of comprehensive events and training programmes open to members and non-members are run by the CSD. These events cover topical subjects in design in the wider business world, and include talks by well-known designers about their work.

In 1991 the Society launched its new quarterly magazine, *Design Review*, which is free to all members, together with the existing regular newsletter, *Preview*.

Through the amalgamation in 1990 of the CSD's Designers' Register and the Design Council's Designer Selection Service, clients may seek the help and advice of specialist designers who can best meet their needs. The new service provides a centralized register of over 1,800 consultancy practices nationwide.

The Society reflects the wide range of disciplines practised by its members. Founded in 1930, its Royal Charter was granted in 1976. In addition to its membership base, four specialist organizations are affiliated to the CSD: The Design Business Association, The Colour Group, The Design Research Society and The Lighting Forum. The British Institute of Interior Design was absorbed by the CSD in 1988.

For further information about the CSD and its services and benefits, please contact:

The Information Services
The Chartered Society of Designers
29 Bedford Square
London WC1B 3EG

Tel: 071-631 1510
Fax: 071-580 2338

DIRECTORY OF **DES** *ign* ERS 1991

Architectural Components
Boats/Marine
Capital and Plant Equipment
Ceramics/China
Domestic/Consumer Goods
Electronic Equipment
Furniture
Glassware
Lighting
Medical/Scientific Equipment
Modelmaking/Prototyping
Office/Business Equipment
Packaging
Silversmithing
Sports/Leisure Equipment
Toys/Games
Transportation
Trophies/Ceremonial Items

ACP Design

19 Southernhay West, Exeter, Devon EX1 1PJ
Telephone (0392) 413328 Fax (0392) 413201

ACP Design is an experienced multidisciplinary practice. We can provide a full or partial service from product concept to production information. We have proven expertise in metal and plastic enclosures for electronic and technical equipment, DIY and household products, the built environment with prefabricated accommodation units and building components, and interior design including space planning, finishes, fixtures and fittings. Offices also at Northaw House, Potters Bar, Hertfordshire.
Clients include: Stag Microsystems, Parametric Technology, Dataman Designs, Heathrow Airport, Nat West Bank, Trojan Structures, Health Authorities.

Contact Mr Graham Knox
Size 6-10
Affiliations CSD, RIBA

Addison

60 Britton Street, London EC1M 5NA
Telephone 071-250 1887 Fax 071-251 3712

We are a worldwide design consultancy with over 200 specialists working in the Far East, USA and Europe. Our expertise covers architecture, ergonomics, graphics, leisure, office and retail, product design and transportation together with design research. While addressing aesthetic and technical issues, we draw from our modelmaking, prototyping and CAD facilities, to offer consolidated approach from concept generation to production.

Contact Mr John Williamson
Size over 100
Affiliations CSD

Applied Products Ltd

68 Thames Road, Strand-on-the-Green, Chiswick, London W4 3RE
Telephone 081-995 8031 Fax 081-742 1307

Applied Products is a consultancy with an innovative approach to all aspects of design. Our team of professionals has considerable experience in product design and marketing requirements. We specialize in, but are not limited to, the design of consumer durables and microprocessor-based equipment. Applied Products produces accurate models and prototypes. This is an excellent method of realizing a product prior to embarking upon full production. We believe in full client involvement at all stages of a project offering a 'phase-by-phase' design approach.
Clients include: BOC (Edwards High Vacuum), GPT, Landis and GYR, Marconi, Mars (Four Square), Mercury, Motorola, Reuter(Wyatts), Servis.

Contact Mr Peter Schmidt
Size 1-5

ASA Designers Ltd

The Clockhouse, 357/359 Kennington Lane, London SE11 5QY
Telephone 071-793 0727 Fax 071-793 0612

ASA is a design studio based in London, working in areas as diverse as electronic and consumer products, furniture and systems, luggage and lighting. Our work has achieved success internationally for small and medium sized UK companies and multinational operations, including Steelcase Strafor, Giroflex, Antler and RTZ.
ASA is a group of ten, listed as a consultant under the DTI Design Initiative.
Additional facilities include in-house CAD and modelmaking.

Contact Mr Adrian Stokes
Size 11-20
Affiliations CSD, DBA

Ashton & Cordell Associates

DESIGN COUNCIL REGISTERED

2 Park Road, Oxted, Surrey RH8 0AL
Telephone (0883) 712746

Specializing in product design, both consumer and capital goods. Past and present clients include: capital goods – Hymac, Blaw Knox, Stothert & Pitt, Winget, Marshall Handling, English Numbering Machines, Hamworthy Engineering, British Steam Specialists, Babcock & Wilcox; consumer goods – Ansafone, Microplas, Milton Bradley (Europe), Prestige, Universal Parking Meters, Offshore Instruments, F C Brown (steel equipment). Particular areas of capability – innovation and development of small mechanisms; design as applied to industrial machinery; general consumer goods; electronic products etc.

Contact Mr Alan Rossi Ashton
Size 1-5
Affiliations CSD

Brian Asquith Design Partnership

DESIGN COUNCIL REGISTERED

Turret House, Church Street, Youlgreave, Derbyshire DE4 1WL
Telephone (062 963) 6204 Fax (062 963) 6759

Multidisciplined practice specializing in product, graphic and exhibition design, with a section working in precious metals. We offer a complete service from concept through development to final production, with offices, workshop and factory in Derbyshire. We have won six Design Council Awards and our clients include Baxi, British Airways, International Tennis Federation, Shell, British Coal and Grand Metropolitan. Many important silver commissions have been undertaken, including international sporting trophies, ecclesiastical pieces, and assignments for government, universities and royalty.

Contact Mr Brian Asquith
Size 11-20
Affiliations RCA, CSD, RSA

Atkinson Design Associates Ltd

DESIGN COUNCIL REGISTERED

12 Abbey Gate, Leicester, Leicestershire LE4 0AB
Telephone (0533) 516260 Fax (0533) 510697

Atkinson Design Associates are a small dedicated design consultancy working in the following areas: lighting and lighting systems, furniture and furniture systems, product design, industrial design, interior design, industrial architectural systems design. The work of the office for clients in the UK, Europe and USA demonstrates an open mind towards materials and manufacturing technology. This openness results in a visually diverse portfolio, where the personality of the client and client requirements are clearly expressed. The only residual concern demonstrated through our work is the consistent pursuit of quality.

Contact Mr Paul Atkinson
Size 6-10

ATKINSON DESIGN ASSOCIATES
Abbey House 12 Abbey Gate Leicester LE4 0AB
Tel: 0533 510509   Fax: 0533 510697

Atlantic Design

DESIGN COUNCIL REGISTERED

7-13 Cottons Gardens, Kingsland Road, London E2 8DN
Telephone 071-729 0082 Fax 071-729 0145

Atlantic Design specializes in product development consultancy, providing product strategy and innovative design skills to support our clients' research and development programmes. Specific areas of knowledge are with telecommunications equipment, marine electronics and several European consumer products. Our studio facilities include: product strategy, human factors, quality analysis, concept design and modelmaking, mechanical design, test prototyping, materials selection; plastics, metals, graphics and packaging.
New products range from navigation sysytems for racing yachts, to mobile telecommunications. Clients include: GEC, Racal, STC, Stowe Marine, Maxon Systems, Low & Bonar and British Rail.

Contact Mr Richard Appleby
Size 1-5
Affiliations RCA, CSD, RSA

Axis Design Europe

2 Cosser Street, London SE1 7BU
Telephone 071-633 9911 Fax 071-620 0238

Over the last decade we have experienced steady managed growth both in the size of our company and in the scale of the projects we have handled.
Effective design solutions require a balance between creativity, quality and cost efficiency. That balance is at the heart of our contract with the client. We provide creative solutions to a wide range of design needs including product design, furniture, intertior architecture and space planning.

Contact Mr Jeremy Harvey
Size 11-20
Affiliations CSD

Bartingale Design Associates

The Hilger Site, Westwood Industrial Estate, Margate, Kent CT9 4JA
Telephone (0843) 296624 Fax (0843) 296623

BDA are product design consultants offering industrial design, engineering design and full model and prototype facilities. Our expertise includes all aspects of product design using the latest materials and processes. Products recently commissioned include domestic appliances, navigation instruments, power and communication management, medical instrumentation, office furniture plus DIY and industrial tools. Some of our products have also received design awards. BDA have a strong team comprising industrial and engineering designers offering a personal efficient and economic service to all manufacturing industry.

Contact Mr Peter Bartingale
Size 6-10
Affiliations CSD

Ken Bell Design

35 The Glen, Green Lane, Northwood, Middlesex HA6 2UR
Telephone (09274) 23908

Ken Bell Design specializes in the design of commercial and consumer products. The service ranges from the development of initial design concepts through to finished product specifications. this also includes product graphics, packaging, photography and modelmaking.
Our clients cover a wide range of industries, whose products include computer terminals, audio and video consumer goods, Ministry of Defence equipment and security products.
Ken Bell has a wide experience in the field of industrial design and has received several major design awards.

Contact Mr Ken Bell
Size 1-5
Affiliations CSD

Bell Wickham Associates

Pittams Farm, Wappenham, Towcester, Northamptonshire NN12 8SP
Telephone (0327) 860236 Fax (0327) 860990

Bell Wickham is a long-established small unit giving a personal product design service to manufacturers of all types of capital and consumer goods. The practice has experience in computing, medical, laboratory, nautical and other electronic equipment, transport, yacht fittings and domestic hardware such as heaters, clocks, tableware and plastic goods. Model and prototype making, together with a graphic design service covering corporate identity, packaging, stationery, brochures etc are also offered. A number of design awards have been won including British Design Awards in 1989 and 1990.

Contact Mr John Wickham
Size 1-5
Affiliations CSD

Bernado R&D Ltd

Erikshällsg. 47, Södertälje, S—151 46, Sweden
Telephone +46-755 86844 Fax +46-755 76131

We are a research and development company performing complete advanced projects in the areas of engineering, automotive, graphic and industrial design, ergonomics, materials-composites and plastics, CAID, CAD, CAM and modelmaking.
Offices in Brazil and Sweden serve clients from three continents with fast, innovative, intelligent, reliable and economical solutions. Holders of several engineering patents. Clients in a wide range of fields, from telecommunications, household appliances and furniture to automotive styling and corporate identity.

Contact Eng Bernado Valiera-Mascarenhas
Size 6-10
Affiliations SAE(USA), CREA(Brazil), CF, SMF, SIF, SF(Sweden)

BIB Design Consultants Ltd

9 Clarendon Cross, Kensington, London W11 4AP
Telephone 071-229 7236 Fax 071-229 6089

BIB is a leading international product design consultancy specializing in consumer durables and capital equipment. With a broad client base in USA, Australia, Japan and Europe. BIB's designs have gained substantial market share and have won many international awards.
Our skills include concept development, appearance design, mechanical engineering, ergonomics, market evaluation; and using our knowledge of the full range of manufacturing technologies we can design and develop projects through to final production. We have excellent CAD facilities and expertise and a full modelmaking and prototype workshop in house to ensure confidentiality.

Contact Profes Nick Butler OBE
Size 11-20
Affiliations RDI, CSD, RSA

Blackbox Ltd

6 Michael Street, Limerick,
Telephone +353 61 310030 Fax +353 61 310029

Blackbox specializes in the design of consumer durables targeted at the home products market. These include small appliances, housewares and hardware, DIY, personal care, garden and leisure products. Services on offer include product design/development, modelmaking, product graphics, graphic design and packaging. Brochures available.

Contact Mr Philip Kenny
Size 6-10

Brauer Associates

20 Dock Street, London E1 8JP
Telephone 071-481 2184 Fax 071-481 3368

Brauer Associates, founded in 1976, are architects specializing in the design, development and marketing of building products. Services include market research, product innovation, design, development and promotion involving product literature, exhibitions and advertising. The practice works with UK and foreign clients, and technical documentation has been prepared for use in the USA, Japan, and the European Community. Current clients include MK Electric, Escol, Norwood Partitions, Ergonom and Quelfire. Products include ceilings, trunking, floors, screens, ironmongery, building fixings, partitions, timber structures, external cladding, roofing, lighting and fire stopping materials.

Contact Mr Irving Brauer
Size 6-10
Affiliations RIBA, CSD

Broadoak Design Partnership

Bowden Hall, Bowden Lane, Marple, Stockport, Cheshire SK6 6NE
Telephone 061-426 0279 Fax 061-426 0281

We see our role as that of both designers and planners, providing a service to our clients which can be involved from feasibility study through to completion. Our group is a balance of design, production engineering and marketing which, when allied to our graphics department, offers total project development, but at a personal level. Our experience covers most sectors and our extensive links with manufacturing industry ensure that design development follows projects through to completion. Brochure available.

Contact Mr Alan Learney
Size 6-10
Affiliations CSD

Anthony R Brookes

14 Lansdown Crescent Lane, Cheltenham, Gloucestershire GL50 2LD
Telephone (0242) 233852 Fax (0242) 227559

Design consultancy – concept to preproduction stage with prototype facility.

Contact Mr Anthony Brookes
Size 6-10
Affiliations CSD

Julian Brown Associates

58c Charlotte Road, London EC2A 3QT
Telephone 071-739 2739 Fax 071-729 5768

Julian Brown was previously a designer with Porsche Design in Austria.
The London studio is structured on a European model, combining creative research with focused commercial product design, and is active within numerous sectors of the modern manufacturing world. As a design-led organization, we enjoy an international reputation for designing clear, fresh and practical products in response to the needs of tomorrow's society, and have had the pleasure of collaborating with clients from the following countries: United Kingdom, Germany, Spain, Norway, Italy, France, USA and Japan.
For Japan, Mr T Noguchi, tel: Tokyo (3) 230 7927.

Contact Mr Julian Brown
Size 1-5

Buxton Wall McPeake Ltd

Cavendish House, 30 Pall Mall, Manchester M2 1JY
Telephone 061-835 1553 Fax 061-832 1902

Working with national and multinational clients, we have provided stylish, practical design solutions for everything from trains to toys, with all the engineering and project management skills that implies. We will work within your specific marketing and production requirements, ensuring that we achieve the optimum solutions for your product range. Our integrated approach to design and our investment in computer technology enables product, packaging and promotional material to be developed in parallel, ensuring optimum project timescales and consistency of image and identity.

Contact Mr Bob Buxton
Size 11-20

Cambridge Consultants Ltd

Science Park, Milton Road, Cambridge, Cambridgeshire CB4 4DW
Telephone (0223) 420024 Fax (0223) 423373 Telex 81481 (CCL G)

CCL designs and develops new products and processes for a wide range of industries. By integrating extensive engineering and industrial design resources under one roof, we can demonstrate an impressive track record of commercially successful products. We employ over 120 graduates covering industrial design, mechanical and production engineering, digital and analogue electronics, software and physics. In liaison with our parent, Arthur D Little, we offer a service which can span all stages of development, from product strategy and market research, right through to advice on manufacture. Please telephone for a brochure.

Contact Mr Howard Biddle
Size over 100

Cambridge Industrial Design

The Old School, 22 High Street, West Wickham, Cambridge, Cambridgeshire CB1 6RY
Telephone (0223) 290888 Fax (0223) 290806

Based in a converted village school, our experienced and enthusiastic team has worked for clients in the medical, scientific and consumer product industries. Our skills have contributed to the success of products ranging from hi-fi (A & R Cambridge, Teledyne Acoustic Research and Celestion) to marine radio and satellite communications equipment (Marconi). Recently we have worked closely with W Vinten redesigning lightweight video camera tripods and pan and tilt heads. Our products have won Design Council Awards (1978, 1986 and 1988), and many international prizes. Other clients: Gould Electronics, J Bibby Science Products, Normalair-Garrett, British Telecom, Sankey Vending, Drayton Controls.

Contact Mr Peter Harries
Size 6-10

Cambridge Product Design Ltd

4 Newton Road, Little Shelford, Cambridge, Cambridgeshire CB2 5HL
Telephone (0223) 845385 Fax (0223) 845480

The company provides comprehensive product design consultancy for European clients from idea to marketplace, backed by over 20 years' award-winning expertise in the design and development of products for consumer and industrial clients. We believe that our careful project planning through costing and detail design can ensure that quality is delivered on time and to cost. Our clients have successful products of worldwide reputation as a result.

Contact Mr Allen Boothroyd
Size 1-5
Affiliations CSD, RSA

Ceramic Modelling Services Ltd

Bush House, Pitgreen Lane, Wolstanton, Newcastle-under-Lyme, Staffordshire ST5 0DL
Telephone (0782)662233 Fax (0782) 744413 Telex 36395 HENBAM G

Ceramic Modelling Services offer a complete service encompassing the design and development of ceramic products involving tableware, giftware, sanitaryware and industrial ceramic products.
The company has a skilled team of designers, and modellers able to originate design, produce prototypes and then progress through to production stages.
Ceramic Modelling Services enjoy a worldwide reputation with approximately 40% export. The services provided are flexible and extensive involving sketch design, presentation, technical drawings, prototypes, models, block moulds (trials) and case moulds (master moulds).

Contact Mr Peter Carr
Size 11-20

Colin Cheetham Design Partnership

The Maltings, Brewery Road, Hoddesdon, Hertfordshire EN11 8HF
Telephone (0992) 464542 Fax (0992) 446086

Design, an analytical and creative exercise, not art. Research, engineering, costing, testing; wedding the product to the needs and emotions of the consumer. Accent on and studies of market acceptance, costing, safety, ergonomics, innovation without risk. Thirty years a company; 250 products, from writing instruments to automatic guided vehicles; major international awards; listed as consultants under the DTI Initiative; 34 such projects completed. Large premises, communicative pleasant staff, complementary design skills. Clients: Advel, Cossor, Dexion, Do-It-All, ITT, GEC, Kodak, London Underground, Marconi, Mercury, Norgren Martonair, STC.
Ask for our book.

Contact Mrs Sandy Chilton
Size 6-10
Affiliations CSD, RSA

Cooper Design Associates

The Old Chapel, Fop Street, Uley, Dursley, Gloucestershire GL11 5TG
Telephone (0453) 860979 Fax (0453) 860977

Cooper Design Associates offers an in-depth design consultancy service covering all areas of corporate graphics. Our clients include manufacturers, retailers and service industries, for whom we design an extensive range of brochures and promotional literature, as well as technical data, catalogues and reports. Our studio also handles a variety of packaging and point-of-sale material for products ranging from FMCG to industrial.

Contact Mr Richard Cooper
Size 1-5

John Cox Associates

8 Berwick Street, London W1V 3RG
Telephone 071-734 4587 Fax 071-734 4586

We are an independent consultancy geared to the needs of firms providing products and services for buildings and the environment. Our design experience ranges from door furniture to steel lintels and complete building systems. We have worked with all principal materials and manufacturing methods, and our service covers all facets of product development and launch: research, concept design, design development including structural and production design, organization of testing and approvals, and technical graphics. We also provide strategic marketing consultancy and carry out marketing research for our clients.

Contact Mr John Cox
Size 1-5
Affiliations CSD, RIBA

Crombie Anderson

16 Comely Park, Dunfermline, Fife, Scotland KY12 7HU
Telephone (0383) 620247 Fax (0383) 620357

Crombie Anderson has a highly creative team of industrial designers forming the core of a multidisciplinary design resource capable of undertaking substantial turnkey product development programmes both nationally and internationally. Crombie Anderson emphasize the crucial importance of product appearance (styling) and human factors (ergonomics) in creating commercial advantage over competitors.
Crombie Anderson's team has over the last ten years demonstrated both creative skill and sound technical ability in identifying and translating market requirements into over 100 commercially successful finished products.
Our portfolio embraces medical and laboratory sectors, consumer electronics, business machines and heavy capital equipment.

Contact Mr Douglas Anderson
Size 21-50
Affiliations BIM, IMC

9

Ian Crook, Chartered Designer

8 Mill Lane, Feckenham, Redditch, Worcestershire B96 6HY
Telephone (0527) 893667 Fax (0527) 857530

Business established 1979 handling both consumer and industrial products. Broad service covering innovation, problem-solving, appearance and manufacturing. Considerable expertise in designing for plastics especially injection-moulding and rotational moulding. Also metalworking processes including extrusion and presswork. Detailed engineering drawings produced on CAD system. Design illustrations (artists' impressions) part of the complete design service and also available as a separate facility. Projects include: Roto-moulded site-huts, site toilet, grit bins, road signs, 'caravan', door furniture, security products, bathroom fittings, garden sprayer, barbecues, rechargeable garden lighting, hologram viewer, road lamp.

Contact Mr Ian Crook
Size 1-5
Affiliations CSD

John David & Associates

The Old Village School, Bishops Wood, Stafford, Staffordshire ST19 9AA
Telephone (0785) 840896 Fax (0902) 26028 Telex G 338490

Our services encompass a wide range of skills from industrial design, concept visualization, prototype models, product support graphics and technical literature.
Our clients include JCB, British Leyland, GEC, Dorman Diesels, ADM Delta, Delta Group.

Contact Mr John David
Size 1-5

Alan Davies Design Projects Ltd

Cannock Road, Hightown, Cannock, Staffordshire WS11 2TD
Telephone (0543) 425720 Fax (0543) 871818

Our product and capital goods design team has a 15-year successful track record with clients including Qualcast, Lucas, Smiths Industries, Parker, Kangowolf, Glynwed, APV, Delta, GEC, Xpelair, Pegler, Swan. Specialists in practical problem analysis and solution with in-house facilities including styling studio, drawing offices, prototype and model workshops and electronics development.

Contact Mr Alan Davies
Size 6-10
Affiliations IED, IIM, DBA

Chris Dawson Associates

18-20 Grand Avenue, Hassocks, Sussex BN6 8DB
Telephone (079 18) 2610 Fax (079 18) 6464

Product design consultancy specializing in a creative and professional approach for new product generation, design development, styling and engineering. Wide experience in product design for major international companies, including Kimberly-Clark, Kenner Parker Tonka, Britains Petite, Rexel. Projects include washroom equipment, toys, office equipment and general consumer products.

Contact Mr Chris Dawson
Size 1-5
Affiliations CSD

DCA Design Consultants

19 Church Street, Warwick, Warwickshire CV34 4AB
Telephone (0926) 499461 Fax (0926) 401134

DCA is a vigorous and highly creative design consultancy with in-house skills and experience in all aspects of product design and development. Our expertise includes: product innovation, industrial design, graphics, electronics, mechanical engineering, ergonomics and product engineering.
Extensive design studios and workshops enable us to build excellent visual models and working prototypes. We pride ourselves on offering a swift and cost-effective design service for both large and small companies involved in a whole range of businesses. Brochures available.
Clients: Stanley Tools, ICI, Sainsbury's, London Transport, Sketchley, Rolls-Royce.

Contact Mr Michael Groves
Size 51-100
Affiliations RDI, RSA, CSD, IMechE, IEE, IOD

Design Acumen

2-10 Magdalen Street, London SE1 2EN
Telephone 071-962 1126 Fax 071-962 1125

Through progressive expansion we have become an independent arm of the multidisciplinary practice Murdoch Associates – established 25 years. Both companies operate from shared premises near London Bridge incorporating full workshop facilities. The company enjoys a reputation for original and innovative solutions resulting in international patents and immediate commercial impact for our clients. Our portfolio comprises many market leaders spanning a diverse range of industries, for example: architectural products, street/interior furniture, boats/marine products, domestic/consumer goods, agricultural products, electrical equipment, transportation, signage/displays, toys/games, capital/plant equipment and lighting.

Contact Mr Ian Dryburgh
Size 6-10
Affiliations CSD, DBA

Design + Development

Bourton Industrial Park, Bourton-on-the-Water, London GL54 2HQ
Telephone (0451) 21446 Fax (0451) 21686

Design and development of furniture, furniture components and allied products, from concept through development to production for UK and overseas clients. Substantial modelmaking, prototyping and pre-production facilities. Advice on materials and material sourcing.
Some clients: Antocks Lairn, Evertaut International, Hille Ergonom, Matthews Office Furniture, Ness Furniture, Leabank, Race Furniture, Steelcase.

Contact Mr Ian Finlator
Size 1-5

Design 4 (Plastics) Ltd

Unit 402, Thorp Arch Trading Estate, Wetherby, Yorkshire LS23 7BJ
Telephone (0937) 845176/842922 Fax (0937) 845419

Designing products and components effectively in plastics requires extensive knowledge of the tooling and processing methods. This is particularly important for injection-moulding, where sympathetic design can drastically reduce tooling costs and simplify assembly procedures. We offer a complete design and development service including concept designs, presentation drawings, technical product development, production of prototypes, detail drawings, advice on assembly techniques and material selection, and the sourcing of both tooling and components. Established in 1979, previous work includes toys, games, electronic and electrical products, domestic appliances, point-of-sale, packaging, engineering components etc.

Contact Mr Peter Viner
Size 6-10

Design House Consultants Ltd

DESIGN
COUNCIL
REGISTERED

120 Parkway, Camden Town, London NW1 7AN
Telephone 071-482 2815 Fax 071-267 7587

Design House product design is part of a leading interdisciplinary consultancy encompassing graphic design, interior design and new product development and is dedicated to the design of innovative consumer durables and development of packaging structures. Project teams are tailored to the specific needs of each client. We work closely with our clients to create products which are stylish, practical to manufacture and commercially effective.
Our client list includes: Boots, Lever France, Potterton International, Rabone Chesterman, and The Post Office.

Contact Mr John Larkin
Size 6-10

Design Marketing

DESIGN
COUNCIL
REGISTERED

Pennine House, Pennine View, Great Eccleston, Preston, Lancashire PR3 0UX
Telephone (0995) 70815 Fax (0995) 71112

Design Marketing is a multidisciplinary design practice operating primarily in product design. Our expertise and experience span the full range of product categories: consumer goods, electrical products, sports/recreational goods, furniture, toys and giftware, automotive products, building products and capital goods. Our clients range from major marketing companies to manufacturers and entrepreneurs. We have facilities to provide a complete product design and development service: design, concept illustration and artwork, mock-ups and prototypes, full technical specification drawings, sourcing of and liaison with component manufacturers and suppliers.

Contact Mr Graham Jones
Size 1-5
Affiliations CSD

DESIGN MARKETING

Design Matters

DESIGN
COUNCIL
REGISTERED

9 Onslow Gardens, Wallington, Surrey SM6 9QL
Telephone 081-773 1933 Fax 081-773 0147

New product conception, product design, product graphics, ergonomics, modelmaking.
In the current economic climate, producing quality products is more important than ever. Manufacturers are becoming increasingly aware of the power design has in influencing the buying public. Consumers are more discerning, no longer willing to accept second-rate products.
By understanding our clients' needs, we have developed exceptional working relationships based on co-operation, flexibility and enthusiasm. This, allied to the application of focused creative flair, has proved to be an ideal recipe for successful design.
Creative solutions accurately targeted.

Contact Mr Clive Solari
Size 1-5
Affiliations CSD

DESIGN MATTERS
PRODUCT DESIGN & ERGONOMICS CONSULTANTS

Design Technology

DESIGN
COUNCIL
REGISTERED

16 High Street, Hadleigh, Suffolk IP7 5AP
Telephone (0473) 823637 Fax (0473) 827389

Design Technology is an industrial design and product development consultancy providing a complete product design service from initial concepts through to production. We work with national and international client companies to improve product appearance, enhance product features, generate innovative marketing strategies, simplify assembly and reduce manufacturing costs. We have a proven track record in the fields of telecommunications, medical products, consumer products and capital goods. Clients include Black & Decker, GEC Plessey Telecommunications, Biorad Corporation, London Stock Exchange, Central Office of Information, BOC, Heatrae Sadia.

Contact Mr John Hawker
Size 1-5
Affiliations CSD

Design Workshop

Lilac Cottage, Pontysaeson, Tintern, Chepstow, Gwent, Wales NP6 6TP
Telephone (0291) 689603

Design Workshop provides a comprehensive design service for clients needing three-dimensional items made with fabrics. Specializing in products aimed at children, we have considerable pattern-making expertise, and the ability to guide ideas to the drawing board, and through the manufacturing process to the marketplace.
Clients include major retail chains, and manufacturers in the UK and abroad.

Contact Ms Susan Samuels
Size 1-5

Dessuro-Dufour Design Inc

3111 Ste-Catherine est, Montreal, Quebec H1W 2C1, Canada
Telephone (514) 521-0732 Fax (514) 521-0732

Located in Montreal, North America's French speaking metropolis, Dessuro Dufour Design definitely has a distinctive and innovative point of view. French culture and traditions blend together with North American values and knowhow resulting in the design of functional and attractive products which meet the needs of a wide variety of consumers.
If you are looking for industrial design expertise for the North American market, look no further. Our firm offers complete design services, from briefing to prototype development, using the flair and methodology that is necessary to create profitable products.

Contact Mr Sylvain Dufour
Size 1-5

DHA Industrial Design

8 Manor Park Business Centre, Mackenzie Way, Cheltenham, Gloucestershire GL51 9TX
Telephone (0242) 232945 Fax (0242) 224275

DHA Industrial Design is a small, efficient design consultancy which provides imaginative solutions to a wide range of product types. We strive for excellence in aesthetics and engineering, achieved realistically in terms of origination and production.
Clients: Yale-Valor, Glynwed, Dowty Electronics, Simon Engineering, Early Learning Centre, ITEK Colour Graphix, Electrolux Group, Redland, Tecalemit Garage Equipment, Linolite Lighting.
Product types: toys, domestic showering equipment, lighting and heating equipment, elderly disabled persons' aids, electronics, in-vehicle information system, office telecommunications equipment, heavy engineering products, domestic conservatory accessories, garage equipment, medical products.

Contact Mr Duncan Adamson
Size 1-5
Affiliations CSD

Dialog Design

32-34 Friars Street, Sudbury, Suffolk CO10 6AG
Telephone (0787) 310177 Fax (0787) 310135

Our objective is to help clients achieve business targets by providing a thorough and effective industrial, professional and consumer product design service which recognizes the benefits of establishing a close working relationship from the earliest stages in a development programme. We work for clients both nationally and internationally, maintaining a very broad product portfolio, and believe that in this way we keep abreast of design, manufacturing, materials and market trends.
Services range from product assessment/market analysis through new product concepts and development prototypes to CAD details and supplier liaison.

Contact Mr Barry Pearson
Size 1-5
Affiliations CSD

DIALOG DESIGN

Diametric Design Associates

City House, 16 City Road, Winchester, Hampshire SO23 8SD
Telephone (0962) 863466 Fax (0962) 842662

For a number of years now Diametric Design has been directly involved in the successful launching of new products in the field of electronic enclosures and capital goods. Our services are tailored to suit individual client requirements and budgets, in terms of merely producing initial design concepts, to offering a more comprehensive package which involves taking those concepts through to production. Our aim is to integrate market demand with what is technically and economically feasible.
Facilities include: CAD, prototyping, modelmaking. Also listed as consultants under the DTI Design Initiative.

Contact Mr John Pierce
Size 1-5
Affiliations CSD

Dimension Design Consultants

19 Jevington Way, Lee, London SE12 9NF
Telephone 081-857 6570 Fax 081-857 2935

A New Design Dimension.
The Offer – the right product at the right time.
The Expertise – from the idea to product launch.
The Service – imaginative, individual and flexible.
The Experience – multinationals to start-up companies.
The Aim – design excellence.
The experience grows through excellence.

Contact Mr Paul Appleby
Size 1-5
Affiliations CSD

Direct Data Design & Development

Unit 4, Barkla Shop, St Agnes, Cornwall TR5 0XN
Telephone (0872) 552784 Fax (0872) 552856

Complete electronic product design for energy-saving systems, computers and industrial control; analogue and digital hardware design, real-time software, communications, computer interfacing. Complete product design and management, feasibility study, planning and design, production lead-in.
Specialist skills include: electronic volume product design, mechanical design, software, statistics, closed loop control, PERT, prototyping and small runs, 'C', 'FORTH' and assembler languages.
Previous project areas include: professional dimmers, lighting control, crane control, thyristor power control modules, power supplies, machine control, computer communications, infra-red remote control, distributed industrial control, petrochemical metering/dispensing.

Contact Mr Andrew Ridyard
Size 1-5
Affiliations IEE, RSS

Dow Design Group Ltd

165 Grange Road, Darlington, Co Durham DL1 5NT
Telephone (0325) 282556 Fax (0325) 380985

A multidisciplined practice combining the skills of fully qualified designers and offering a full range of design services which include product design, modelmaking – both architectural and prototype, photography and graphic design. The interior and environmental design facility is extended by working in tandem with a firm of chartered and landscape architects. In addition the consultancy is listed under the DTI Design Initiative scheme. During 1990 the practice has gained experience in exhibition work and most recently in creative design for the workplace.

Contact Ms Joanna Straiton
Size 1-5
Affiliations CSD

Henry Dreyfuss Associates

423 West 55th Street, New York, New York 10019, USA
Telephone 212-957-8600 Fax 212-265-5839 Telex 237699WWBUS

For over 60 years a leading inustrial design consultancy, providing all aspects of product development including planning, design, CAD, human factors, prototyping, graphics and market testing. We have helped our clients realize successful introductions of consumer and business products, transportation interiors, industrial and medical equipment, corporate identity and packaging. Long term clients include: AT&T, American Airlines, Polaroid, John Deere, Hyster, Falcon Jet, Singer, Emerson Quiet Kool, Astra Jet Corporation, Valmont Industries, Boehringer Mannheim Corporation and Hill Refrigeration.

Contact Ms Juanita Alexander
Size 51-100
Affiliations IDSA, HFS, AIGA, ASAE, CMG, CAUS, APDF, DMI

Durbin Associates

2-3 Priory Wharf, Priory Street, Hertford, Hertfordshire SG14 1RJ
Telephone (0992) 550535 Fax (0992) 550584

A comprehensive industrial design and prototype service for manufacturers of business, consumer, telecommunications and scientific products. Our objective is to produce visually appealing products which are comfortable to use, launched on time and make money.
CAD is used to produce detail drawings, and our own fully equipped workshop produces models, prototypes and pre-production runs. We have established links with specialists in graphic design, electronic design and human factors.
Winners of 1990 British Design Award, 1990 Industrie Forum Design Hannover, and a product in Design and Art Direction '90 Annual.

Contact Mr Paul Durbin
Size 1-5
Affiliations CSD

Warwick Evans Design

132 Science Park, Milton Road, Cambridge, Cambridgeshire CB4 4GD
Telephone (0223) 420515 Fax (0223) 423922

Based on the Cambridge Science Park, we offer industrial design, ergonomics, mechanical engineering, electronic design, software and prototype development, taking projects from concept to production with colour visuals, engineering drawings, models, mock-ups and prototypes. We have designed domestic products, sports equipment, scientific instruments, telecommunications equipment, computer workstations, automotive products and mechanical handling machinery. Our main skill is in producing imaginative, functional products, which can be practically manufactured and look great!
Catalogue available from Warwick Evans on the above number.

Contact Mr Warwick Evans
Size 1-5
Affiliations CSD

John Ewans Design

Park Royal Business Centre, 9-17 Park Royal Road, London NW10 7LQ
Telephone 081-961 8980 Fax 081-961 2346

Involving outside designers can only be justified by the results achieved from their input into a project. The fact that we have established long term working relationships with numerous companies demonstrates that our services do give genuine benefits. We specialize in the design of non-consumer products. These range from commercial lighting and office equipment through to medical products and machine tools. The strength of our service is that we back up our visual design skills with qualified mechanical engineering expertise. We also offer full modelmaking and prototyping services.

Contact Mr John Ewans
Size 6-10
Affiliations CSD, DBA

JOHN EWANS DESIGN

FIRA (Furniture Industry Research Association)

Maxwell Road, Stevenage, Hertfordshire SG1 2EW
Telephone (0438) 313433 Fax (0438) 727607 Telex 827653 FIRA G

FIRA's product design and development service – for British and international furniture clients – links uniquely to their production, quality, testing, marketing and materials technology skills. From the leading international furniture technology centre, FIRA designers continually evolve new products for companies from a host of countries worldwide. Services cover conception and detailed design, prototyping, evaluation: all to achieve defined production and marketing targets. The design process is also supported by qualified staff in ergonomics, material specifications, product costing, packaging. UK and overseas clients include manufacturers, furniture specifiers, interior designers and retailers.

Contact Mr Jack Moses
Size over 100
Affiliations CSD, BIM, IMechE, PRI

Fitch RS Design Consultants

4 Crinan Street, London N1 9UE
Telephone 071-278 7200 Fax 071-833 1014 Telex 22826

Fitch RS product design is a truly rounded and international skill. Many of our projects involve the creation of joint US/UK teams and the blending of product, graphic and architectural disciplines. As well as our team in the UK, which has particular expertise in consumer goods, computer and telecoms products, office and street furniture and retail systems, we have one of the largest product design and development practices in North America. They have complementary skills in capital goods, medical equipment, software interfaces, office and computer equipment and household products.

Contact Mr David Rivett
Size over 100

Fleming Thermodynamics Ltd (FTD)

1 Redwood Court, Peel Park, East Kilbride, Glasgow, Scotland G74 5PF
Telephone (03552) 26600 Fax (03552) 26210

FTD provides a fully integrated engineering and industrial design and development service covering all the normal engineering disciplines, styling and full size modelling, component machining and working prototype manufacture. Testing and development using computerised data acquisition and control is carried out in-house. FTD has in-house CAE capability, including analytical software and VersaCAD full colour 3-dimensional CAD system.
Clients include Alcatel, Sumitomo, General Motors, Ford, National Standard, Austin Rover Group, EIMCO, Burmah, Renold Group, Syltone.
BS5750 Part 1 quality assurance submission in preparation.

Contact Ms Elaine Catton
Size 11-20
Affiliations IMechE, RAeS, IProdE, CSD, ICAS, CIMA, FEANI

FM Design Ltd

1a Lonsdale Square, London N1 1EN
Telephone 071-700 3333 Fax 071-700 0597 Telex 27950 ref 3114

Product/environmental/transportation/furniture: FM Design (part of Fether Miles Group) provides the full range of design and development services major industry requires from an international design consultancy. Additionally, involvement in broader issues enables us to respond to geographic market variations, develop corporate product identities and identify and design for segmented markets.
Programmes are structured precisely to reflect the strategic aims and resources of clients. We work with major international organizations and companies interested in developing export markets.
Clients: Samsonite, Sanyo, British Rail, Remploy, Project, Yale, Tupperware, London Transport, Map, Jotul.

Contact Ms Melinda Ross
Size 21-50
Affiliations CSD

Form Factor

68 Knaves Hill, Linslade, Leighton Buzzard, Bedfordshire LU7 7UD
Telephone (0525) 371972

A small consultancy with low overheads, we are extremely competitive on price, and highly effective in achieving design flair and style through simple and economical tooling.
Projects from styling concept through to engineering drawing are handled by the same designer, ensuring that proposals are always practical and functional.
Eye-catching form has been a key factor in creating successful communications products for Epson, Gestetner and GPT, EPoS equipment for Checkout Computers and Thorn EMI, and spirometers, including the British Design Award-winning 'Compact' for Vitalograph.

Contact Mr Julian Abrams
Size 1-5
Affiliations CSD

Form Foundry

Carrington Business Park, Carrington, Urmston, Manchester M31 4DD
Telephone 061-776 4240 Fax 061-775 8995 Telex 667678 Carbus G

Product design by Form Foundry combines innovation, originality and style to solve critical aesthetic and ergonomic problems. Close co-operation with the client, from concepts to final development, ensures that new products are finalized within demanding timescales.
The consultancy has worked on a diverse range of products for national and international manufacturers, including: Audioline, Berol, Britax Weathershields, Cleco, GEC Avery, Goblin, Kalmar UK, Sarasota Instrumentation, Narrow Aisle UK and Sony.

Contact Mr Philip Cook
Size 1-5
Affiliations CSD

Forth Product Design

32 Bernard Street, Leith, Edinburgh, Scotland EH6 6PR
Telephone 031-554 2626 Fax 031-554 2443

We are a consultancy which combines creativity with experience resulting in innovative yet budget-conscious solutions. Conceptual design, ergonomics, high-quality aesthetic design, creative engineering, design for manufacture (DFM), EMC capabilities, CAD/CAM techniques, and modelmaking – used as a complete product design service or as individual disciplines. Our main area of activity is in injection-moulded plastics.
We have a proven track record of successful products for clients which include Digital, Fortronic, Spider Systems, Bank of Scotland and De La Rue.

Contact Mr Stephen Duddy
Size 1-5
Affiliations IED

Frazer Designers

6 Hampstead West, 224 Iverson Road, London NW6 2HL
Telephone 071-624 6011 Fax 071-328 6085

Frazer Designers offers an exciting blend of industrial design talent and experience. The combination of imaginative ideas and styling together with high technology skills has led to a large proportion of our designs being successfully manufactured.
Our principal designers personally direct a project from initial concepts through specification to final production. Supporting the design team are specialists in ergonomics, CAD, modelmaking, engineering and electronics. Products include computers, domestic appliances, telecommunications, toys and games, lighting and instrumentation for Psion, Philips, Braun, Boots, Xpelair, NEC, Mercury, Hasbro, JSB, M&S and Digitron.

Contact Mr Stephen Frazer
Size 11-20
Affiliations CSD, DBA, D&AD

The Furniture Consultancy Ltd

DESIGN COUNCIL REGISTERED

1 Clarendon Street, London SW1V 2EH
Telephone 071-233 7043 Fax 071-233 7038

We design furniture for retail and contract use. Stag Meredew, Hypnos and Litton Furniture are just three of a wide client list which extends to Sweden, Italy and the USA. We do some marketing consultancy and our own product promotion, but most of our work is for furniture producers who need strong commercial designs. Products we have designed are currently on sale in Conran's (USA), Habitat, Heal's, IKEA, MFI, Easthope & Co, Roche Bobois. Please write or telephone for a brochure which explains our activities in more detail.

Contact Mr Richard Entwistle
Size 1-5
Affiliations CSD

Gerrard and Medd

DESIGN COUNCIL REGISTERED

Quadrant, 17 Bernard Street, Edinburgh, Scotland EH6 6PW
Telephone 031-555 0670 Fax 031-554 1850

Product design and styling, commercial interior and contract furniture design including specialist and custom pieces. The practice works for major industrial and commercial clients as well as start-up companies which are enjoying commercial and critical success. The practice has particular expertise in medical electronics.
Clients include: BAA, Carron Phoenix, Ferranti, Glasgow Royal Concert Hall, Grant Westfield, MacTaggart and Mickel, Medical Laser Technology, North Sea Compactors, Racal Guardall, Reynolds Medical and Standard Life.

Contact Mr David Gerrard
Size 1-5
Affiliations CSD, STD

Goodwin Emck

DESIGN COUNCIL REGISTERED

Barn House, Home Farm, Warren Lane, Pyrford, Woking, Surrey GU22 8XD
Telephone (0483) 722686 Fax (0483) 755212

We have undertaken, commercially and technically, projects in the following areas:
Architectural: cubicles, ceilings, raised floors, office furniture, sign systems, conservatories. Electronics: marine equpment, GPS receivers, broadcasting control panels, cabinets. Consumer: hi-fi, fridges, lighting, cookers, boilers, artists' equipment, showers. Electrical: trunking, wire management systems, hospital trunking, floor boxes.
Clients: Thrislington, Herman Miller, Martin Roberts, BICC Group, British Telecom, Aiwa, Formwood, Signco, Lec, Winsor & Newton, Brookes & Gatehouse, Valor, Chaffoteaux.
Awards: nine in ten years.

Contact Mr David Goodwin
Size 6-10
Affiliations CSD, DBA

Grey Matter Design Consultants plc

DESIGN COUNCIL REGISTERED

28 Scrutton Street, London EC2A 4RJ
Telephone 071-247 1887 Fax 071-377 9909

Grey Matter is an independent multidisciplinary design team specializing in product design, graphic design and packaging. This broad range of skills provides our clients with a complete design programme from concept through to launch. The industrial design facilities, which include computer-aided draughting and computer-aided manufacturing, enable products to be developed from concept through prototyping to full production including liaison with toolmakers and production management.
Our client list is broad, ranging from small start-up companies through to multinationals. Grey Matter were awarded a 1988 British Design Award for durable consumer and contract goods.

Contact Mr Kevin Thompson
Size 11-20
Affiliations RSA, DBA, D&AD

Martin Grierson

22 Canham Road, London W3 7SR
Telephone 081-749 5236 Fax 081-749 5236

Designer of all categories of furniture. Past commissions include designs for manufacturers of contract office and boardroom furniture and upholstered office and domestic seating. In addition, our own workshops can prototype ideas and manufacture one-off commissions. The design style of the practice is classically modern but often draws inspiration from beautiful design ideas from the past. Major clients include: British Rail, Collins & Hayes, ESB Ireland, The Home Office, Croydon Borough Council, Arflex SpA, Irish Export Board.

Contact Mr Martin Grierson
Size 1-5
Affiliations CSD, RSA

martin grierson

Designer and manufacturer
of special project furniture

Gripgold Ltd

20 Guernsey Farm Lane, Felpham, Bognor Regis, West Sussex PO22 6BU
Telephone (0243) 585944 Fax (0243) 584032

Gripgold Ltd is an independent design consultancy offering specialist product design services – mechanical, electro-mechanical and electronics disciplines. Designing for production is the aim in order to produce cost effective products. We provide from concept to manufacture, with modelmaking
facilities. Our small but successful team has completed projects including: data recorder power supplies, lighting products, connector systems, data switches, ethernet tap system, control equipment, shower equipment projects, product value engineering.
Our client list includes: Duracell Batteries, AB Electronics, Aqualisa Products, Futters (London), Lorlin Electronics, MDS Medical, Eurotherm Systems.

Contact Mr Roger Virgo
Size 1-5

GRIPGOLD

GVO, Inc

2470 Embarcadero Way, Palo Alto, California 94303, USA
Telephone 415-858 2525 Fax 415-493 8105

GVO, founded in 1966, one of the most prominent and largest US design and development firms, provides design research, industrial design, user interface design, product graphics and packaging, engineering analysis, modelmaking, prototyping, mechanisms engineering and CAD documentation. Operating internationally, GVO offers clients access to latest technologies, world market trend expertise and award-winning designs. GVO's clients include Hewlett Packard, Thompson CSF, John Deere, Kimberly Clark, McKesson, Syntex, Apple, Johnson and Johnson and Alps Electric.
'Fusion of art and engineering' and 'time-based parallel development' are trademarks of GVO's performance.

Contact Mr Robert Abler
Size 21-50
Affiliations IDSA, ASME, PE, RSA

Haley Pearson Design

99 St Albans Avenue, London W4 5JS
Telephone 081-995 9225 Fax 081-995 9225

We are a small company which aims to provide our clients with a friendly and cost-effective service. Our solutions are creative, market relevant, technically resolved and value engineered. Our expertise ranges from toys through mainstream consumer products, to complex electronic products.

Contact Mr Ian Pearson
Size 1-5

HALLRichards

94 Leonard Street, London EC2A 4RH
Telephone 071-729 1880 Fax 071-739 1862

Working throughout Europe, in America and the Middle East, HALLRichards gives a comprehensive service in products, graphics, packaging, furniture, lighting, interiors and exhibitions. Market-orientated, innovative concepts are taken through detail design, development, prototyping and testing, utilizing our CAD system and fully equipped workshops. We are experienced in sourcing sub-contractors and supervising production. Design of literature, packaging, corporate and brand identity completes the service. Clients include American Express, AGB, British Rail, Courtaulds, Exxon, National Bank of Kuwait, Next, Philips and TSB.

Contact Ms Stella Gilleberg
Size 11-20
Affiliations CSD, IEE

Hampf Industridesign AB

Stenslyckevagen, Box 32, S-4430 40 Särö, Sweden
Telephone (46) 031-937130 Fax (46) 031-936891

Hampf Industridesign are product design consultants. We provide design strategy, industrial design, human factors, mechanical engineering, product graphics, modelmaking and prototyping.
We have more than 20 years of wide experience in information technology products, using modern CAD equipment for cost effective solutions for our clients. One of the founders of Design Management Center in Sweden is a member of our board. The success we have achieved together with our clients has been proven by profitable products and recognized by many awards in Sweden, Germany, USA, Yugoslavia and Italy.

Contact Jan Kampf
Size 1-5
Affiliations CSD

J W Hand & Partners

Greendock Street, Longton, Stoke-on-Trent, Staffordshire ST3 2NZ
Telephone (0782) 311452 Fax (0782) 599513

Hand & Partners provides a specialist service in: shape design, surface pattern design, technical, presentation and visualization drawing, expert modelling, master mould making, casing in resin, rubber and plaster, die making, ram press work, production working moulds for the ceramic and allied industries. This includes   tableware, giftware, figurines, technical ceramics and architectural mouldings – for bone china, earthenware, porcelain, stoneware and high grade alumina production. We work closely with industrial ceramic manufacturers worldwide combining the highest standards of design and craftsmanship with competitive fees and reliability of service.

Contact Mr Jeffrey Hand
Size 21-50

Malcolm Hastings Design

184 Church Street, Wolverton, Milton Keynes, Buckinghamshire MK12 5JS
Telephone (0908) 321895

Malcolm Hastings Design provides a bold, fresh approach to solving design problems by successfully combining creative flair with technical ability and commercial awareness. Services include: product origination, development design, styling, product corporate identity, modelmaking/prototyping, production liaison, applied graphics. Clients range from start-up to multinational for design projects including plastic household and garden products, electronic and technical equipment, architectural and office products, and professional/DIY tools. Design studio and workshop facilities are conveniently based in Milton Keynes for easy access to clients all over the country.

Contact Mr Malcolm Hastings
Size 1-5
Affiliations CSD

Haydon Williams International Ltd

121 Mortlake High Street, Mortlake, London SW14 8SN
Telephone 081-392 1444/5/6/7 Fax 081-876 9661 Telex 936268 COLOUR G

Consultants in design, colour and style: embracing automotive industry, textiles, carpets, plastics, consumer products, white goods. Specialists in product development opposite the volume market. Involvement also in sporting goods market and luggage.
International involvements in: Japan/Australia/New Zealand/USA/Europe/UK. Expertise in market development and presentation and colour for the consumer and contract markets.

Contact Mr Haydon Williams
Size 6-10
Affiliations DBA

David Hayward Product Design

139 Leckhampton Road, Cheltenham, Gloucestershire GL53 0DQ
Telephone (0242) 570314 Fax (0242) 528947

David Hayward Product Design offers a professional design service from initial concepts through to prototypes, packaging and production. We work with manufacturers of domestic household products having specific expertise in plastics, metals and glass. We also offer design management services to organizations involved in training and development.
Clients include: Next, Armitage Shanks, A & J Gummers, Samuel Heath, Stuart Houghton, Rushbrookes, Dartington Crystal, Open University/BBC, Worshipful Company of Pewterers, International Tin Research Institute. Additionally we now manufacture and market a range of products in pewter under the name of David Hayward English Pewter.

Contact Mr David Hayward
Size 1-5
Affiliations CSD, RSA

Heights Design

Wainstalls, Halifax, Yorkshire HX2 7TJ
Telephone (0422) 240914 Fax (0422) 240589

Heights Design has built its reputation for high quality creative products on the basis of true integration of industrial and engineering design with a clear understanding of the needs of manufacturing. Original expertise in the development of specialist mechanical products has expanded to cover electronic testing and processing equipment. Heights Design Group's manufacturing section provides the support to take a project through modelmaking and prototyping to production. Clients who have benefited from integrated design include Du Pont, STC, Bulldog Tools, Provident Financial Group, Nestlé, Stanley Bostitch and BOC.

Contact Mr Neil Owen
Size 51-100
Affiliations CSD

Derek Henden & Co Ltd

Fullwoods Mews, 23a Bevenden Street, London N1 6BH
Telephone 071-251 5752 Fax 071-490 0363

A design company with considerable in-house facilities for product development, modelmaking and one-off manufacture.
We offer specialist skills in the fields of toys, small consumer durables and visual effects systems for film, television and exhibitions.

Contact Mr Derek Henden
Size 6-10
Affiliations CSD, Modmkrs Assoc

Heritage Design

204 The Chandlery, 50 Westminster Bridge Road, London SE1 7QY
Telephone 071-721 7523 Fax 071-721 7524

We design products that are aimed to be leaders in their marketplace through innovation in form, technology and use of materials. Our experience covers a wide range of projects in lighting and furniture, for contract and domestic markets. In the field of lighting, recent work has ranged from linear systems to track spotlights and domestic fittings. Furniture projects include an office system, conference tables and designs for various forms of seating. The design service is supported by full modelmaking and prototyping facilities. Clients include Concord GTE, Newman Tonks Hardware, Tecnolyte and Open Plan.

Contact Mr Paul Heritage
Size 1-5
Affiliations RCA

Hodges & Drake Design

North Mills, Frog Island, Leicester, Leicestershire LE3 5DH
Telephone (0533) 513357 Fax (0533) 514573 Telex 342200 REF L146

Hodges and Drake is a product design consultancy with an established reputation for aesthetic and technical creativity. Our client list includes international and UK companies of all sizes, and is evidence of our ability to provide cost-effective design services resulting in commercially successful products. Clients include: Legrand SA, ACCO Europe, Plessey, Barron McCann Computer Systems, Holmen Hygiene (Sweden), Calor Gas, Royal Mail. Modelmaking/prototyping facilities are in-house. Specialised interaction design experience is provided by Human Factors Solutions, who with Hodges and Drake form the North Mills Group of companies.

Contact Mr Christopher Drake
Size 1-5
Affiliations CSD

Derek Hodgson Associates

17 Willow Street, London EC2A 4QH
Telephone 071-729 2976 Fax 071-729 5110

In 1991, Derek Hodgson Associates celebrates ten years of designing successful products that improve our work, travel and leisure environments. When London Underground embarked on the redesigning of the entire signing of the underground, it commissioned the practice to develop the product system that supports its new corporate graphics. Although unique in its scale, this project typifies the complex, problem-solving design work undertaken.
Derek Hodgson Associates is ideally placed, with internationally recognized products and quality clients, to provide further excellence in product design in the UK and central Europe.

Contact Mr Derek Hodgson
Size 1-5
Affiliations CSD, RSA

Nick Holland Design Group Ltd

The Bank, 10 Mount Stuart Square, Cardiff, South Glamorgan, Wales CF1 6EE
Telephone (0222) 490293 Fax (0222) 471225

A high-quality multidisciplinary design group, internationally recognized for contemporary products, both industrial and consumer. We offer a comprehensive service in product, graphic and surface design and, as a consultancy registered with the Chartered Institute of Marketing, full marketing and market research consultancy.
Our services include comprehensive product design facilities, including new product concepts, research, design, development, modelmaking and engineering through to product launch. Clients include both large and small companies throughout the UK and overseas, and the services we offer are practical, professional and cost effective.

Contact Mr Nick Holland
Size 11-20
Affiliations CSD, DBA, RSA, IM

Hollington Associates

66 Leonard Street, London EC2A 4QX
Telephone 071-739 3501 Fax 071-739 3549

Hollington Associates has an international reputation for aesthetic, functional and technical innovation. The practice is intentionally small, but efficient through the use of CAD – each designer has a computer workstation. Clients typically are those for whom design excellence is essential, such as Herman Miller (USA), Filofax, NAD and Gordon Russell. Product engineering development can be undertaken in-house if required. Brochure available.

Contact Ms Jane Rawson
Size 1-5
Affiliations RSA

Hothouse Product Development Partners

Merton Abbey Mills, London SW19 2RD
Telephone 081-543 0034 Fax 081-543 2250

We have established the partnership to provide an efficient, advanced and innovative product development consultancy. One that is highly creative but also realistic because we understand the constraints that our clients work under.
Computers, integrated with traditional techniques throughout the business from the initial design stages right through the product engineering process, permit efficiency, speed and the application of progressive techniques.
Close teamwork, the handling of large development programmes, good communications with clients and key specialists has proved to be a major strength, and a key factor for success.

Contact Mr Richard Thom
Size 6-10
Affiliations CSD

Industrial Design Consultancy Ltd

The Portland Business Centre, Manor House Lane, Datchet, Berkshire SL3 9EG
Telephone (0753) 47610 Fax (0753) 49224 Telex 849932 IND UK G

Industrial Design Consultancy offers the manufacturing industry a complete product service. Our multidisciplinary capabilities incorporate creative design, mechanical and electronics engineering, electro-optical and microprocessor systems, design backed by fully equipped workshops producing block models, prove-outs and fabricated working prototypes manufactured in most materials. A low-volume resin injection moulding facility enhances batch manufacturing together with post-design toolmaking liaison. IDC's total flexibility to project strategy gives the consultancy a unique approach to client demands and satisfaction offering a full or in-part service tailored to client needs.

Contact Mr John Stimpson
Size 51-100

Innes Design

6 Church Road, Auchencairn, Castle Douglas, Kirkcudbrightshire, Scotland DG7 1QS
Telephone (055 664) 270 Fax (055 664) 381

Projects typically in the following categories: automotive, marine, agricultural, caravan, electrical, heating, airport service equipment, sanitation and refrigeration equipment. Design, styling, engineering and mock-ups completed in these categories for many companies including the following: Ford Motor Company, Sekura A/S, Heatrae Sadia Heating, JCB Research, Dronningborg A/S, Massey Ferguson Tractors & Industrial, ABI Caravans, Portasilo, Versatech Incorporated, Kubota, Penman Engineering, A/S Vestfrost, John Deere, RSC Equipment.

Contact Mr Ray Innes
Size 1-5

Isherwood Design Associates

10 Richmond Hill, Richmond, Surrey TW10 6QX
Telephone 081-940 0473 Fax 081-940 0473

Our strong, creative industrial and product design originates from the understanding of market needs as well as technological possibilities, materials and processes, developing innovative, functional and appropriate designs for profitable manufacture and suitable for mass production or low-volume programmes. We're a small group with a highly individual approach capable of working with concept engineers, product planning teams, research and production engineers. We've designed products for a range of industries: medical, domestic consumer, electronics, telecommunications and marine and have created exhibition systems and won international design prizes for street furniture and office furniture systems. Successful, profitable, creative design.

Contact Mr Peter Isherwood
Size 1-5
Affiliations CSD, RSA, RCA

Isis UK Ltd

Utopia Village, 7 Chalcot Road, London NW1 8LH
Telephone 071-722 6155 Fax 071-722 4921

Effective thinking.
Clear answers.
Total solutions.

Success in the making.

Contact Mr David Edgerley
Size 6-10
Affiliations CSD, RSA

Ben Johnson Design Consultancy

Mill Cottage, Barcombe Mills, Near Lewes, East Sussex BN8 5BP
Telephone (0273) 400353

The consultancy has particular experience in the design of products for public use in shopping centres, public transport and leisure. The wide range includes all kinds of furniture, street furniture, lighting, signs, canopied or glazed structures and special kinetic wind and water features.
We have comprehensive knowledge of the manufacture and use of many materials, and will carry the project through from inception to manufacture, through presentation scheme, production of working drawings, modelmaking and prototyping. Clients include many local authorities, London Regional Transport, London Underground, O&Y, Woodhouse.

Contact Mr Ben Johnson
Size 1-5
Affiliations CSD

Jones Garrard Ltd

116 Regent Road, Leicester, Leicestershire LE1 7LT
Telephone (0533) 542390 Fax (0533) 556658

Our customers require creativity and innovation to help them develop differentiated products/added-value services. The objectives of increased sales, improved profitability, greater market share and lower manufacturing costs are critical in our design approach.
We have truly specialist groups of designers and engineers working in the areas of transportation, pharmaceutical/medical products and innovative packaging.
Our careful integration of engineering and industrial design is working well for Boots, British Rail, English Glass, ICI, London Underground, 3M, Unilever and others.

Contact Mr Roger Smith
Size 21-50
Affiliations CSD, IED, RSA

JONES GARRARD

Kasabov Associates

Unit 4, 6 Erskine Road, London NW3 3AJ
Telephone 071-586 9237 Fax 071-586 9670

Kasabov Associates, a multidisciplinary practice with an international client base and wide-ranging expertise, can develop an idea, design a product, produce documentation and arrange for manufacture.
We cover industrial design, human factors, engineering details and graphics. Close links with local modelmakers and other consultants mean we can provide a fast, economical and comprehensive service.
Designs include medical diagnostic instruments for Amersham International and Serono (Switzerland), muscle stimulators for BMR (Ireland) and Ultratone, rangefinder for Sonic Tape and networked computer imaging systems for Medinet (USA).

Contact Mr George Kasabov
Size 1-5
Affiliations CSD, RIBA

Kinneir Dufort Design Ltd

7 Cumberland Grove, Bristol, Avon BS6 5LD
Telephone (0272) 554376 Fax (0272) 540915

Kinneir Dufort demonstrate their businesslike results with designs spanning: telecoms, computing, radio, TV, X-Ray, games, toys, medical, vending, white goods, gardening, kitchen, DIY, hobby, sports, yachting, education, R&D, office equipment, security, babycare, motoring, industrial equipment for:
British Telecom, British Coal, BBC, the AA, Rolls-Royce, Inmos, Reinshaw, Dow Corning, Lever Bros, Esselte, DRG, Creda.
Our highly qualified and motivated team is at your disposal, backed up with Macintosh CAD. Our prototype workshops help to prove exactly how the product will work and what it will look like.

Contact Mr Ross Kinneir
Size 6-10
Affiliations CSD, RCA

Kirkbride Payne Rick Partnership

The Studio, 31 Sancroft Road, Harrow Weald, Middlesex HA3 7NX
Telephone 081-863 7721 Fax 081-861 1917

Also at 18 Dublin Crescent, Henleaze, Bristol, BS9 4NA. Tel: 0272 623195.
We offer clients in both capital and consumer product markets a tailored design service that can produce cost-effective design solutions, based upon sound engineering and strong aesthetic awareness. By working for both large and small companies and liaising closely with our clients' design personnel, we have developed many longstanding, successful working relationships. We offer an economic service from concept through to production, including modelmaking and prototyping, together with related technical illustrations, corporate identity and promotional literature.

Contact Mr Peter Payne
Size 6-10
Affiliations CSD

Landmark Design & Consult bv

Watertorenweg 172, Rotterdam, 3063 HA, The Netherlands
Telephone 010-4118540 Fax 010-4523120

Landmark Design & Consult is one of the leading Dutch product design consultancies. Landmark designs products with innovative concepts, distinctive features and strong market potential. We provide industrial design in relation to market position and corporate identity, human factors, engineering and production technology. Landmark works in commission for a growing number of international clients. Our approach is towards close co-operation with clients, development teams and industries.
Landmark has at its disposal a team of more than ten designers, attuned to a great diversity of commissions, and substantial modelmaking facilities.

Contact Mr Theo Groothuizen
Size 11-20
Affiliations KIO, IoN, ICSID

Design & Consult

L A N D M A R K

Landmark Product Design

DESIGN COUNCIL REGISTERED

27 Hoxton Street, London N1 6NH
Telephone 071-729 7166 Fax 071-729 7489

Landmark Product Design is a consultancy of four partners, whose work is internationally renowned. We have combined our skills and experience to create a consultancy with a reputation for producing exciting and successful designs for clients throughout the world.
We aim to design products which delight the visual and tactile senses, and are easy to understand. Our creative skills, coupled with our ability to develop products quickly and efficiently through to production utilizing our CAD system, have made us attractive to both large and small corporations.
Our recent work has included the design of power tools, hair styling products, telephones, audio equipment, fizzy drinksmakers and bathroom ceramic ware.

Contact Mr Clive Grinyer
Size 6-10
Affiliations CSD, RSA

Lane Design

DESIGN COUNCIL REGISTERED

Henrietta House, 17/18 Henrietta Street, Covent Garden, London WC2 8QX
Telephone 071-836 9991 Fax 071-497 2633 Telex 265354

We are an award winning consultancy experienced in working internationally on products ranging from packaging to medical and scientific equipment and domestic consumables. We believe there is no product that cannot be improved. We can help to make your more attractive, more economical, more cost effective; we can give your product a distinction. We speak English, German, French and Italian; and work for large concerns like Grundig, Philips and Orient Watch, but also enjoy working for many smaller companies covering a wide range of products.

Contact Lars Townson
Size 6-10
Affiliations OIF

Lane Design

Langley Design Associates

DESIGN COUNCIL REGISTERED

Arthur House, Petersfield Avenue, Slough, Berkshire SL2 5DU
Telephone (0753) 31248 Fax (0753) 824076

A small, highly professional design consultancy, specializing in consumer product development through to production. Our design services include new product development, modelmaking, packaging, point-of-sale design, shop furniture design and manufacture. In ten years of designing for both multinational and small manufacturing companies we have gained a wealth of experience in materials and production methods, particularly injection moulding of plastics. Our long term relationship with many of our clients is proof of the innovative, cost-effective solutions which we have produced.

Contact Mr John Langley
Size 1-5
Affiliations RSA, CSD

Level Six Design Consultants Ltd

DESIGN COUNCIL REGISTERED

1 Wedgwood Court, Pin Green, Stevenage, Hertfordshire SG1 4QR
Telephone (0438) 740164 Fax (0438) 742606

Level Six is a multidisciplinary design consultancy that can demonstrate a wealth of expertise across many market sectors with a broad portfolio of clients at home and abroad. Flexibility is the key note, with emphasis on the pursuit of aesthetic excellence matched with proven manufacturing experience. Selecting the correct processes for materials ensures trouble-free manufacture and cost-effective products that outsell the opposition. Our specialities are product design and graphic communication offering a management service from concepts to product launch, working with multinationals producing global products for global markets.

Contact Ms Rosemary Mills
Size 6-10
Affiliations CSD

LEVEL SIX

London Associates

103 High Street, Berkhamsted, Hertfordshire HP4 2DG
Telephone (0442) 862631 Fax (0442) 874354

London Associates is a leading product design consultancy working for UK and international companies. We have the creative flair needed to provide innovative design solutions for competitive consumer markets combined with the discipline and experience necessary for designing complex capital goods for specialist applications. Our project management systems are excellent, incorporating all the facilities essential for creative product development and prototyping, including CAD and desktop publishing. Our ability to design well-coordinated competitive products is reflected by our design awards and long-term working relationships with clients.

Contact Mr Will Bentall
Size 11-20
Affiliations CSD, DBA, IED

Patrick H Lynch

16 The Centre, Weston-super-Mare, Avon BS23 1UW
Telephone (0934) 635513 Fax (0934) 641072 Telex 449897 NEWTCO

Expertise in the design and application of glassfibre reinforced plastics. Recent projects have been in the small boat industry: jet water scooters, rigid inflatables, five and six metre sportsboats. Clients: Aqua Marketing, Chinook Inflatables, Dateline Boats, Freelance Marine and Hustler Power Boats. Applications in transport have included: insulated freight containers and vehicle bodies (clients: Concargo, Lex Tillotson). Capability to take designs through from drawing board to pattern, mould making and prototypes, subject to size.
Overseas projects undertaken

Contact Mr Patrick Lynch
Size 1-5
Affiliations BIM, ISMM, IBCAM, IOEx, CIM, IIM

Lyons Ames

63 Farringdon Road, London EC1M 3JB
Telephone 071-404 0407 Fax 071-405 0365

Lyons Ames is a creative and practical consultancy combining innovative solutions with cost-effective production methods. We have designed products in the areas of: childcare, consumer electronics, DIY and industrial tools, domestic air-conditioning, information technology, kitchen equipment, luggage and lighting. Our clients include: Asahi, Astracat, Boots, Dixons NCR, NSP Group, Plasplugs, Power Adhesives, Sony, Tomy and Trane. We work closely with our clients to achieve their commercial objectives, providing a comprehensive design management service including strategic planning and product development.

Contact Mr Kerrin Lyons
Size 6-10
Affiliations CSD

MacGregor Associates

1 Beech Avenue, Sherwood Rise, Nottingham, Nottinghamshire NG7 7LJ
Telephone (0602) 691787 Fax (0602) 691788

MacGregor Associates is a multidisciplinary consultancy specifically set up to help companies develop and manufacture commercially successful products, better, faster and cheaper.
The design division offers a comprehensive new-product development service including help with design strategy, planning and management. We undertake product design and development from concept proposals through all stages to manufacturing implementation, either as a total project or strengthening your in-house team with our specialist skills.
We have successfully created products in many aresa including: electric vehicles, disabled/elderly, engineering, consumer, household and toys.

Contact Mr Chris Boyett
Size 21-50
Affiliations CSD, IMechE, IProdE, IQA, AQMC

Maddison Ltd

Holly Oak, Gay Street, West Chiltington, Pulborough, Sussex RH20 2HJ
Telephone (0798) 812877 Fax (0798) 812698

Maddison are a highly creative design team with the skills and experience to develop products from concept through to production.
Our work and client list are international and include developments for Fisons Horticulture, Aqualisa, Ferrero SA, Parker Pen, Spinlock, Van Geel, Duracell, Unipath, Hunter International, SKC Inc and Eli Lilly. Facilities include computer-aided design, modelmaking and prototype tooling. We also have an office in the Far East to assist clients with sourcing and manufacturing.

Contact Mr David Maddison
Size 6-10
Affiliations CSD, DBA

Colin Marsh Design Consultant

13 Kent Road, East Molesey, Surrey KT8 9JZ
Telephone 081-979 4177 Fax 081-979 4177

The Studio has a broad range of product designing. Our speciality is new concepts, often for existing products, and developing these with the client to full production. We have an extremely high proportion of our designs on the market, because we understand cost, product value and manufacuring techniques. Our work ranges from heavy engineering autoclaves, to housing and ergonomics for the microelectronic alarm industry.
We find that our client/designer relationship is long lasting, and two in particular, Leeds & Bradford Boiler Co and Modern Alarms, have been with us for 15 years.

Contact Mr Colin Marsh
Size 1-5

MFD Design

Bell House, 32 Bell Street, Romsey, Hampshire SO51 8GW
Telephone (0794) 516171 Fax (0794) 524460

A company of industrial designers and engineering consultants providing highly creative design that is fully integratred with the requirements of engineering design and profitable production. We provide a total product design, development and management package: alternatively we complement our client's design team as required. Facilities include: modelmaking, graphics, prototype development, ergonomics and consultancy in market research, marketing, materials and design management. Supporting services: CAD, DTP, FEA and microfilm technical references.
Product experience includes capital goods, industrial plant, machinery and equipment, mobility/healthcare, electrical/electronics, transportation, marine and architectural.

Contact Mr Chris Wesson
Size 11-20
Affiliations CSD, IMechE, IStructE, IED, RIBA

Clyde Millard Design

Lane End House, Bowling Green Lane, Buntingford, Hertfordshire SG9 9BT
Telephone (0763) 71173 Fax (0763) 71439

We provide a comprehensive product design service with creative solutions carried through into successful products, which combine essential market, engineering and production requirements. Emphasis is on providing a flexible service tailored to client needs. We have long-standing working relationships with clients ranging from small companies to large corporations, across a wide range of industries producing consumer and industrial products. Winners of British Design Award 1989 and Gute Industrieform Awards1984 and 1988.
Services include: feasibility studies, concept design, development design, detailing and model and prototype making.

Contact Mr Clyde Millard
Size 1-5
Affiliations CSD

Minale Tattersfield & Partners Ltd

The Courtyard, 37 Sheen Road, Richmond, London TW9 1AJ
Telephone 081-948 7999 Fax 081-948 2435

Established in 1964, Minale Tattersfield's international design work has received numerous awards and has been the subject of many prestigious exhibitions worldwide. Clients include: Aqualisa, Armitage Shanks, Giorgio Armani, Healthdyne, London Transport, Kansai Paint, BP Oil, Tetra Pak, Zannotta, Irish Distillers, Action GT, Johnnie Walker, Boots, Elida Gibbs, Harrods, Zoeftig, Johnson & Johnson, Milton Bradley, Merck Sharp & Dohme, Unilever, Boehringer, Wella and many more.
With design studios in London, Paris Brussels and Australia and offices in Milan, New York, Hong Kong, Osaka, Barcelona, Casablanca, Cologne and Madrid, Minale Tattersfield is able to provide a truly international design service.
Brochures available.

Minale, Tattersfield & Partners Limited

Contact Ms Liza Honey
Size over 100
Affiliations CSD, DBA, JIDA, CA, RIA, RAIA

Moggridge Associates

7/8 Jeffreys Place, Jeffreys Street, London NW1 9PP
Telephone 071-485 1170 Fax 071-482 3970

Moggridge Associates are product design consultants with offices in London, San Francisco, Hannover and Denmark. We provide industrial design, mechanical engineering, human factors, interaction design, innovation design, product planning, product graphics and packaging, modelmaking and prototyping either as specialist or an integrated service.
Operating internationally offers clients access to new technologies and worldwide market knowledge. Our company has won many design awards in Europe and USA.
Clients: Apple, Boots, Ford, Hoover, Tokyo Gas, Xerox, Yeoman Marine.

Contact Mrs Ingelise Nielsen
Size 21-50
Affiliations RDI, RSA, CSD, HFS, DBA, IOD, IMechE, IED, IDSA, VDID

David Morgan Associates

10 Broadbent Close, 20/22 Highgate High Street, London N6 5JP
Telephone 081-340 4009 Fax 081-348 6478 Telex 8951182 GECOMS G

David Morgan Associates is internationally renowned for the design and development of commercially successful products. We are world leaders in the design of luminaires and lighting systems. We are also experts in consumer, commercial and industrial product design and development. Projects are progressed from research, strategy, concept and development stages to a full production specification. We offer in-house CAD, modelmaking, prototyping, photography and thermal testing facilities. International awards include Braun, Gute Industrieform, Philips Lighting and British Design in Japan.
Clients include Acorn Computers, Boots, GEC, FKI, Tefal, Marconi, Megger, Thorn, Potterton, Panasonic, Sheaffer, Valor, Philips, Strand Lighting, Ingersol Rand.

Contact Mr David Morgan
Size 1-5
Affiliations CSD, DBA

MRDC Ltd

Parndon Mill, Harlow, Essex CM20 2HP
Telephone (0279) 641090 Fax (0279) 641085

MRDC Ltd provides a product design service from original concept, through product development to complete product specification, particularly for the plastics industry. Substantial prototyping facilities are available with special expertise for producing accurate models of plastics components and packaging, and full graphic design facilities covering corporate identity, packaging and promotional literature. The consultancy has received eight Design Council Awards and many from overseas. Design programmes have been carried out for many companies including: BICC, BP, Betts, Boots, BT, Cannon Babysafe, A C Edwards, Fisons Pharmaceuticals, Harcostar, Kimberly-Clark, Marley, Opella Mouldings, Reed Plastic Containers, Salter Housewares, Stafford-Miller.

Contact Mr John Calvert
Size 1-5
Affiliations CSD, PRI

David Muston Design Ltd

GMS Building, Rockingham Drive, Linford Wood East, Milton Keynes, Buckinghamshire MK14 6QB
Telephone (0908) 676605 Fax (0908) 691234

We specialize in creating designs that work, by which we mean attractive, innovative products that are easy on the eye of the consumer, the hand of the operator and the pocket of the manufacturer. We cover product styling, CAD, engineering design, ergonomics, modelmaking, prototyping and initial batch production.
You – the client – simply buy the parts of the service you need, or alternatively we handle the whole project; and when you're happy with it, we can also help pack it, publicise it, and even upgrade your corporate identity to match it.

Contact Mr David Muston
Size 1-5
Affiliations CSD, BPS, MKCC

Myatt Design

6 St Mark's Mews, St Mark's Road, Leamington Spa, Warwickshire CV32 6EJ
Telephone (0926) 451092 Fax (0926) 832762 Telex 311794 CHACOM G

Myatt Design offers a complete service from industrial design through styling and product engineering to graphic design for products, exhibitions and literature.
We have wide experience in transportation fields ranging from cars, trucks, tractors and vehicles for the physically handicapped to marine products and vehicle hardware.
In industrial plant and equipment fields we have designed packaging machinery, industrial and scientific laser systems, machine tools and overland ore conveyors. We also cover certain domestic and contract goods.

Contact Mr Reg Myatt
Size 1-5
Affiliations CSD, IMechE

The New Product Unit

Teeside Polytechnic, Borough Road, Middlesborough, Cleveland TS1 3BA
Telephone (0642) 231386 Fax (0642) 226822

Established in 1987, The New Product Unit is an industrial design consultancy, located within Teeside Polytechnic. We provide a product design service from original concept, through product development to complete product specification. Substantial prototyping facilities are available.
Although our portfolio includes a number of market leaders within the domestic products market, the NPU have completed numerous industrial, leisure, display and scientific products for national and international clients. We are particularly concerned with new product innovation and are currently pursuing patents on a number of totally new product concepts.

Contact Mr Tim Dear
Size 1-5

Ninaber/Peters/Krouwel

Noordeinde 2d, Leiden, 2311 CD, The Netherlands
Telephone 071 141341 Fax 071 130410

Industrial design consultancy with 25 employees. Services: industrial design, user interface design, engineering, tooling, CAD-CAM, modelling and prototyping. Knowhow and experience in all kinds of materials and production technologies: plastics, metal and woodworking, extrusion, low-cost micro-electronics, precision mechanics and advanced assembly technology.
Products: mass products and capital goods.
Recent Awards: Design Selection Award – ID Magazine NY and nine IF awards – Hanover Fair 1990. Many designs are in the collections of the Stedelük Museum, Amsterdam, Neue Sammlung, München and MOMA, New York.

Contact Ms Ria Bloemberg
Size 21-50
Affiliations KIO, ICSID

P-E International

692 Warwick Road, Solihull, West Midlands B91 3DX
Telephone 021-705 8238 Fax 021-704 1078 Telex 334755

Experienced management and technical consultancy specializing in least-cost manufacturing designing. Our work consists mainly of developing innovative designs and processes which result in reliable products being manufactured within acceptable cost, time and investment limits. Capability includes mechanical, electrical and electronic design, CAD, modelmaking and prototyping. Recent successes include agricultural products, special purpose machinery, compressors, business machines, food and drinks vending, automotive products and access equipment.
Service includes design project management, CAD.

Contact Mr Bill Cox
Size over 100
Affiliations MCA, JMC, IMechE

Packaging Innovation Ltd

1-5 Colville Mews, Lonsdale Road, London W11 2AR
Telephone 071-727 3226 Fax 071-727 4831 Telex 946240

We specialize in designing packaging, with emphasis on creating new packaging forms. Clients involve us right from the start, identifying market opportunities through innovative packaging. Our creative team combines product and graphic designers and our understanding of packaging technology means we exploit the full potential of new packaging.
In-house CAD development and prototyping facilities ensure rapid development of concepts in complete secrecy, resulting in the successful implementation of new packs. Clients include: Procter & Gamble, Nestlé, Glaxo, Conoco, Heinz, Monsanto, Total Chimie, RHM, Wellcome Foundation, Rowntrees.

Contact Ms Sheila Clark
Size 21-50
Affiliations CSD, DBA, D&AD, IoP, Mktg Soc, RSA

Pankhurst Design & Developments Ltd (PDD)

286 Munster Road, London SW6 6AP
Telephone 071-381 6155 Fax 071-381 9475

1989 and 1991 British Design Awards, together with 11 other awards gained in as many years, endorse our reputation for the design excellence of products which are innovative, stylish, commercially successful and which demonstrate a substantial return on our clients' consultancy investment.
CAD and excellent CAM equipped workshops complement our total product development service from concepts and prototypes through to full production engineering.
Clients include: British Airways, British Telecom, Dunhill, Duracell, GEC Plessey Telecommunications, Marconi, Philips, Racal, Rexel, Russel Hobbs Tower, Technophone, and Unilever.
PDD are listed as consultants under the DTI Design Initiative. Our new brochure is available on request.

Contact Mr Stephen Williams
Size 11-20
Affiliations CSD, DBA, RSA

Pape Woodward Partnership

2 Walsworth Road, Hitchin, Hertfordshire SG4 9SP
Telephone (0462) 433977 Fax (0462) 433030

The Pape Woodward Partnership specializes in the design of toys, games, and play equipment. We work on commissions for inventive design, new concept development and prototype modelmaking. The Pape Woodward Partnership is one of Europe's leading design consultancies operating exclusively in the toy industry.
Clients: Berchet, Boots, Britains Petite, Fisher Price, Hasbro Bradley Kiddicraft, Texas Instruments and Tomy.

Contact Mr John Pape
Size 6-10

Parker Stratton

6 Rossetti Studios, 72 Flood Street, London SW3 5TF
Telephone 071-376 5215 Fax 071-352 7551

A brand development and design consultancy concerned with all aspects of consumer brands including NPD, packaging, three-dimensional design and retail design for a variety of client companies.
We are a team of 12 designers and writers, supplemented as necessary by associate specialists in marketing and research.
We believe good design should be effective design and we have the success stories to prove it.
Clients include: Aquascutum, Bass, Coca-Cola Schweppes, Geemarc, Guinness, Halifax Building Society, Harvey Nichols, Holsten, Napolina, RHM, Ritz Paris, Smiths Foods, Unilever NV, Valentino.

Contact Mr Terry Stratton
Size 11-20
Affiliations CSD, IM, D&AD, DBA

John Payne Industrial Designers

Hampton Mill, Corn Mill Road, Evesham, Worcestershire WR11 6LL
Telephone (0386) 442902 Fax (0386) 765183

Experienced consultant and designers of technically orientated products – where improved marketability, costs, aesthetics as well as function are prerequisites. Industrial machines, electronic enclosures, control rooms, trailers, consumer items, plastic products, medical and photographic equipment etc. Size of product or range immaterial.
Consultancy service only available if required or selection from full industrial design service of feasibility advice, design generation, models, detail drawings, production supervision etc. Integration with client's own team if required. Prompt turnaround. Industrial lecturer. Far East experience.

Contact Mr John Payne
Size 1-5
Affiliations CSD

Pearson Design

108 Fulham Palace Road, Hammersmith, London W6 9PL
Telephone 081-741 7491 Fax 081-748 7210

Pearson Design concentrates mainly on medical, technical and scientific projects, such as the design of blood assay equipment, neutron dosemeters, light boxes, through to security and consumer products of a technical nature.
We adopt a practical approach using our in-house modelmaking, prototyping and production facilities wherever possible to complement the design process.
Clients include: Unipath (Unilever), Siemens Plessey, Mono Equipment, Procter & Gamble, Vinten Instruments.

Contact Mr Mike Pearson
Size 1-5
Affiliations CSD

Pemberton Dear

Parndon Mill, Parndon Mill Lane, Harlow, Essex CM20 2HP
Telephone (0279) 434868 Fax (0279) 434875

Pemberton-Dear is centrally placed to provide a comprehensive design and development service for the UK, Scandinavia, Europe and the USA. From totally new design concepts to the revitalisation of existing ranges Pemberton Dear has the graphic and product design experience of working with small companies and multi-nationals. Major clients include: ITT Fluid Technology, Standard Radio & Telefon, Alcatel Austria, Norwegian Telecom, Cambridge Computer, Chubb Fire, Swann-Morton, Flygt Pumps AB, Jabsco Pumps.

Contact Mr John Pemberton
Size 1-5
Affiliations CSD

PEMBERTON·DEAR
CHARTERED DESIGNERS

Pentagram Design Ltd

11 Needham Road, London W11 2RP
Telephone 071-229 3477 Fax 071-727 9932 Telex 8952000 PENTA G

Pentagram has a unique international reputation. It offers product design, graphics, architecture and interior design.
Product design is carried out by partner Kenneth Grange, probably covering the widest range of products of any consultancy in Europe. A large number of these are in continuous quantity production, many well known in the domestic scene. These include Kenwood and Bendix appliances, Kodak cameras, Wilkinson Sword razors and British Rail's InterCity 125 train.
The consultancy is widely employed in Japan for a diversity of products from bathrooms to spectacles, car seats to cookers.

Contact Mr Kenneth Grange
Size 51-100
Affiliations RDI, CSD, RA

PERA

Nottingham Road, Melton Mowbray, Leicestershire LE13 0PB
Telephone (0664) 501501 Fax (0664) 501264 Telex 34684 PERAMM G

The Product Design Group is a team of specialist industrial designers and mechanical engineers within the multidisciplined PERA consultancy. Our aim is to balance the needs of the market with cost-effective creative design input. We are able to facilitate communication between design and the manufacturing disciplines, leading to reduced design and development timescales. Computer software tools are used to generate innovative concept design solutions capable of thorough visual and mechanical analysis. Our industrial design portfolio includes consumer goods and capital plant equipment spanning both large and small companies.

Contact Mr Alvin Wiggins
Size 51-100

Pirate Design Associates

30-40 Dalling Road, Hammersmith, London W6 0JB
Telephone 081-741 0706 Fax 081-748 6683 Telex 94070294 PIRAG

Pirate Design is a new product development consultancy specializing in innovative, pragmatic product design solutions. Senior consultants have a wide range of professional experience in marketing, engineering and the applied arts.
The West London headquarters house fully integrated CAD/CAM prototyping facilities, whilst the North London site is equipped with modern CNC machine tools and injection moulding equipment for low-cost tooling development and batch moulding.
Although a British company, Pirates's main focus is currently the Far East, particularly Japan, where the company is well known and widely employed.

Contact Mr Michael Ganss
Size 21-50
Affiliations CSD, RCA, IEE, IMechE, IProdE, IM

The Plastics Development Centre

3 Carnbane Industrial Estate, Newry, County Down, Northern Ireland, BT36 6QJ
Telephone (0693) 67938 Fax (0693) 63203

The Plastic Design Centre is a product design consultancy specializing in the Rotational Moulding process. Using the latest computer aided technology we provide a design service from original concept through product development to complete product specification.
Our advice covers the following: evaluation and redesign of existing products, new product design and development, state-of-the-art computer aided design, finite elements analysis, mould selection and manufacture, product placement and product testing.

Contact Dr J Scott
Size 1-5
Affiliations IMechE, PRI

Priestman Associates

8 World's End Place, Kings Road, London SW10 0HE
Telephone 071-376 4890/4899 Fax 071-376 4837

Priestman Associates are a small energetic team of product and industrial designers, with a record of award-winning designs. We enjoy working with both large and small clients on products as diverse as cookers (for Belling), toys (Hasbro and Tri-ang), heaters (Runtal Italia), office furniture (Speyhawk), racing car fascias (General Motors) and golfball cleaners. Partners work closely with clients throughout the project: from conception through development and modelmaking to detailed production drawings and manufacture. We strive for inspired, effective design which has both wit and simplicity.

Contact Mr Nigel Goode
Size 6-10

Product First

10 Barley Mow Passage, Chiswick, London W4 4PH
Telephone 081-994 6477 Fax 081-994 1533 Telex 8811418

Product First specializes in the creation, design and development of manufactured goods. By combining the disciplines of design, design engineering and marketing, we are able to offer a total new product development and product design service in the areas of consumer durables, structural packaging and industrial products.
Our clients, some of the world's most respected and product-innovative companies, include Apple, GEC, Kango, Unilever, 3M, Ross Electronics. We also work with many small, new companies who also see design as essential to their development and growth.

Contact Mr John Boult
Size 6-10
Affiliations CSD, Mktg Soc, CBI, RCA

The Product Group

20 Brandling Park, Jesmond, Newcastle upon Tyne, Tyne & Wear NE2 4RR
Telephone 091-281 1889 Fax (06977) 3814

The Product Group (Product Development Consultants).
Formed by designers who want to produce work at the forefront of their field, where quality of thought is paramount. A small team of talented professionals. From concept generation to the shelf. A truly turnkey operation. Clients: furniture, electronics, sports, medical, FMCG – packaging, security, marine, domestic equipment, marketing, banking computers, automotive, building products. Our experience: developing well-engineered products, in a very short time and to a budget, that are innovative and, most important of all, consumer orientated.

Contact Mr Mike Corcoran
Size 1-5

Profile Design

The Dock Office Building, Trafford Road, Salford Quays, Manchester M5 2XB
Telephone 061-872 8148 Fax 061-848 7885

Profile Design is a creative and energetic design consultancy with experience in all aspects of product design and development. Through close liaison with the client at all stages of development we can maximise the product's market potential whilst minimising design costs. Creating innovatory design solutions yet at the same time giving an efficient, value-for-money service, undertaken within a guaranteed time scale. Since our establishment in 1984, we have utilized our extensive knowledge of materials and processes to produce visually attractive, cost-effective products for all types of industrial manufacturers.

Contact Mr Stephen Booth
Size 1-5

P S D Associates Ltd

The Studio Workshops, 5 Swan Street, Old Isleworth, Middlesex TW7 6RJ
Telephone 081-569 9333 Fax 081-569 9100

PSD Associates is a rapidly developing, broadly-based design practice, specializing in 3-dimensional design – product, furiniture and environmental. We are working with a growing body of international clients across a wide range of industries. Current projects include office furniture sytems, enviromental furniture, seating, airport interiors, service environments, signage systems, telecommunications equipment and domestic appliances.
PSD believes in design that provides tangible commercial results that contribute effectively to our clients' overall business performance. At the same time, we consistently produce work that meets the highest design standards.
Creative design for successful, profitable companies.

Contact Mr Paul Stead
Size 11-20
Affiliations CSD, FIRA

The Arthur Quarmby Partnership

83 Fitzwilliam Street, Huddersfield, Yorkshire HD1 5LG
Telephone (0484) 536553 Fax (0484) 514199 Telex 51458 COMHUD G

Product innovators and designers, especially for the building industry. Originally in R&D for British Rail. Responsible for: Europe's first range of interchangeable shell structures, in many locations including Antarctica; Melaphone speech transfer unit in mainline stations throughout Britain; and range of tube-boat assault craft for Rotork Marine. BP Chemicals International consultant designers for 12 years: over 60 projects into production including Europe's first inflatable furniture.
DTI/EEC grant-funded research projects: new ceramic building materials; microbiology in building. Also involved in illustration and research for British Clayware Land Drain Industry and Sports Council.

Contact Mr Kevin Drayton
Size 6-10
Affiliations RIBA, RSA

Queensberry Hunt

24 Brook Mews North, London W2 3BW
Telephone 071-724 3701 Fax 071-723 0508

We design domestic products and have a CAD facility. Our aim is good design for the mass market. We try to understand the consumers' requirements and the reality of the commercial world. We do not believe there is an unresolvable conflict between design and the market place. Many Queensberry Hunt products have achieved very high volume sales. The Queensberry Hunt partners have between them won six Design Council Awards and the German Bundes Preiz (Gute Form). A number of our products are in the permanent collection of the Victoria & Albert Museum. Brochure available.

Contact David Queensberry
Size 11-20
Affiliations CSD, DBA

Q
H

Raffo Design Associates

H3 Chester Enterprise Centre, Hoole Bridge, Chester, Cheshire CH2 3NE
Telephone (0244) 320820 Fax (0244) 320843

The aim of new product development is to drive the germ of an idea through production and into success in the market place. At Raffo Design Associates we meet this goal with exciting but commercially aware design, based on sound marketing and engineering knowledge. Since 1978 we have worked in partnership with our clients developing products ranging from computers to tractors. We provide a complete, flexible and professional service. Winners of a 1990 Design Award.

Contact Mr David Raffo
Size 6-10
Affiliations CSD, DBA

The Rainford Partnership

115 Slade Lane, Levenshulme, Manchester M19 5EF
Telephone 061-257 2866 Fax 061-257 2867 Telex 629735

The company: with offices in Toronto and Manchester we are tightly run, efficient and able to react quickly and effectively to your product design requirements. Expertise: established within the field of electronic products and enclosures, consumer goods and office furniture. A broad understanding of the related technical aspects, strong commercial awareness and practicality with design flair. Service: concepts through modelling to prototype and production documentation, working with you closely to give the best results. Clients include: international – IBM, MacDonald Dettwiler; national – Pirelli, Genrad, Ingersol Rand, Sansui, ICI Pharmaceuticals, Zero Corporation, Racal Vodafone.

Contact Mr Jonathan Warren
Size 11-20
Affiliations CSD

THE RAINFORD PARTNERSHIP

Peter Ralph Design Unit

40 High Street, Kimbolton, Huntingdon, Cambridgeshire PE18 0HA
Telephone (0480) 860448 Fax (0480) 860318

Internationally recognized industrial design consultancy, specializing in transport, machine tools and capital, commercial and light engineering products. We serve multinational and small local firms alike, providing a creative concept to production service, backed by human factors skills, engineering design, CAD and prototyping services. Our work is rooted in user need and expressed, with style, through an imaginative and cost-effective exploitation of modern materials and manufacturing methods. We aim to serve both manufacturer and user through the creation of profitable excellence.
Design Council Awards 1982-1985. Gute Industrieform Awards 1987-1989.

Contact Mr Peter Ralph
Size 1-5
Affiliations CSD

Random Ltd

326 Kensal Road, London W10 5BZ
Telephone 081-969 7702 Fax 081-960 3035

Random delivers a broad range of product design and development services to clients ranging from start-up companies to 'top 100' multinationals. Designers with manufacturing experience produce highly creative solutions optimized to client's market, technical, production and commercial requirements. Random also provides a substantial infrastructure. A computer network of (UNIX) CAD stations, linked to CNC millers, enables cost-effective design and development, documented to the highest standards set by global manufacturing. Staff qualifications include: industrial design, mechanical engineering, electronics engineering, software/systems engineering, modelmaking, toolmaking and English literature. Brochures on request, slide presentations by arrangement.

Contact Mr Gus Desbarats
Size 11-20
Affiliations CSD

Renfrew Associates

Rutland House, 33 Rutland Street, Leicester, Leicestershire LE1 1RE
Telephone (0533) 531961 Fax (0533) 539827

A design group specializing in new product development for the consumer, electronics, medical and industrial markets. Research, design development, prototype manufacture and production engineering services are complemented by an in-house batch production facility –flair comes as standard.
Clients include: Bridgeport Machines, Esso, Esselte, Flymo, Fisco, GEC, Glynwed, ICI, Linwood, Micrelec, Normond Instruments, Pumptronics, Qualcast, Scientific Generics, Triton and Torus Computers.

Contact Mr Bruce Renfrew
Size 11-20
Affiliations CSD, BIM, RSA

Ricardo — AS&A Ltd

Unit 25, The Business Centre, Avenue One, Letchworth, Hertfordshire SG6 2HB
Telephone (0462) 481056 Fax (0462) 481057 Telex 827547 CG BUS G

Ricardo — AS&A is an engineering and industrial design consultancy providing a total product development service. We look at all aspects of manufacture and customer finance, bringing both design and engineering skills to the task of increasing efficiency, lowering costs and ensuring a successful product. Great emphasis is placed on ergonomics, aesthetics, materials selection, manufacturing alternatives and every aspect of the product to achieve the right balance.

The company is part of and can draw upon the diverse engineering skills of Ricardo International. The group has a worldwide reputation in automotive engineering, aerospace and robotic systems.

Contact Mr Mark Holland
Size 11-20
Affiliations CSD

Riley & Reay

110 Blackfriars Foundry, 156 Blackfriars Road, London SE1 8EN
Telephone 071-721 7085 Fax 071-721 7109

Responsibility for quality, market suitability, profitable manufacture and the environment are probably what make Riley & Reay the most sought-after design group in Britain. Part of our creative mix is an understanding of home and international markets. We apply the exacting requirements of competitive market-led design with detailed production knowledge. Our interest and commitment ensure that our clients' design needs are managed strategically from concept through to prototype. Our experience in a diverse range of product areas has been built up from a broad range of clients which include British Rail, Formica, British Gas, Haagen-Dazs and Hoover.

Contact Mr Gavin Reay
Size 1-5

Roberts Design Associates

St Michaels Court, St Michaels Square, Ashton-Under-Lyne, Lancashire OL6 6XN
Telephone 061-343 2074 Fax 061-343 2074

We have an excellent professional reputation for working closely with client organizations from initial design concepts to preparation of final manufacturing details. Experience in liaison with marketing and engineering personnel, and in negotiating with modelmakers, toolmakers and suppliers to ensure that the product fulfils all aesthetic, user, technical, patent and cost requirements. Design expertise covers large scale textile machinery, medical equipment, garden and water hose related products, coin-operated equipment, and industrial and commercial light fittings. Sound understanding of low and high volume production methods, especially for plastics mouldings and sheet metal items.

Service includes design mangement.

Contact Mr Simon Roberts
Size 6-10

Rodd Industrial Design

Green House, Emery Down, Lyndhurst, Hampshire SO43 7DY
Telephone (0703) 282456 Fax (0703) 282020

Rodd provides a complete high quality industrial design service. Our clients span Europe and range from small sunrise businesses to multinationals like IBM. Recent work includes binoculars, advanced computer concepts, kettles, toasters, sanitary ware, hotel security systems and VT editing suites. We have a string of design awards, most recently winning the coveted D&Ad award for 'The most outstanding British product design 1990'. Rodd works closely with clients, applying creativity, practicality and flair to produce outstanding solutions to meet real needs.

Contact Mr Tim Rodd
Size 1-5
Affiliations CSD

John Ryan Design

13 Castle Green, Weybridge, Surrey KT13 9QL
Telephone (0932) 847111 Fax (0932) 857035

Design of consumer and industrial products from concept stage through design development to detailed production specification and the supply of appearance models or working prototypes, depending on client requirements. Considerable experience working for both large and small organizations in most areas of product design, especially electronic consumer products industry. In private practice since 1975 with proven record for progressive commercial design solutions, including a Design Council Award. Companies worked for include ITT Domestic Consumer Products, Bristol-Myers, Ansafone, GEC Video Systems, Racal-Decca, Drallim Telecommunications, Spong Manufacturing and Pillar Electrical.

Contact Mr John Ryan
Size 1-5
Affiliations CSD

Ryland Davis Associates

22a Wentworth Road, Harborne, Birmingham, West Midlands B17 9SG
Telephone 021-427 5096 Fax 021-766 8744

We provide a comprehensive design service from development of brief and preparation of initial designs through to detail drawings, visuals and prototypes. Our clients include Ibstock Building Products, Redland Engineering, ECC Quarries, The Family Planning Association, Rabone Chesterman & Merrythought. Work covers three main areas of design activity: products – with expertise in metals, plastics, clay, concrete and wood; graphics – primarily publicity and point-of-sale display; interiors – commercial and domestic with a 'Design and Build' service. Our technical facilities include: model/prototype workshop, and darkroom for preparation of camera-ready artwork and halftone screening.

Contact Mr Tim Davis
Size 1-5
Affiliations CSD

Howard Davidson Ryles Design Associates

Fern Cottage, Haighton Green Lane, Haighton, Preston, Lancashire PR2 5SR
Telephone (0772) 863046

The expertise of Howard Davidson Ryles Design Associates, established in 1982, covers all aspects of furniture, kitchen, bedroom, living room, office upholstery, bathroom, occasional objects and toys. Other specialist areas include fittings/component/handle design, value engineering and quality control and design management (for small furniture companies).
24-hour answering service, quotations/fees on request. Companies worked for include Bernstein, Bridgecraft, Stag and Gresham Bennett (office furniture).

Contact Mr Howard Davidson Ryles
Size 1-5
Affiliations CSD

Sadler Associates

Milnwood, 13 North Parade, Horsham, West Sussex RH12 2BT
Telephone (0403) 211622 Fax (0403) 60936

SA is a multidisciplinary consultancy resource specializing in the innovative design and integrated development of new products.
SA was established in 1973 and operates internationally in five market sectors – consumer, industrial and environmental products, transport systems and communications.
SA's unique experience in these markets is combined with creative and technical skills to enable the practice to offer a comprehensive range of product design services from research and concept innovation to prototypes and production drawings.
British Design Awards – 1984, 1987, 1989.
Clients include: Ford of Europe, Crosby Sarek, De La Rue, Rediffusion Simulation.

Contact Mr Kenneth Sadler
Size 11-20
Affiliations RCA, CSD, RSA

Salford University Business Services Ltd

DESIGN COUNCIL REGISTERED

Salford Tramways Building, PO Box 50, Frederick Road, Salford, Manchester M6 6BY
Telephone 061-736 8921 Fax 061-737 0880

Salford University Business Services is a commercial consultancy based within the University of Salford, employing the expertise of full time in-house design consultants supported by academic and industrial associates. As a university-based company, Business Services offers exceptional resources in the field of product design. The Product Design Group offers a wide range of experience in design projects embracing the fields of capital equipment, consumer durables, leisure and medical products. Clients range in size from business start-ups to multinational companies such as ICI, British Aerospace and BICC.

Contact Mr Alan Postill
Size over 100
Affiliations IMechE, IProdE, IEEE, IEE, IED, IMet, RAeS, IOA, InstP

Sams Design

103 Friern Barnet Road, London N11 3EU
Telephone 081-361 8845 Fax 081-361 4305

Sams Design has won the following awards for design:
1990 BBC Design Awards, Products. 1990 BBC Design Awards, overall winner. 1990 Forma Finlandia International Design Competition, second place in 'The World's Best Plastic Products' category. 1990 Institute of Packaging, Gold Star. 1990 Institute of Packaging, World Star. 1990 Institute of Packaging, Technical Innovation Award. 1990 Finalist in Prince of Wales Award for Innovation and Production, BBC's 'Tomorrow's World' (result 1992). 1988 British Plastics Federation Horners Award for top plastics product. 1983 Design Council Award.
CAD draughting, in-house modelmaking, component checking.

Contact Mr Bernard Sams
Size 1-5
Affiliations CSD

Satherley Design

DESIGN COUNCIL REGISTERED

The Old School, Exton Street, London SE1 8UE
Telephone 071-928 9377 Fax 071-928 5642 Telex 28604G ATT: SATHERLEY

Satherley Design makes intelligent use of design to help clients achieve their business objectives, particularly product identity, quality, innovation and added value.
In-house resources include: CAD: Anvil and Autocad software for 2 & 3D geometry, solid modelling (release 11) with IGES and DXF transfer. 5¼" and 3½" disk data format and 2400 Baud modem. Ergonomics: hardware and soft ware (detailed under Human Factors). Modelmaking: prototypes and small batch production.
We aim to find solutions which help our clients present a coherent product image, maximize sales, and capitalize on new business opportunities. Clients include BT, Esselte, ICI/Fujitsu, Hasbro Europe, Kodak, Northern Telecom, Rowenta.

Contact Ms Fran Chism
Size 21-50
Affiliations CSD, BIM, IOD, ES

Sector Design

DESIGN COUNCIL REGISTERED

Golley Slater Group, 9-11 The Hayes, Cardiff, South Glamorgan, Wales CF1 1NU
Telephone (0222) 388621 Fax (0222) 238729

Sector Product Design is a multidisciplinary design and engineering team providing expertise in product design, product engineering, CAD, modelmaking and prototyping. Additional consultancy services include marketing, corporate communications and graphic design. We have extensive experience in consumer durables, telecommunications, high technology packaging, medical technology products and FMCG products.
Please call for a copy of our brochure, or to arrange an initial meeting.

Contact Ms Jane Ellis
Size 11-20

Seymour Powell

The Chapel, Archel Road, Fulham, London W14 9QH
Telephone 071-381 6433 Fax 071-381 9081

Seymour Powell is possibly Britain's most high-profile product design group and has a worldwide reputation for highly creative work in the consumer goods and transport design sectors. The company has built its reputation on design excellence without compromising creativity to meet the needs of a diverse international client base which includes British Rail, Casio, Clairol, Curver, Hasbro, London Transport, Norton, Philips, Racal, Tefal and Yamaha. The consultancy offers complete design management from strategic planning, through to full product development including CAD, prototyping and modelmaking.

Contact Mr Graham Brett
Size 21-50
Affiliations DBA

Slany Design Team

Heilbronner Str. 50, Stuttgart-Esslingen, 7300, Germany
Telephone 010499-711-31 2079 Fax 01049-711-31 2040

Slany design is an international design team that has supported market leaders in Europe, the USA and Japan for over three decades. Currently the German 'Design Team of the Year' (Design Innovations '90), we hold over 800 national and international design awards, giving us a track record unique in Europe. We offer some of the world's most demanding clients the professionalism and flair required to create winning designs for products with a total annual turnover of over DM 8 billion.
Professional development of consumer and capital goods.

Contact Mr Slany
Size 11-20
Affiliations VDID

Smallfry

2 Southam Road, Dunchurch, Rugby, Warwickshire CV22 6NL
Telephone (0788) 812133 Fax (0788) 521581

Smallfry is an enthusiastic industrial design consultancy with an international clientèle. The Duke of Edinburgh's Designer's Prize and Design Council Award reflects the team's creative ability to innovate without disregarding the manufacturing details. The consultancy offers a sophisticated design and management service for new product development from strategic planning and feasibility through prototype to production.

Contact Mr Steven May-Russell
Size 6-10

Marcus Smith — Industrial Design

126 Milton Road, Cambridge, Cambridgeshire CB4 1LD
Telephone (0223) 60788 Fax (0223) 60788

Independent design consultancy offering a wide range of skills and services particularly suited to innovative product development. Present areas of activity include: DIY equipment, electronic/electrical goods, toys/puzzles/games. Many products currently in manufacture have included origination of ideas as well as subsequent design development. Design Council Awards 1982 and 1983. Considerable experience in high-volume injection moulded plastics. Flexible approach to solving design problems allied with attention to detail and the ability to progress them through all stages of a design schedule.

Contact Mr Marcus Smith
Size 1-5
Affiliations CSD

Roger Smith Design

Timbers, Woodhouses, Yoxall, Staffordshire DE13 8NR
Telephone (0543) 472677

A well established industrial design consultancy with a reputation for flair and innovation. These qualities, combined with knowledge and practical experience at home and internationally, are offered to benefit our clients. Our service includes expertise in conceptual design, styling, model making, prototypes and design for production.

Contact Mr Roger Smith
Size 1-5

Somerfield Design

10 Barley Mow Passage, Chiswick, London W4 4PH
Telephone 081-994 6477 Fax 081-995 0113

Product consultants – Consultants concepteurs produits – Produkt-Berater. Visual and technical innovation – the unique link.
Transport, automotive accessories, castors, handwashers, hand tools, cycle alarms, Stoplock, projectors, tipping trailers, yacht vangs, jugs, radiator keys, keyfobs, fire extinguishers, flushing syphons, urinals, watering cans, proximity lighting, planfiles, personal care . . . so far. Briefing, advance quotations, market research, brainstorming, product origination, sketches, visuals, exploded views, modelmaking, engineering, electronics, supplier sourcing, costing, tooling drawings, CAD, sample approval, assembly, production, launch.
Three professionals about 15 minutes from Heathrow. Please call in.

Contact Mr Alan Somerfield
Size 1-5
Affiliations CSD

Source Product Design

10 Barley Mow Passage, Chiswick, London W4 4PH
Telephone 081-994 6477 Fax 081-995 0113

We know the importance of appearance, quality and cost in selling a product. To suit our clients' needs, we cover all or a selection of the following stages: concept design, development, engineering detailing/drawing, model/prototype making, production coordination.
Our clients range from sole traders to corporations in Great Britain and abroad (Spanish spoken and ready to travel). Previous work on consumer and office products includes: toys, telephones, torches, intruder detectors, office furniture, heaters and promotional goods. Brochure available.

Contact Mr Fred Diaz
Size 1-5

Springboard Design Group

5 Nine Tree Hill, Bristol, Avon BS1 3SB
Telephone (0272) 244408 Fax (0272) 428943

Springboard Design is a multidisciplinary group with a wide range of experience in product/industrial design, graphic communication and interior/environmental design. In the products department our portfolio includes projects for clients ranging from top architects to contract furnishers and retailers and from multinational businesses to start-up entrepreneurs.
We base our design on a thorough knowledge of materials engineering and manufacturing techniques. With the additional back-up of prototyping, marketing and graphic communication expertise, we can offer a total design package of project development encompassing our clients' design needs.

Contact Mr Michael Hoddell
Size 6-10
Affiliations CSD, DBA

Stable Block Design Consultants Ltd

P O Box (South Bank) 25, Middlesborough, Cleveland TS6 6YT
Telephone (0642) 468140 Fax (0642) 460323

Our multilateral approach to product design is harmonized through product styling, range demarcation, engineering and client liaison, culminating in the production of a corporate physical identity.
Clients include: Adam Leisure, Berol, Flymo, GPT, Grorud Industries (Norway), Heatrae Sadia, Ideal Standard, Singer Industries Taiwan, Tunstall Telecom.

Contact Mr Ian Davis
Size 6-10

Systems Technology Consultants

PO Box 5, Toft Road, Knutsford, Cheshire WA16 9DU
Telephone (0565) 652911 Fax (0565) 650950 Telex 668371 ATT: SYTECH

Specialists in use of computers to support product design and manufacture. Independent, impartial advice and implementation assistance covering feasibility, justification, specification, evaluation and acceptance testing. Scope covers all aspects of CIM including: design (CAD), manufacturing (CAM), production management (CAPM), process planning (CAPP), production engineering (CAPE), testing (CAT), quality control (QA/QC), maintenance management (CAMM), plus integration of functional systems using common databases and open networks using MAP, TOP and MMS. Listed under Design Enterprise Scheme.
Subsidiary address, Southern Region: Wiltown Place, Wiltown, Curry Rivel, Langport, Somerset TA10 OHZ.

Contact Dr Frank Taylor
Size 6-10
Affiliations BCS, IEE, IDPM

TACP Design

South Harrington Building, Brunswick Business Park, Sefton Street, Liverpool, Merseyside L3 4BQ
Telephone 051-708 7014 Fax 051-709 1503

Multi-award-winning practice with considerable experience in all aspects of design from town planning to graphics has resulted in a design discipline of working *from* brief, objectives and client satisfaction *towards* aesthetic fitness-for-purpose and the market. Industrial design projects in both multi-production and small-run items anywhere in the UK, and we offer the enormous advantages of working north of Watford. Economic, realistic, responsible, effective.

Contact Mr Joseph Parker
Size 11-20
Affiliations CSD, RIBA, ABTT

Tedder Associates

37 Westbourne Road, West Kirby, Wirral, Merseyside L48 4DQ
Telephone 051-625 1498 Fax 051-625 2548

Twenty four years' experience of industrial design across a broad spectrum of products enables us to generate fresh, competitive and successful designs within realistic budgets. Our clients range from highly successful niche market specialists through familiar brand name manufacturers to individual innovators. We are listed as consultants under the DTI Design Initiative.

Contact Mr John Tedder
Size 1-5
Affiliations CSD

3T Ltd

7 Ladbroke Park, Millers Road, Warwick, Warwickshire CV34 5AE
Telephone (0926) 411422 Fax (0926) 492780

3T – The Art of Industry – Innovative support for commercial and manufacturing companies. 3T's objective is to ensure success in designing, developing, manufacturing and promoting products, processes and services. Whether a client requires new products, special machinery, manufacturing advice, corporate development or graphic design, 3T have the necessary skills. Embodying design management within an enthusiastic team of industrial designers, production engineers and graphic designers, 3T ensure that the best concepts are developed, achieving maximum product performance at least cost. 3T also assist to initiate and sustain successful and profitable manufacture.

Contact Mr Michael Beard
Size 11-20
Affiliations CSD, IMechE, RSA

Alan Tilbury Associates

Old Farm House, West Farm, Preston, Chippenham, Wiltshire SN15 4DX
Telephone (0249) 890870 Fax (0249) 891045

We are a design practice working with the furniture and ceramic industries. We seek quality, integrity and pleasure in our designs and work closely with our clients to achieve these aims efficiently.
We have a purpose-built workshop for prototype-making and development where we also make special one-off pieces and batches of furniture.

Contact Mr Alan Tilbury
Size 1-5

Tomporcon Ltd

55 Westmorland Road, Urmston, Manchester M31 1HL
Telephone 061-748 2230

Multidisciplinary and versatile, Tomporcon provides a design and investigation service within mechanical engineering, including proven expertise in fluid-handling systems, small heat exchangers and packaged refrigeration systems. From conceptual ideas, brainstorming sessions and product feasibility studies through to quality engineering, technical articles, product and training manuals, we can adapt our programme to meet specific requirements.

Contact Dr Tom Porter
Size 1-5
Affiliations InstR, IOB, PRI

TST Associates

98 Sydney Place, Bath, Avon BA2 6NE
Telephone (0225) 460404 Fax (0225) 444540

LOCATION: Bath-based with good road/rail links to major UK centres. CAPABILITY: wide design experience with large and small companies for both mass and low-volume production. High technical awareness. SERVICE: close co-operation with client, from formulating brief through to production; concept visuals, detail drawings, artwork, finish specification and sourcing for manufacture; excellent mock-up and pre-production prototyping; links with other services for marketing, graphics, etc. CLIENTS: American Spray, Blick, Drinkmaster, GEC, Honeywell, Initial, Medphone USA, Monsanto, Radiation Dynamics, Securitas/Group 4, ZIG/Peter Everard, Autonumis.

Contact Mr David Sibbald
Size 1-5
Affiliations CSD

Alan Tye Design RDI Ltd

Great West Plantation, Tring, Hertfordshire HP23 6DA
Telephone (044 282) 5353 Fax (044 282) 7723 Telex 826715 AERO G

Our combination of architectural qualification and Royal Designer for Industry is probably unique. Evidence of success are products sold in 80 countries and 25 Design Awards. 'This design is far ahead of its time and now 20 years after its launch is still unsurpassed' – Classics of Design Exhibition. Our specialized approach using only Senior Designers, and payment-on-results fee structure have achieved success throughout 25 years of professional practice on projects from conservatories to systems furniture, light fittings and computer hardware to kitchen utensils. Past clients include: Concord International, Herman Miller (USA), Messin (Finland), Pilkington, Polycell, Plessey.

Contact Mr Alan Tye
Size 1-5
Affiliations RDI, RIBA, CSD, RSA

Paul Usher Design

Clare Lodge, 41 Holly Bush Lane, Harpenden, Hertfordshire AL5 4AZ
Telephone (0582) 766449 Fax (0582) 765619

A broadly experienced consultancy providing a complete product design service from innovation and creative design, models and illustration to graphics, colour, artwork and production drawing. Through our close association with Wulstan Designs & Controls Ltd we are also able to offer mechanical engineering and electronics expertise.
Past work includes office machines for Alcatel Business Systems; electronic equipment for GEC, Metal Box, Lansing Bagnall and Reuters; machine tools for Wickman; hand tools for Tucker Fasteners. Winners of one Italian and two German design awards, we pride ourselves on our exciting, innovative and practical design solutions.

Contact Mr Paul Usher
Size 1-5
Affiliations CSD, InstPI

Anthony van Tulleken Associates

88 Brook Green, London W6 7BD
Telephone 071-603 7649

With 15 years as a consultancy, we are a well-qualified, experienced industrial design team, sharing two recent Design Awards with our clients. The practice is deliberately small and flexible, enabling us to maintain a close personal relationship with our clients, several of whom have been with us since the practice started. A fee proposal with quotation and detailed outline of each stage is submitted to the client for approval before design work begins. All completed work is presented in brochures, reinforced by models and artwork if required. Our clients have included world leaders in several fields, such as Solid State Logic, Neve Electronics (a Siemens Company) and Elga.

Contact Mr Anthony van Tulleken
Size 1-5
Affiliations CSD

Warwick Design Consultants Ltd

Unit 12 Waterloo Park Estate, Bidford on Avon, Warwickshire B50 4JH
Telephone (0789) 490591 Fax (0789) 490592

Winner of the DTI Small Firms Merit Award for Research and Technology (SMART) two years running, Warwick Consultants has a reputation for developing new products which in addition to styling require a high degree of technical innovation. Comprehensive studio, laboratory and workshop facilities exist to support a complete service in product and transportation design.
Industrial design skills include: mechanical engineering, electronics, software, modelmaking and prototyping.
Major clients: GEC, Electrolux, Kraft General Foods, Lucas, Pepsico, Pifco Salton Carmen.
Associate companies: Design Resource (Australia), Transport Design International.

Contact Mr Martin Pemberton
Size 11-20
Affiliations CSD, RSA

Wharmby Associates

1 Bonny Street, London NW1 9PE
Telephone 071-482 4866 Fax 071-267 7925

International award-winning practice with growing reputation for product design with flair and practicality. Design management, strategy and full product development, including packaging and graphics. Recent work includes: housewares, toys and baby products, telephones and audio equipment for Sony (Japan), OUN Corporation (Japan), LEC Incorporated (Japan), STC Telecommunications, DRG Sellotape, Esselte Dymo, Stig Ravn (Denmark), Marks & Spencer, Bluebird Toys and Thorn EMI.

Contact Mr Martin Wharmby
Size 1-5
Affiliations CSD

Wiggins Electronics

23 St George's Avenue, Grays, Essex RM17 5XB
Telephone (0375) 384841

Our small company works in the consumer product originating industry, producing designs for mass production. We listen to client's brief on market 'slot', manufacturing price and manufacturing methods. Past clients include Pullway, Mecury/Telecraft, Spillers Milling, Marten Partnership and Gant Enterprises. Working with both analogue and digital techniques, recent projects include a balanced splitter combiner design for UHF TV extension reeler, any-leg-in, any-leg-out, complete range of cost-effective high performance TV aerials, including compact 'E', and a highly successful telephone call blocking device, key controlled.

Contact Mr David Wiggins
Size 1-5

Wigram Tivendale Associates

Dolphin House, Albany Park, Camberley, Surrey GU15 2PL
Telephone (0276) 63256 Fax (0276) 24162

WTA is a team of experienced industrial designers with the skills and facilities to assist companies in creating well designed products. WTA produces concept visuals, carefully researched design proposals, styling models, and full production drawings. The Camberley studios have a well equipped drawing office and workshop with CAD and graphics workstations.
WTA works with a large number of companies on products for the domestic, communications, medical, scientific, defence and industrial markets. With two Design Awards, WTA has a good record of successful work. Contact us for a brochure.

Contact Mr Richard Wigram
Size 1-5

Elaine Williamson Design Consultancy

29 Branksome Court, Western Road, Canford Cliffs, Poole, Dorset BH13 7BD
Telephone (0202) 700142 Fax (0202) 700142

The consultancy has 25 years' experience designing in all areas, including surface pattern and shape, for the ceramic and related industries both at home and abroad, including amongst its clients bone china, earthenware and porcelain manufacturers. Many of the consultancy's clients are recognized leaders in these fields.
We aim to give a complete service from conception to finished product and work with the manufacturer closely to this end.

Contact Ms Elaine Williamson
Size 1-5
Affiliations CSD

Gordon Wilson Design

Moor Lodge, Bradfield Dale, Sheffield, Yorkshire S6 6JA
Telephone (0742) 851400 Fax (0742) 851560

We aim to create products which are successful through being innovative, good to use, simple and elegant. We have extensive experience of products in all materials together with associated graphics and exhibitions. The practice is intentionally small in the sincere belief that it produces better design; partners being involved with clients and their projects from beginning to end.
Current projects include electrical and electronic products, kitchen equipment, furniture, domestic appliances, building products, scientific equipment, street furniture, capital equipment, consumer goods, bathroom products, tools, technical literature, corporate identities and environmental projects.

Contact Mr Gordon Wilson
Size 1-5
Affiliations CSD, RCA

York Electronics Centre

University of York, York, Yorkshire YO1 5DD
Telephone (0904) 4432323 Fax (0904) 432335 Telex 57933 (YORKUL)

The University of York's design, development and prototype construction service for industry.
Instruments, sensors and controllers incorporating embedded microcomputers. EMC (Electromagnet Compatibility) design advice for testing for 1992 European Directive. Fast throughput, optical inspection systems. Enterprise Initiative feasibility studies. Intensive short courses on EMC, VSATs, Flight Control, OCCAM, Neural Computing etc.
National design commendations received for projects making substantial savings for clients.
Clients include: Ben Johnson & Co, Bonar & Flotex, Boots, BNFL, British Telecom, Courtaulds, Dale Electric, Elida Gibbs, FKI, IBM, Rowntree Mackintosh, STC.

Contact Mr Graham Long
Size 11-20
Affiliations IEE

DIRECTORY OF DESIGNERS 1991

Acoustics

Aerodynamics

Architectural Products

Automation/Robotics

Biotechnology

CAD/CAM

Chemical

Civil

Combustion

Communications

Computing/Software

Control

Drawing Office Services

Electrical

Electronics

Filtration

Fluid Mechanics

Heating Ventilation

Hydraulics

Instrument

Machine Tools

Magnetics

Marine

Mechanical/Mechanisms

Medical

Mining

Offshore

Optics Lighting

Plant

Pneumatics

Process

Production

Pumps/Valves

Quality

Refrigeration

Reliability

Safety

Stress

Structural

Testing/NDT

Thermodynamics

Transducer

Transmission

Tribology

Value Engineering

Vehicles

Vibration/Sound

Zygology

Alpha Thames Engineering Ltd

Essex House, Station Road, Upminster, Essex RM14 2SU
Telephone (04022) 29229 Fax (04022) 51273

Alpha Thames Engineering is registered with the Designer Selection Service, Design Council, the DTI Design Initiative and is a member of the Federation of Engineering Design Companies. Alpha Thames specializes in project management and engineering design of processing systems, special-purpose machinery and product development. A contracting service is also provided, offering full CAD, draughting to BS308, Parts 1, 2 and 3, and modelmaking, backed up by DIP for manuals, technical and commercial literature. The company implements and maintains a quality management system in compliance with BS5750, Part1 .

Contact Mr David Appleford
Size 6-10
Affiliations IEng, IED, REng Des, InstPI

Developing Technology
For Europe's Future

AMTRI

Hulley Road, Macclesfield, Cheshire SK10 2NE
Telephone (0625) 425421 Fax (0625) 434964 Telex 668020

AMTRI offers an unrivalled depth of technical expertise and practical experience in the successful application of quality design to production, process and manufacturing industries. Our objective is to provide clients with innovative and cost-effective solutions appropriate to their needs. The design group is able to draw upon the abilities and expertise of highly trained consultants whose proven skills are complemented by advanced research and development facilities at its base in Macclesfield. AMTRI's clients include British Airways, British Aerospace, ICI, Ilford and CEGB.

Contact Mr Neil Parkin
Size 51-100
Affiliations IMechE, IProdE

APV Baker — Special Projects Division

Westfield Road, Peterborough, Northamptonshire PE3 6TA
Telephone (0733) 262000 Fax (0733) 263570 Telex 32311

APV Baker's Special Projects Division offers clients a complete engineering service for all stages of a project, from feasibility study prototyping and custom design work, to manufacture, installation and commissioning. Special Projects expertise ranges from bulk handling and distribution of liquid and solid raw materials through process to packaging and product handling systems. With many years' experience in a wide range of industries, including food, pharmaceutical, soaps, paper conversion and defence, Special Projects can custom design, manufacture and install unit machines, full production lines or complete processing plants.

Contact Mr Geoff Midgley
Size 51-100

Associated & Marine Technology Ltd (A.MTEC)

Six Oaks House, Rudd Lane, Upper Timsbury, Romsey, Hampshire SO51 0NU
Telephone (0794) 68988 Fax (0794) 68967

A.MTEC is an independent company operating as technology, engineering, design and commercial consultants.
For all sectors of industry we specialize in the design and analysis of all types of lightweight and unique structures, product design management, stress analysis, finite element analysis and the application, engineering and design of fibre reinforced polymers (FRP) and structural plastics.
Our marine work is centred on providing engineering, management and marketing consultancy to industry, operators and owners, covering commercial and leisure vessels, with an emphasis on those vessels requiring a high input of engineering.

Contact Eur. Ing Anthony Marchant
Size 1-5
Affiliations RINA, ICE, IMechE, RAeS, CSD, IMet

M A Banham & Company

'Rhencullen', Thetford Road, Coney Weston, Bury St Edmunds, Suffolk IP31 1DN
Telephone (0359) 21217 Fax (0359) 21825

We are a multidisciplinary team specializing in all aspects of engineering, industrial and product design. We are able to design industrial machinery and consumer products, both styling and engineering. Recently, we have had projects in the packaging, distribution, electronics, and materials handling industries. Our clients include blue-chip household names as well as those aiming to be. We offer a service geared to the needs of our clients from paper designs to working prototypes to production machinery. From concept to production.

Contact Michael Banham
Size 6-10
Affiliations IED, IMechE, IOP

Anthony Best Dynamics Ltd

Holt Road, Bradford-on-Avon, Wiltshire BA15 1AJ
Telephone (02216) 7575 Fax (02216) 4912 Telex 265871 MONREF G

We provide design, consultancy and development services specializing in noise, vibration and engineering dynamics. Facility for prototype manufacture of miniature mechanisms to complete vehicles. We undertake work on vehicles, aerospace, nuclear, industrial machinery, computer and domestic equipment, building acoustics and services. Mathematical modelling of machines and processes, finite element analysis, prediction of resonant frequencies, mode shapes and stresses. In-house vibration testing facilities for components and elastomers. Portable equipment available for on-site testing and measurement of noise and vibration. Supply of special purpose computer-based equipment for noise and vibration test and analysis.

Contact Mr Anthony Best
Size 11-20
Affiliations IMechE, IOA, ANC

Birt Electronic Systems Ltd

5 Bassett Court, Newport Pagnell, Buckinghamshire MK16 0JN
Telephone (0908) 618289 Fax (0908) 613162

The company provides electronic system design services including feasibility study, design, production engineering and production to companies wishing to utilise electronic systems in their products and processes. It provides both analogue and digital design capability and has considerable experience in microprocessor, programmable logic array and surface mount technologies. The company specialises in real-time control applications and has built up considerable expertise on effective sensor and actuator interfacing for such applications. It also runs an assembly facility which can be used to provide clients with fully production-engineered solutions.

Contact Mr Leslie Birt
Size 1-5
Affiliations IERE, IEE

Bonas Griffith Ltd

12a Southwick Industrial Estate, Sunderland, Tyne & Wear SR5 3TX
Telephone 091-548 4808 Fax 091-548 0086

The company's expertise consists of design, prototype manufacture and development of engineering products, and in particular textile machinery, machines with high speed mechanisms and interfacing electronic controls with mechanisms. The company's principal clients are: Sulzer Ruti of Ruti (Switzerland), Scapa Porritt, Unaform, Hugh Mackay, General Hybrid, Thai Silk Company (Thailand), Fine Art Developments, Eltex of Sweden, Bonas Machine Company, Detexomat and Bentley Engineering.

Contact Mr John Griffith
Size 11-20
Affiliations MTech, IMechE, ATI

L N Burgess

Charlham House, Charlham Way, Down Ampney, Cirencester, Gloucestershire GL7 5RB
Telephone (0793) 750660

We design for the food industry. Plant: automatic machinery for all products. Complete factories to incorporate the following: automatic in-line production of pastry, confectionery, bread and any specialized products. Our systems are flowline and control stores, dispensing, mixing, baking, cooling, freezing to dispatch.
All designs to the highest standards of hygiene.

Contact Mr Leslie Burgess
Size 1-5

Cambridge Consultants Ltd

Science Park, Milton Road, Cambridge, Cambridgeshire CB4 4DW
Telephone (0223) 420024 Fax (0223) 423373 Telex 81481 (CCL G)

CCL designs and develops new products and processes for a wide range of industries. By integrating extensive engineering and industrial design resources under one roof, we can demonstrate an impressive track record of commercially successful products. We employ over 120 graduates covering industrial design, mechanical and production engineering, digital and analogue electronics, software and physics. In liaison with our parent, Arthur D Little, we offer a service which can span all stages of development, from product strategy and market research right through to advice on manufacture. Please telephone for a brochure.

Contact Mr Howard Biddle
Size over 100

Cambridge Engineering Design Ltd

Abington Hall, Abington, Cambridge, Cambridgeshire CB1 6AL
Telephone (0223) 891270 Fax (0223) 892622 Telex 81183 WELDEX G

CED offers a team of design engineers with skills in mechanical, electrical, electronic and software engineering. We provide a service which includes conceptual studies through to detailed design and prototype manufacture. Specialities include equipment for rugged environments such as industrial monitoring and control, optical measurement, automatic on-site pipe line welder, inspection and test equipment, demagnetizers, sea-wave turbine generator.
Clients include: Castrol, CEGB, Cementation, Ciba Corning, Dunlop, Norsk Hydro, Rolls-Royce, TI, Tiede. CED provides in-house design services for The Welding Institute and RAPRA Technology.

Contact Dr Philip Blakeley
Size 11-20
Affiliations InstP, WeldI, IMechE, IMet

Camtech Systems Ltd

The Grain Store, Heath Road, Warboys, Huntingdon, Cambridgeshire PE17 2UW
Telephone (0487) 823813 Fax (0487) 823812

Camtech Systems is a multidisciplinary engineering and design consultancy specializing in product development. Our technical expertise includes electronics, software and mechanical engineering and industrial design. We place a strong emphasis on ingratating these skills with those of marketing and production to develop commercially successful products.
We undertake all stages of the product development process from feasibility studies and concept development to detail design, manufacture of prototypes and production engineering. Product areas include laboratory instrumentation, consumer durables, high technology industrial products and instrumentation.

Contact Mr Keith Douglas
Size 6-10
Affiliations IEE, IMechE, IED

Cheshire Engineering and Design Consultant

17-19 Buxton Road, Buglawton, Congleton, Cheshire CW12 2DW
Telephone (0260) 271445 Fax (0260) 278194 Telex 665256 INTENG G

We offer a broad range of expertise, extending from the design of special-purpose machinery to the design and development of industrial and domestic products. Specialist knowledge exists with regard to manufacturing processes and techniques. The knowledge available is being used frequently to optimize the manufacturing costs of a product. Die and mouldmaking are included in our range of experience in industrial processes and the expertise available has been used widely in connection with the design of rugged plastic enclosures for industrial electronic equipment. The company has a wide range of contacts within industry and academic establishments.

Contact Mr Peter Gough
Size 6-10
Affiliations AMTRI, RAPRA, PERA, IEE, InstP, IMechE, IED

Cosine Ltd

Rhyd-y-Fantwn Bach, Monington, Cardigan, Dyfed, Wales SA43 3BL
Telephone (0239) 86696 Fax (0239) 86634

Cosine offers to manufacturers and designers technology support and creative engineering. We can create new products or assist with structure, materials, production strategy, heat, light, sound, bearings, motors, computer or electronic interfaces, detailed analysis or general technology audit, market comparisons. Recent work includes environmental impact, harmonization to standards, noise mechanisms, fully tooled products from scratch, complex trouble-shooting.
We work regularly with award-winning designers and companies of all sizes.

Contact Mr Colin Stanwell-Smith
Size 1-5

Cosine
CONCEPTS IN CONTEXT
TECHNOLOGY FOR DESIGN

John Cox Associates

8 Berwick Street, London W1V 3RG
Telephone 071-734 4587 Fax 071-734 4586

We are an independent consultancy geared to the needs of firms providing products and services for buildings and the environment. Our design experience ranges from door furniture to steel lintels and complete building systems. We have worked with all principal materials and manufacturing methods, and our service covers all facets of product development and launch: research, concept design, design development including structural and production design, organization of testing and approvals, and technical graphics. We also provide strategic marketing consultancy and carry out marketing research for our clients.

Contact Mr John Cox
Size 1-5
Affiliations CSD, RIBA

Cranfield Engineering and Technology Enterprise Ltd (CREATE Ltd)

Building 244, Cranfield Institute of Technology, Cranfield, Bedfordshire MK43 0AL
Telephone (0234) 752710 Fax (0234) 750054 Telex 825072

CREATE is a professional engineering design consultancy specializing in product design and manufacturing technology. In-house skills include mechanical, electronic, software and analytical engineering, CAD/CAE, industrial design, prototype development and project management. Where appropriate, CREATE also draws on the resources of the Cranfield Institute of Technology, to provide an unrivalled capability. CREATE's portfolio includes innovative projects ranging from consumer goods to machine systems, and clients from almost every sector of industry. A particular speciality is the combined development of both new designs and their design tools, to transfer expertise to the client.

Contact Mr Kelvin Davis
Size 11-20
Affiliations BIM, IChemE, IOD, IProdE, IMechE, IEE

Crombie Anderson

16 Comely Park, Dunfermline, Fife, Scotland KY12 7HU
Telephone (0383) 620247 Fax (0383) 620357

Crombie Anderson has a substantial in-house resource capable of undertaking total product development on a turnkey basis. We offer extensive expertise in design for manufacture, in particular the integration of modern materials and processes to ensure the lowest possible cost and highest quality of finished product. Our services embrace product enclosures, mechanisms, electro-mechanics and electronics hardware and software. We have specialist expertise in high-voltage and high-frequency work. Extensive CAD facilities are utilized on all project work. Prototype and pilot manufacture also catered for.
Our portfolio embraces heavy capital equipment, integrated business systems, consumer products and healthcare.

Contact Mr Douglas Anderson
Size 21-50
Affiliations BIM, IMC

CTS Design Ltd

Celtic House, Langland Way, Reevesland Industrial Estate, Newport, Gwent, Wales NP9 0PT
Telephone (0633) 271202 Fax (0633) 270702

Design services are provided within two main areas: microprocessor based product design and software development with systems integration using personal computers. Within this range of disciplines, we provide a total design and development package from feasibility study through to design and final production.
Microprocessor applications: design of consumer, automotive and industrial electronics using the most efficient and cost-effective components to realize the final product. Systems design: our systems engineering team has a wide range of experience in the development of PC-based equipment including: image processing, production data collection and processing, radio systems control.

Contact Mr Steve Clarke
Size 6-10
Affiliations IEE

Datum Appropriate Technology Ltd

Hellesdon Park Road, Norwich, Norfolk NR6 5DR
Telephone (0603) 414411 Fax (0603) 423906 Telex 975452 REDPACK G

Datum is engaged in the research, design and manufacture of inspection techniques, packaging machinery systems, robotic handling and feeding systems, and special purpose assembly machines. The Datum Group has an advanced CAD system enhancing its expertise in such disciplines as mechanical, electric, electronic, ultrasonic, pneumatic, PLC and computer controlled systems. Using the combined resources of a prototype workshop and the larger production facilities of its own subsidiaries, Datum can manufacture finished designs as well as provide a spectrum of services from investigative research to the commissioning of turnkey projects.

Contact Mr Oliver Chastney
Size 21-50

Designex

Woodpeckers, Ash Lane, Down Hatherley, Gloucester, Gloucestershire GL2 9PS
Telephone (0452) 730503 Fax (0452) 730913

Designex specializes in the design of extruded aluminium/UPVC and thin gauge steel products: conservatories, porches, doors/windows, shower cubicles, smoke ventilators, commercial vehicle bodies, ladders, lintels, picture frames etc, including associated components and equipment (plastic mouldings, metal pressings, mechanical pneumatic operating mechanisms). We take the product from its initial design concept through to production by preparing: detailed design layout drawings, detailed manufacturing drawings, technical specifications/literature/manuals, product testing and prototype manufacture when necessary. Current clientèle: British Alcan, Halls, Abacus, Nu-Aire, Amari Plastics, PHS, Beldray, Youngmans, Ellbee, Magnet.

Contact Mr Roger Emsley
Size 1-5

Destech (UK) Ltd

10 Sun Street, Waltham Abbey, Essex EN9 IEE
Telephone (0992) 714962 Fax (0992) 717810

Specializing in consumer, lighting and commercial goods, our fully equipped design office, model shop, development and test laboratories work from concept through to production for a number of famous companies as well as offering individual services such as design and detail draughting (manually or using CAD), laboratory testing to national and international standards (including preparation of products for export evaluation) and modelmaking in most materials. Clients from domestic appliances, lighting, catering equipment, electronic goods, small appliances and toys.

Contact Mr Peter Bennett
Size 6-10
Affiliations BSI, IMechE, IEE

J M Dickenson

229 Beverley Road, Kirkella, Hull, Humberside HU10 7AG
Telephone (0482) 655091

Marine design consultancy dealing with the design – including conversion and refitting – of all types of marine vessels up to 150 metres in length and built in steel, aluminium and glass reinforced plastic. Clients include major marine consultancies, shipowners, shipbuilders, engineering companies, design departments. Computer facilities available for ship design calculations. Unusual marine craft and stability data a speciality. Preparation of design and construction plans, specifications, overseeing of build, costing, liaising with contractors and classification societies. Vessels designed or converted include twin screw motor yachts, research vessels, fishing vessels, coasters, fast patrol craft.

Contact Mr John Dickenson
Size 1-5
Affiliations RINA

Dudley Designs & Equipment

Pensnett House, Pensnett Trading Estate, Kingswinford, Dudley, West Midlands DY6 7PP
Telephone (0384) 291139 Fax (0384) 292785 Telex 333198 (DDE)

Dudley Designs & Equipment offer a complete design consultancy, draughting and technical illustration service. Our main areas of expertise are in mechanical/hydraulic materials handling equipment and special-purpose machines. Some of the projects that we have recently completed include special-purpose trucks for narrow aisle warehouse applications, hydraulic man platforms for fire fighting, hydraulic scissor lifts, various types of conveyors, moving equipment, agricultural machinery, steel strip rolling and handling lines. Also special machines for cutting keys, thread grinding, robot welding fixtures, and endurance test rigs of various types.

Contact Mr Maurice Arnold
Size 21-50
Affiliations IMatM, IAgrE

Geoffrey Duff Associates Ltd

Kings Head House, High Street, Kirton, Boston, Lincolnshire PE20 IEG
Telephone (0205) 722221 Fax (0205) 722221

Geoffrey Duff Associates is a small practical consultancy which was established in 1971. It provides a full service from technical market research to production engineering including the manufacture of working models, prototypes, test equipment and process machinery. The company is based at Kirton in Lincolnshire and Lichfield in Staffordshire, from where it services its clients both nationally and internationally. The company is small and has low overheads. The charges are commensurately small and projects are estimated before work is started to enable the client to assess his outlay accurately. Estimates are free of charge.

Contact Mr Geoffrey Duff
Size 11-20

Philip Dunbavin Acoustics Ltd

Vincent House, 212 Manchester Road, Warrington, Cheshire WA1 3BD
Telephone (0925) 418188 Fax (0925) 417201

Philip Dunbavin Acoustics Ltd is an independent company providing expert analysis, advice and design on all aspects of noise and vibration control and audio-engineering. PDA offers a wide range of services including initial design work and problem solving of fault diagnosis in the following categories: mechanical services, environmental noise, transportation noise, architectural acoustics, vibration isolation, new product engineering, industrial noise control, electro-acoustics.

Contact Mr Philip Dunbavin
Size 6-10
Affiliations IOA, ISCE, SEE, IOSH, AES, APRS, IBS, ANC

E & L Instruments Ltd

Rackery Lane, Llay, Wrexham, Clwyd LL12 0PB
Telephone (0978) 853920 Fax (0978) 854564 Telex 61556

Electronics designers with substantial experience in products for small and medium size volume production. Analogue, digital and microprocessor hardware and software design. Full CAD facilities. Particular expertise in simulators for training purposes in electronic subjects but also using electronics to simulate non-electronic systems. Expertise also in control electronics for industry; test and measurement electronic instruments.

Contact Mr Idris Price
Size 21-50
Affiliations IEE, IEEIE

Elgood & Dye Services Ltd

3-8 Redcliffe Parade West, Bristol, Avon BS1 6SP
Telephone (0272) 293051 Fax (0272) 262451

Elgood and Dye Services provide a comprehensive in-house design and draughting service with the facilities and experienced staff of engineers, designers and draughtsmen needed to undertake specific projects, large or small. These projects can range from complete design and feasibility studies within turnkey, product design and value engineering exercises to commissioning or final account and marketing advice. Our engineering expertise and projects that we have worked on range from mechanical, electrical, electronic, special-purpose machinery, petro-chemical plant, buildings and building services (M&E), to architecture. We would be pleased to discuss any project large or small, anytime, anywhere – just call.

Contact Mr Anthony Murfitt
Size 11-20

Engineered Design

Units 10 & 11, Martor Industrial Estate, Marshfield, Chippenham, Wiltshire SN14 8JQ
Telephone (0225) 891912 Fax (0225) 891913

Engineered Design is a partnership specializing in the design of special purpose machines and automation, and the manufacturing of this equipment. We offer a design service from concept to full manufacturing drawings by CAD or manually, additionally offering manufacturing and test at our works. We have wide experience in the design of specialized production machines, including punching machines and precision multi-axis machines, and including the application of pneumatics, hydraulics, electrics, electronics, PLCs, detectors, drives etc.

Contact Mr Henry Collier
Size 1-5
Affiliations IEng IED, REngDes, IMechIE

Engineering Innovations

18 Porteous Crescent, Chandler's Ford, Eastleigh, Hampshire SO5 2DH
Telephone (0703) 269508 Fax (0703) 255225

Engineering Innovations are consulting engineers and designers with a wide range of experience in design and development of products, tools and machines. Our business is solving engineering and design problems using a theoretical approach tempered by practical experience. We use computer techniques and CAD as appropriate. Engineering Innovations can provide a complete design and prototype service from conception to production drawings. However we can assist at any stage of any project in a specialist capacity, ie assessment of mechanisms, suitable materials, structural analysis or thermal performance.

Contact Mr Martin Jones
Size 1-5
Affiliations IMechE

ENGINEERING
INNOVATIONS

Engineering Research Centre

DESIGN
COUNCIL
REGISTERED

Cambridge Road, Whetstone, Leicestershire LE8 3LH
Telephone (0533) 750750 Fax (0533) 750774 Telex 341626 GECERC G

The GEC Engineering Research Centre provides specialist technical services and consultancy in engineering design, analysis and testing to a wide range of clients in both private and public sectors. Services cover provision of basic design data, specialist analysis and testing, instrumentation, new product innovation design and development. Expertise is available in the following disciplines: acoustics and vibration, stress and structural analysis, thermodynamics and heat transfer, fluid mechanics, aerodynamics, control, fluid power, tribology, metallurgy and information services. A brochure is available on request.

Contact Dr Eddie Pink
Size over 100
Affiliations IMechE, IEE, IMet, IMC, BSI, BCS

Fleming Thermodynamics Ltd (FTD)

DESIGN
COUNCIL
REGISTERED

1 Redwood Court, Peel Park, East Kilbride, Glasgow, Scotland G74 5PF
Telephone (03552) 26600 Fax (03552) 26210

FTD provides a fully integrated engineering and industrial design and development service covering all the normal engineering disciplines, styling and full-size modelling, component machining and working prototype manufacture. Testing and development using computerised data acquisition and control is carried out in-house. FTD has in-house CAE capability, including analytical software and VersaCAD full colour 3-dimensional CAD system. Clients include Alcatel, Sumitomo, General Motors, Ford, National Standard, Austin Rover Group, EIMCO, Burmah, Renold Group, Syltone. BS5750 Part 1 quality assurance submission in preparation.

Contact Ms Elaine Catton
Size 11-20
Affiliations IMechE, RAeS, IProdE, CSD, ICAS, CIMA, FEANI

Fulmer Systems Ltd

DESIGN
COUNCIL
REGISTERED

227 Berwick Avenue, Slough, Berkshire SL1 4QT
Telephone (0753) 71356 Fax (0753) 36617 Telex 849374

Fulmer Systems is the research and development arm of Fulmer Materials Technology concerned with automation, mathematical modelling and robotics.
Fulmer is particularly active in the healthcare, aerospace and manufacturing automation sectors, and offers services in CAD, design and build of prototype machines, mathematical modelling, stress analysis and advanced robotics.

Contact Dr Patrick Finlay
Size 51-100
Affiliations IMechE, IProdE

Gill Electronic Research & Development

Solent House, Cannon Street, Lymington, Hampshire SO41 9BR
Telephone (0590) 679955 Fax (0590) 676409

Innovative electronic engineering complements industrial design expertise to create the complete product design service. Consultancy and feasibility studies, all classes of electronic, software and industrial design, project management, manufacturing facilities for prototypes and production.
Design expertise: cost-effective design for high and low volume, consumer equipment, high functionality intelligent instruments, sensing and measurement techniques, batch and real time software, moulded plastic packaging, design for harsh environments, thorough design documentation. Our project experience embraces large and small projects across a diverse range of industries, gaining international patents and UK and overseas awards.

Contact Mr Michael Gill
Size 11-20
Affiliations CSD, IEE

Grad Ltd

DESIGN
COUNCIL
REGISTERED

Aberdeen Science and Technology Park, Campus Three, Balgownie Drive, Bridge of Don, Aberdeen, Scotland AB22 8GW
Telephone (0224) 703570 Fax (0224) 704233

Robotics, automation and remote intervention. Research, design and development of equipment utilizing electronic, mechanical, software and laser/electro-optics expertise to provide multidisciplined services, ie feasibility studies, contract research and design, product development, computer aided design, prototype build and operational trials and tests.

Contact Mr Chris Peterson
Size 21-50
Affiliations NARRC

Grove Design

DESIGN
COUNCIL
REGISTERED

The Grove, Pembridge, Leominster, Hertfordshire HR6 9HP
Telephone (05447) 8901 Fax (05447) 8901

Grove Design provides a mechanical engineering design and draughting services employing CAD techniques.
Projects handled include: plastic injection moulding; agricultural and industrial handling machines; mining equipment; automotive looms; industrial heaters; general fabrication.
Please call to discuss projects of any size.
Also an office in South Wales.

Contact Mr Austin Owens
Size 1-5
Affiliations CEng, IMechE, RAeS, BIM

GVO, Inc

2470 Embarcadero Way, Palo Alto, California 94303, USA
Telephone 415-858 2525 Fax 415-493 8105

GVO, founded in 1966, one of the most prominent and largest US design and development firms, provides design research, industrial design, user interface design, product graphics and packaging, engineering analysis, modelmaking, prototyping, mechanisms engineering and CAD documentation.
Operating internationally, GVO offers clients access to latest technologies, world market trend expertise and award winning designs.
GVO's clients include Hewlett Packard, Thompson CSF, John Deere, Kimberly Clark, McKesson, Syntex, Apple, Johnson & Johnson and Alps Electric.
'Fusion of art and engineering' and 'time-based parallel development' are trademarks of GVO's performance.

Contact Mr Robert Abler
Size 21-50
Affiliations IDSA, ASME, PE, RSA

Harland Simon

Torrington Avenue, Coventry, West Midlands CV4 9XQ
Telephone (0203) 473748 Fax (0203) 474196 Telex 312355

A multidisciplinary team of professionals drawn from John Brown and Harland Simon Automation Systems, providing total solutions to a wide range of industries. Our consultants, supported by additional in-house engineering resources, have over 100 man-years of experience in simultaneous engineering covering product design, design for manufacture and assembly, production and process engineering, assembly evaluation and simulation, group technology, computer integrated manufacture (CIM) and implementation. Strategically located, we offer economic, efficient and practical services. We specialize in providing the catalyst to improve your operation whether it's to reduce product cost, enhance process safety or provide better control and management information.

Contact Mr Tony Shale
Size 6-10
Affiliations IMechE, IProdE, IED, IEE, BIM

University of Hull

Department of Engineering Design and Manufacture, Cottingham Road, Hull, Humberside HU6 7RX
Telephone (0482) 466222 Fax (0482) 466533 Telex 592592

The department has been undertaking consultancy work since its inception in 1979. All 13 members of the academic staff are active in consultancy and have expertise in the following areas: engineering design, component failure diagnosis, tribology, material selection and testing, finite element analysis, acoustics and vibration, vehicle dynamics, computer-aided design and manufacture, flexible manufacturing and assembly, automated inspection and quality control, expert systems. Equipment and other facilities exist to support these activities fully.

Contact Prof Chris Brookes
Size 11-20
Affiliations IM

Huxley Bertram Engineering

F3, Brookfield Centre, Twentypence Road, Cottenham, Cambridge, Cambridgeshire CB4 4PS
Telephone (0954) 50809 Fax (0954) 51991

Versatile design and development engineers (primarily mechanical), taking projects from concept to commissioning. Special-purpose equipment and new product design. CAD and good workshop facilities. Wide in-house expertise plus collaboration with local computer/electronics expertise and industrial design skills allow total solutions in many areas. Automatic assembly machinery; research and test equipment; miscellaneous projects involving mechanisms, pneumatics, servo-hydraulics, high pressure technology, nano-technology, motion control etc. Clients range from major oil companies to manufacturers for the disabled; electronic components to tape measures; multi-nationals to the smallest of businesses.

Contact Mr William Bertram
Size 11-20

Ingenion Design Ltd

Davey House, 31 St Neots Road, Eaton Ford, St Neots, Huntingdon, Cambridgeshire PE19 3BA
Telephone (0480) 75217 Fax (0480) 75228

Ingenion is a professional consultancy providing electronics and mechanical design and manufacturing experience to the general engineering and process control industry.
Company skills include the design of intelligent portable instruments, telecommunications and modems, temperature measurement and data logging, optical and light analysis.
Ingenion is listed as a subcontractor under the DTI Design Initiative scheme and has completed a number of projects sponsored by the scheme. We can also provide a manufacturing service from prototype to final product once the design is complete.

Contact Mr John Williams
Size 6-10
Affiliations IEE, IED, IERE

Isis UK Ltd

Utopia Village, 7 Chalcot Road, London NW1 8LH
Telephone 071-722 6155 Fax 071-722 4921

Effective thinking.
Clear answers.
Total solutions.

Success in the making.

Contact Mr David Edgerley
Size 6-10
Affiliations CSD, RSA

Jekyll Electronic Technology Ltd

Unit 3, Zephyr House, Calleva Park, Aldermaston, Berkshire RG7 4QW
Telephone (0734) 817321 Fax (0734) 814743

Jekyll is a specialist electronic product design company offering services covering initial product conception and feasibility evaluation, detailed design, production and through life support, using appropriate technology. The services are backed by in-depth skills in: design of commercial, industrial and consumer products; electronic design (digital and analogue); design of software; computer and communications engineering; instrumentation; the use of computer-aided engineering techniques; design of semi-custom integrated circuits; aesthetic and mechanical design; production engineering; manufacturing. Innovation, quality, flexibility and a fast response to client needs have ensured Jekyll's success.

Contact Mr Martin Grossman
Size 6-10
Affiliations IEE, BSI

Jones Garrard Ltd

116 Regent Road, Leicester, Leicestershire LE1 7LT
Telephone (0533) 542390 Fax (0533) 556658

Our customers require creativity and innovation to help them develop differentiated products/added-value services. The objectives of increased sales, improved profitability, greater market share and lower manufacturing costs are critical in our design approach.
We have truly specialist groups of designers and engineers working in the areas of transportation, pharmaceutical/medical products and innovative packaging.
Our careful integration of engineering and industrial design is working well for Boots, British Rail, English Glass, ICI, London Underground, 3M, Unilever and others.

Contact Mr Roger Smith
Size 21-50
Affiliations CSD, IED, RSA

Loughborough Consultants Ltd

University of Technology, Loughborough, Leicestershire LE11 3TF
Telephone (0509) 222597 Fax (0509) 231983 Telex 34319

This company markets the expertise and technical facilities of Loughborough University of Technology. We have available specialists in all engineering design areas from large departments of mechanical, civil, electrical and chemical engineering, transport technology and manufacturing engineering, and from postgraduate Institutes of Engineering Design and Polymer/Materials Technology. There are very strong design groups in automation/robotics, mechatronics, special-purpose machinery, laser technology, underwater acoustics, computer-aided electronics, electronic component technology, vacuum coating technology, biotechnology, particle technology, vibration/sound, heavy electrical engineering and structural engineering, with significant computing capability in all areas.

Contact Dr Tony Ward
Size 21-50

Anthony Manners & Associates, Consulting Mechanical Engineers

DESIGN COUNCIL REGISTERED

Coombe Willows, Noss Mayo, Plymouth, Devon PL8 1EN
Telephone (0752) 872671 Fax (0752) 665414

Design of structures using FEA techniques. Design of fire appliance vehicles to CAA or Home Office specifications and specialist vehicles. Design of hydraulic and electro-hydraulic actuating and control systems. Productionizing and component sourcing. Quality management systems to BS 5750 and BS Stockist Registration requirements. Diagnosis of engineering malfunction and failures. Clients: Merryweather & Sons, Westwood Engineering, PTG Precision Engineers, London Fire and Civil Defence, IDS Aircraft, GSC Engineering, ADAERO Precision Components and other precision engineering companies.
Subsidiary address: Little Brittons, Spring Woods, Virginia Water, Surrey GU25 4PW.

Contact Dr Tony Manners
Size 1-5
Affiliations IMechE, RINA, BIM, IQA

Marvell Consultants Ltd

DESIGN COUNCIL REGISTERED

Draycott Hall, Derwent Street, Draycott, Derbyshire DE7 3NF
Telephone (03317) 5666 Fax (03317) 5547

MCL was established in 1985 to provide a custom software and hardware design service. Every engineer has 10+ years' hands-on experience developing 'specials': one-offs, prototypes, part or complete products. Expertise includes: image processing, video, embedded controllers, specialist interfaces, DSP systems, medical and pharmaceutical process/physiological monitoring, analysis and custom databases.
Designs include: single chip to 32 bit multiprocessors and ASICs, low to high level languages. We not only give practical advice, but can then follow this through by developing the required software and/or hardware.

Contact Ms Beverly Poole
Size 6-10
Affiliations IEE, BCS

MATRIX Systems

23 Grove Road, Leighton Buzzard, Bedfordshire LU7 8SF
Telephone (0525) 851030

MATRIX Systems is a Stage 1 winner of a DTI Small Firms Award for Research and Technology to develop an incubator for use in medical laboratories. The work involves innovation in heat exchanger and control system design leading to a fully developed product.
MATRIX specialized skills are in the use of microelectronics, software and sensors. Strict design rules for coding, configuration and testing are applied to software development to ensure a quality product.
MATRIX also recognizes the importance of Innovation Management and can help organize your internal systems.

Contact Mr Peter Cox-Smith
Size 1-5
Affiliations IED, CGI

Alan McCombie

DESIGN COUNCIL REGISTERED

1 Oak Hill Way, London NW3 7LR
Telephone 071-435 7239

A one-man company working in collaboration with a selection of associated companies which provide multidisciplinary support as required. Consequent low overheads allow modest charge rates. Specialist in the design and development of novel manipulative or process machinery, especially when such machines are to be produced in quantity against competition. Also active in the conceptual design and redesign of simple mass products together with the machinery for their manufacture. Established 12 years. Clients include Alfa-Laval, Auto Wrappers, Marconi, Molins, Rotaprint, Trebor-Sharp, VG Scientific, Wiggins Teape.

Contact Mr Alan McCombie
Size 1-5
Affiliations IMechE

MEJ Electronics Ltd

Alan Turing Road, Surrey Research Park, Guildford, Surrey GU2 5YF
Telephone (0483) 505895 Fax (0483) 61555

Independent professional electronics system design consultancy established for over 14 years, involved in the development of new electronic products for client companies. Areas of expertise include: complete product design capability, often incorporating customized integrated circuits developed using in-house vendor-independent CAE and simulation facilities; low-level device-driving software; operating systems; CAE software tools; diagnostic test units; feasibility and design studies; project scheduling and management; 'project rescue' services. Clients range from consumer electronics companies – household names manufacturing millions of designed units – through to semiconductor manufacturers and university research departments.

Contact Mr Michael Scase
Size 6-10
Affiliations IEEE, IOD, IEE

Memotrace Controls Ltd

13 The Avenue, Spinney Hill, Northampton, Northamptonshire NN3 1BA
Telephone (0604) 642808 Fax (0604) 29858 Telex 311165 CHACOM G

An engineering design and build service with micro-electronics, assisted by Autocad and Micro-Cadcam, Plus software. Factory layout; electrical diagrams: engineering drawings. Mould tools for rubber and plastic. Designs for machine tools and automatic assembly on shaving systems and electronic components. Programming for Allen Bradley 8600 CNC and SLC 500 PLC etc. PCB design and software for Texas Instruments microprocessors such as TMS 9990/9995 for special applications. Clients include Aston Martin Lagonda, British Timken and overseas contacts in China and Turkey.

Contact Mr Raymond Howard
Size 1-5
Affiliations IMechE, IProdE

MFD Design

Bell House, 32 Bell Street, Romsey, Hampshire SO51 8GW
Telephone (0794) 516171 Fax (0794) 524460

We are a multidisciplinary group providing expertise in the areas of mechanical and structural engineering, stress analysis, pneumatics and hydraulics design, materials technology and industrial design. Services include consultancy, feasibility studies, design, development and project management, through design to fully working prototype, but our flexible resources are always tailored to the client's needs. Projects include special-purpose machines and test equipment, handling equipment, telecommunication structures and electronics packaging. Industries served range from marine and sub-sea to aerospace and from food machinery to defence.
See also Product Design entry.

Contact Mr Chris Wesson
Size 11-20
Affiliations CSD, IMechE, IStructE, IED, RIBA

Microsys Consultants Ltd

Milburn Hill Road, University of Warwick Science Park, Coventry, Warwickshire CV4 7HS
Telephone (0203) 414241 Fax (0203) 410428

Microsys Consultants is a privately owned and funded British company specializing in the application of microelectronics to industry. The company was formed in 1989 through management buyout from a subsidiary of GEC Plessey Telecommunications Ltd. We are professional problem solvers, able to identify technological solutions, develop them and introduce them to the commercial world.
The services available are consultancy, design and development and product management. A fundamental element of the Microsys philosophy is quality, and all work is undertaken in accordance with BS5750 Part 1.

Contact Mr David Sykes
Size 11-20
Affiliations IEE

Micro Tech Ltd

Plumb Centre, Hawks Road, Gateshead, Tyne & Wear NE8 3BL
Telephone 091-477 4755/ 5623 Fax 091-477 6678 Telex 53440 CHAMCO G

The company specializes in the design of power electronics and microprocessor control systems. The company has extensive modelling and control simulation experience in servo system and motor drive designs. Together with Nada Electronics, Micro Tech forms The Nada Consulting Group and offers a full service in the field of power management.

Contact Mr Tony Lakin
Size 11-20
Affiliations IMC, IEEE

Moggridge Associates

7/8 Jeffreys Place, Jeffreys Street, London NW1 9PP
Telephone 071-485 1170 Fax 071-482 3970

Complementary to the other skills in our design consultancy, our engineers are experts at designing and developing products through to production. Clients include multinationals, Ford and ICI; industry sector leaders, Gilbarco and Dancall; new companies, Yeoman Marine (Qubit) and Anotec Separations (Alcan); and inventors, Technomed and Willy Johnson.
We can research, design, develop, build and test prototypes, source vendors, prepare production documentation and manage development programmes from conception to production. We have particular expertise in the application of plastics and the packaging of electronics.

Contact Mrs Ingelise Nielsen
Size 21-50
Affiliations RDI, RSA, CSD, HFS, DBA, IOD, IMechE, IED, IDSA, VDID

MPC Data Ltd

Pentagon House, 52 Castle Street, Trowbridge, Wiltshire BA14 8AU
Telephone (0225) 760231 Fax (0225) 777225

MPC Data undertake a wide range of bespoke software development projects, particularly: low level systems software, such as device drivers; networking and communications software, with an in-depth knowledge of many network operating systems and communications protocols; microcontroller firmware for dedicated equipment control (many years' experience of microcontroller system design and development); software auditing and QA evaluations.
We will take complete project responsibility from concept through to completion, or for any part of the design and development process. Our customers are happy to testify to the quality of service which we provide.

Contact Mr Alan Rowe
Size 6-10

Myatt Design

6 St Mark's Mews, St Mark's Road, Leamington Spa, Warwickshire CV32 6EJ
Telephone (0926) 451092 Fax (0926) 832762 Telex 311794 CHACOM G

Myatt Design offers a complete service from industrial design through styling and product engineering to graphic design for products, exhibitions and literature. We have wide experience in transportation fields ranging from cars, trucks, tractors and vehicles for the physically handicapped to marine products and vehicle hardware. In industrial plant and equipment fields we have designed packaging machinery, industrial and scientific laser systems, machine tools and overland ore conveyors.
We also cover certain domestic and contract goods.

Contact Mr Reg Myatt
Size 1-5
Affiliations CSD, IMechE

Michael Neale & Associates Ltd

43 Downing Street, Farnham, Surrey GU9 7PH
Telephone (0252) 722255/723295 Fax (0252) 737106 Telex 858623

Michael Neale & Associates are expert at solving problems with machinery and in providing design advice on new or complex products. They have particular skills in tribology and in mechanical engineering in general. They have provided a completely independent consulting service for over 25 years and have worked on all kinds of products and equipment, from small mass-produced consumer goods to very large items of process plant, mining and marine equipment and aircraft. Our philosophy is to work with your engineers and leave them able to solve the problem themselves next time.

Contact Mr Sandy Polak
Size 6-10
Affiliations IMechE

NNC Ltd

Booths Hall, Chelford Road, Knutsford, Cheshire WA16 8QZ
Telephone (0565) 633800 Fax (0565) 633659 Telex 666000

NNC offers a full range of engineering design and build services backed up with its own comprehensive R&D facilities at Risley, Warrington. NNC's range covers systems engineering for complete processes in the chemical, nuclear and micro-electronic industries, wind-tunnels, laboratory design, power generation, waste treatment systems, environmental control, risk analysis and safety assessments. Extensive CAD facilities and a CONVEX C120 mini supercomputer support a full engineering capability in all disciplines, thermodynamics, tribology, chemistry, corrosion, equipment qualification, seismic analysis, acoustics and vibration and fluid dynamics are some of the specialist capabilities available.

Contact Mr Frank Woodhead
Size over 100
Affiliations IMechE, IEE, INucE

Northern Electronic Technology Ltd

Unit K5 BEC, Eldon Street, South Shields, Tyne & Wear NE33 5JE
Telephone 091-455 4300 Fax 091-455 1847

NET provides a complete design and development facility for electronics and computer-related products and equipment. The company's strength is in producing high quality, technically advanced products to commercial timescales. This is achieved by professional engineers who lead multidisciplinary teams including mechanical and industrial designers to complement their expertise in software and electronic engineering.

Contact Mr Ewan Croucher
Size 1-5
Affiliations CEng, IEE

Pankhurst Design & Developments Ltd (PDD)

286 Munster Road, London SW6 6AP
Telephone 071-381 6155 Fax 071-381 9475

1989 and 1991 British Design Awards, together with 11 other awards gained in as many years, endorse our reputation for innovative, commercially successful engineering solutions which demonstrate a substantial return on our clients' investment. Excellent CAM equipped workshops used extensively alongside CAD offer a total development service including research, materials selection, design, prototyping, testing, production engineering and assistance through manufacture. Clients include: British Airways, British Telecom, Dexion Electronics, Duracell, GPT, Lotus Engineering, Marconi, Philips, Racal, Technophone, Unilever, West Instruments. PDD are listed as consultants under the DTI Manufacturing Initiative and our new brochure is available on request.

Contact Mr Stephen Williams
Size 11-20
Affiliations CSD, DBA, RSA

Pathway Systems

Suite 2, Brooklands, 46 Kneesworth Street, Royston, Hertfordshire SG8 5AQ
Telephone (0763) 248352 Fax (0763) 241350

We offer a range of technical services relating to the design and development of electronic and microcomputer-based equipment for use in industrial and scientific applications. In addition to hardware design development facilities, we offer a full range of software development facilities supporting Assembler, Forth and C for a wide range of microprocessor and PC computers. Our particular areas of expertise include: radio-based computer communication, image capture systems, ruggedized computer equipment, industrial weighing systems, high resolution graphics display systems, factory data collection and reporting, and custom machine control systems.

Contact Mr Tom Hogan
Size 1-5
Affiliations IEE, IERE

Peamore Electronics Ltd

Unit 17, Martlets Trading Estate, Martlets Way, Goring-by-Sea, Worthing, Sussex BN12 4HF
Telephone (0903) 506781 Fax (0903) 506785

Peamore helped win a Queen's Award for Technology in 1989. Edwards High Vacuum International's award winning Drystar System includes a microprocessor controller and electrical sub-system designed by Peamore Electronics. Profile: inventive, rapid-response electronics company offering crisp, clever and cost-effective design of analogue and digital electronics, digital signal processing, microprocessors and software. Proven expertise: PID control, Autotune, ASIC design, consumer electronics, ultrasonics, motor control, PLCs, servos, avionics, EMI/RFI and electro-mechanical systems.
Clients include: EHVI, Rieter-Scragg, British Steel, Vosper Thornycroft, Beechams Pharmaceuticals.

Contact Mr Tony Ware
Size 6-10

PERA

Nottingham Road, Melton Mowbray, Leicestershire LE13 0PB
Telephone (0664) 501501 Fax (0664) 501264 Telex 34684 PERAMM G

PERA's design service, approved to defence standard AQAP1, combines the skills of engineering design, industrial design, value engineering, special-purpose equipment design, materials engineering and man/machine interfacing. The design service is backed by wide-ranging facilities including materials and environmental testing, manufacturing, component/product testing, and prototype development. PERA's expertise in production technology, electronics, quality assurance and computer applications can also be fed into the design service when required. PERA's broad client base covers most manufacturing sectors including defence, medical, automotive, food and drink processing, electronics and transport.
See also PERA's entry in the Product Design Section.

Contact Mr Alvin Wiggins
Size 51-100

Pinkney Byatt Associates

154 St Neots Road, Eaton Ford, St Neots, Huntingdon, Cambridgeshire PE19 3AD
Telephone (0480) 74344 Fax (0480) 76300

Pinkney Byatt apply practical, creative and innovative expertise from concept industrial design through to in-house product assembly. Our skills encompass design, development, production engineering, modelmaking, prototyping and manufacture. Projects range from volume consumer goods to special purpose machines and process development.

Contact Mr Dave Byatt
Size 11-20
Affiliations IED

Pirate Design Associates

30-40 Dalling Road, Hammersmith, London W6 0JB
Telephone 081-741 0706 Fax 081-748 6683 Telex 94070294 PIRAG

Pirate Design is a new product development consultancy specializing in innovative, pragmatic product design solutions. Senior consultants have a wide range of professional experience in marketing, engineering and the applied arts.
The West London headquarters house fully integrated CAD/CAM prototyping facilities, whilst the North London site is equipped with modern CNC machine tools and injection moulding equipment for low-cost tooling development and batch moulding.
Although a British company, Pirate's main focus is currently the Far East, particularly Japan, where the company is well known and widely employed.

Contact Mr Michael Ganss
Size 21-50
Affiliations CSD, RCA, IEE, IMechE, IProdE, IM

Rakar Ltd

98 Commercial Road, London E1 1NU
Telephone 071-480 7341 Fax 071-481 2197

Rakar is a fast growing consultancy, keen to provide a cost effective electronic design service. We supply specialized equipment to a well established client base in the UK and USA, and have expertise in the following areas: microprocessor control and instrumentation; film, TV and video systems; domestic and sports alarm systems and consumer electronics. Well equipped sub-assemblies to total product development.
We encourage working to tight budgets and timescales to bring projects forward with close customer liaison on costs and specifications.

Contact Mr William Windham
Size 1-5
Affiliations IEE, BKST

Random Ltd

326 Kensal Road, London W10 5BZ
Telephone 081-969 7702 Fax 081-960 3035

Random delivers a broad range of product design and development services to clients ranging from start-up companies to 'top 100' multinationals. Designers with manufacturing experience produce highly creative solutions optimized to client's market, technical, production and commercial requirements. Random also provides a substantial infrastructure. A computer network of (UNIX) CAD stations, linked to CNC millers, enables cost-effective design and development, documented to the highest standards set by Global Manufacturing. Staff qualifications include: industrial design, mechanical engineering, electronics engineering, software/systems engineering, modelmaking, toolmaking and English literature.
Brochures on request, slide presentations by arrangement.

Contact Mr Gus Desbavats
Size 11-20
Affiliations CSD

Reliability Consultants Ltd

Fearnside, Little Park Farm Road, Fareham, Hampshire PO15 5SU
Telephone (0489) 885252 Fax (0489) 885038

RCL provides management and technical consultancy, information systems and training in relation to quality, reliability and safety aspects of product design and development. We offer advice on the product itself, the processes of design, manufacture, test and product support. Our principal services cover both hardware and software, helping our clients to achieve better products in a shorter timescale with the ultimate benefit of improved profitability.

Contact Mr Arthur Roberts
Size 51-100
Affiliations IQA, BIM, BCS, SRS, IEE, IMechE, RAeS, SEE

John Reynolds and Associates

39 Greenfield Drive, Great Tey, Colchester, Essex CO6 IAA
Telephone (0206) 211642 Fax (0206) 210314 Telex 9312133487 JR G

Specialists in design of products for use in developing countries, particularly handpumps/other equipment for rural water supply. Extensive experience in development and testing of Afridev Village Level Operation and Maintenance (VLOM) handpump, but also of wide range of consumer products manufactured in developed world. Able to advise on design, research and development and manufacture.
Experience of working with developing country governments, manufacturers, national and international aid agencies, non-governmental organizations in UK, Europe, USA, Kenya, Malawi, Sudan, Ethiopia, India, Bangladesh, China. Able/willing to undertake overseas consultancies at short notice.

Contact Mr John Reynolds
Size 1-5
Affiliations IMechE

Ricardo — AS&A Ltd

Unit 25, The Business Centre, Avenue One, Letchworth, Hertfordshire SG6 2HB
Telephone (0462) 481056 Fax (0462) 481057 Telex 827547 CG BUS G

Ricardo — AS&A is an engineering and industrial design consultancy providing a total product development service. We look at all aspects of manufacture and customer finance, bringing both design and engineering skills to the task of increasing efficiency, lowering costs and ensuring a successful product. Great emphasis is placed on ergonomics, aesthetics, materials selection, manufacturing alternatives and every aspect of the product to achieve the right balance.
The company is part of and can draw upon the diverse skills of Ricardo International. The group has a worldwide reputation in automotive engineering, aerospace and robotic systems.

Contact Mr Mark Holland
Size 11-20
Affiliations CSD

Robelen Products Ltd

Unit 35, First Avenue, Westfield Industrial Estate, Midsomer Norton, Bath, Avon BA3 4BS
Telephone (0761) 414884 Fax (0761) 414884

Small but well-endowed with design and machine shop facilities, together with the experience that has earned us the reputation for innovation, precision and quality in the engineering design field. Intimate knowledge of the engineering and plastics moulding industries has resulted in a range of products designed and managed by us for a clientèle of international stature down to one-man operations. A design package embracing product, tooling, jigs and fixtures, with product management up to pre-production, is commonplace to us.

Contact Mr Ron Stevenson
Size 1-5

Rubber Consultants

Brickendonbury, Hertford, Hertfordshire SG13 8NL
Telephone (0992) 554657 Fax (0992) 554837 Telex 817449 MRRDBL G

Rubber Consultants advises on design, development and production of rubber articles ranging from latex goods to off-shore engineering components. Backed by one of the world's largest rubber research organizations, recently given the PRI's Prince Philip Award for the successful development and implementation of rubber bearings for earthquake protection of buildings, Rubber Consultants offers a full design service for mechanical and civil engineering applications. Extensive facilities are available for physical testing of components and materials, analytical testing and industrial trouble shooting. Information retrieval, bibliographic and market research facilities are also available.

Contact Dr Brian Tidd
Size over 100
Affiliations PRI, RSC, IOP

Sadler Associates

Milnwood, 13 North Parade, Horsham, West Sussex RH12 2BT
Telephone (0403) 211622 Fax (0403) 60936

SA is a multidisciplinary consultancy resource specializing in the innovative design and integrated development of new products. SA was established in 1973 and operates internationally in five market sectors – consumer, industrial and environmental products, transport systems and communications. SA's unique experience in these markets is combined with creative and technical skills to enable the practice to offer a comprehensive range of product design services from research and concept innovation to prototypes and production drawings. British Design Awards – 1984, 1987, 1989.
Clients include: Ford of Europe, Crosby Sarek, De La Rue, Rediffusion Simulation.

Contact Mr Kenneth Sadler
Size 11-20
Affiliations RCA, CSD, RSA

Salford University Business Services Ltd

Salford Tramways Building, PO Box 50, Frederick Road, Salford, Manchester M6 6BY
Telephone 061-736 8921 Fax 061-737 0880

Salford University Business Services Ltd is a commercial consultancy based within the University of Salford, employing the expertise of full-time in-house design consultants supported by academic and industrial associates. As a university-based company, Business Services offers exceptional resources in the field of engineering design. The Product Design Group offers a wide range of experience in design projects embracing the fields of capital equipment, consumer durables, leisure and medical products. Clients range in size from business start-ups to multinational companies such as ICI, British Aerospace and BICC.

Contact Mr Alan Postill
Size over 100
Affiliations IMechE, IProdE, IEEE, IEE, IED, IMet, RAeS, IOA, InstP

Sheffield University

Commercial & Industrial Development Bureau, 2 Palmerston Road, Sheffield, Yorkshire S10 2TE
Telephone (0742) 768555 Fax (0742) 725004 Telex 547216 UGSHEF G

Facilities and staff are available for advice and contract work covering most aspects of the design, manufacture, control, improvement and operation of all classes of machinery, vehicles, plant, structures, processes and also electronic components. Advice is available where complex components and systems require finite element analysis. Measurements can be made on operating machinery and specialist advice is additionally available on heat transfer, fluid creep mechanics, pumps, hydraulics, fluidic control devices, fatigue, fracture, gearing, refrigeration, air-conditioning, plastics and composite materials, fasteners, lubrication wear and friction, bearings, noise and acoustics, concrete.

Contact Dr Robert Handscombe
Size over 100

Siemens Plessey Assessment Services Ltd

Segensworth Road, Titchfield, Fareham, Hampshire PO15 5RH
Telephone (0329) 844440 Fax (0329) 853234 Telex 869489

Plessey Assessment Services (PAS) is the foremost independent environmental and EMC test house in the UK and one of the most advanced in Europe, offering climatic, pyrotechnic, vibration, shock, reliability, EMC/Tempest and dust testing and dynamic structural modelling. With the backing of over 30 years' experience PAS offers a consultancy service dedicated to providing specialist advice and support on specifications and test programmes, and the design and management of major test facilities. PAS provides a service to both the military and commercial markets. NAMAS accredited; BS9000, BSCECC, IECQ and CAA approvals.

Contact Mr Chris Brett
Size over 100

Sira Ltd

South Hill, Chislehurst, Kent BR7 5EH
Telephone 081-467 2636 Fax 081-467 6515 Telex 896649

Sira is an independent applied research, design and development organization specializing in instrumentation and control equipment for scientific and industrial use, and for military and aerospace applications. Clients range from small companies to major multinationals. Facilities include design, manufacture and testing of optics, electronics, software and mechanics and prototyping of complete equipment and systems. Computer-aided design of optics is a particular specialization.
Our subsidiary company, Sira Safety Services, specializes in safety of electrical equipment in potentially explosive atmospheres and also in medical applications. The address is Saighton Lane, Saighton, Chester CH3 6EH.

Contact Mr John Hother
Size over 100
Affiliations AIRTO

Sound Research Laboratories Ltd

Holbrook House, Little Waldingfield, Sudbury, Suffolk CO10 0TH
Telephone (0787) 247595 Fax (0787) 248420

SRL is an independent company specializing in all areas of acoustics, both at design and trouble-shooting stages. The company has a large and experienced staff of qualified engineers. SRL's consultancy activity is complemented by a test laboratory. The company is well known for its training courses and publications. As well as SRL's head office at Colchester, they have subsidiary addresses at Sunbury-on-Thames, Manchester and East Kilbride.

Contact Mr Richard Bines
Size 21-50
Affiliations ANC

Staffordshire Polytechnic

College Road, Stoke-on-Trent, Staffordshire ST4 2DE
Telephone (0782) 744531 Fax (0782) 744035

Design Research Centre/Department of Design.
Research, development, training and consultancy in all areas of design including audiovisual, ceramics, glass, graphics, photography, product design and surface pattern.
Design management consultancy and computer-aided design.

Contact Mr David Weightman
Size 21-50

Nicholas Syred, Consultant

4 The Woodlands, Lisvane, Cardiff, South Glamorgan, Wales CF4 5SW
Telephone (0222) 758816

Expertise includes fluid flows, thermodynamics, fluidics, combustion problems, general process engineering, particle movement/flows in gases and liquids. Specific software can be produced. Projects include gasfired brazing torches, solenoid valve design, wood-burning stoves, cremators, combustion of low calorific valve gases, swarf-removing systems for machine tools, gas driven pumps, diffusers for a range of applications, flow-controllers, cyclone-separators, classifiers, fluidic, swirl-burners, water models/flows of unusual fluids (ie steel etc), heat exchangers.

Contact Prof Nicholas Syred
Size 1-5
Affiliations IMechE, InstE

T-Cubed Consultants Ltd

Orion House, 49 High Street, Addlestone, Surrey KT15 1TU
Telephone (0932) 850070 Fax (0932) 858761

T-Cubed Consultants provide consultant and contract electronic hardware and software design services. We are able to offer fixed price contracts for the design, manufacture and test of electronic based products. Our chartered engineers have many years experience in project development for both MOD and commercial clients, and are familiar with various design and quality requirements. T-Cubed have built up a faultless track record for the design and delivery of various pieces of electronic equipment, within budget and on time.

Contact Mr A Flowerday
Size 6-10
Affiliations IEE

TDC Ltd

The Old Maltings, 135 Ditton Walk, Cambridge, Cambridgeshire CB5 8QD
Telephone (0223) 244133 Fax (0223) 248947

Competitively priced electronics and computing – a complete design, development and consultancy service is available from Cambridge based TDC. We developed from datacomms market leaders Tandata, and we offer a wealth of hardware and software experience gained from successful designs for many clients, including: AB Electronics, British Telecom, Hogg Robinson, ITT, Rockwell.
All aspects of the product cycle are available, from feasibility advice and low production-cost designs, to a complete product service including literature and manuals. Design experience covers: user interfaces, network and system software, data-broadcast equipment, modems, terminals.

Contact Mr Ian Redhead
Size 21-50
Affiliations IEE. BCS

Team Consulting Ltd

DESIGN
COUNCIL
REGISTERED

Barkway, Royston, Hertfordshire SG8 8EF
Telephone (0763) 848959 Fax (0763) 84668

Team's engineers and designers specialize in the application of practical technology and management consulting skills to solve clients' problems. We are a multidisciplinary organization with capability across the board in mechanical, electronic and electrical engineering, control and software.
Particular areas of interest include medical, automation and robotics, test equipment, product development and microprocessor application. Our clients include Arther Lee & Sons; Simon Engineering; Rank Xerox, Stuarts & Lloyds Plastics; Dupont; GKN Technology; Printed Forms Equipment and Bonas Machine Company.

Contact Mr Perran Newman
Size 21-50
Affiliations IMechE, IEE, IED, IIndM, IM, EIA, BRA

Technology Concepts Ltd

DESIGN
COUNCIL
REGISTERED

Raglan House, Llantarnam Park, Cwmbran, Gwent, Wales NP44 3AB
Telephone (0633) 872611 Fax (0633) 872329 Telex 94011765

Consultancy services for computer systems, hardware and software. Hardware services include designing; stand-alone controllers using single-chip microprocessors, 8, 16 and 32-bit microprocessor based hardware, for process control, serial communications and office automation systems, interface cards for the PC-AT and PS/2 MCA bus architectures. The software department can provide bespoke programs/drivers and documentation for a client. Microcomputer operating systems supported are: ZENIX, UNIX, AIX, Concurrent DOS and PC-DOS. Computer systems experience includes planning corporate MIS strategies for IBM users, designing network systems for mainframe, minicomputer, and PCs.

Contact Mr Peter Farrar
Size 11-20
Affiliations IEE, BCS, IDM

The Technology Partnership Ltd

Melbourn Science Park, Cambridge Road, Melbourn, Royston, Hertfordshire SG8 6EE
Telephone (0763) 262626 Fax (0763) 261582 Telex 818896

We provide the following range of services to our clients: the identification of strategic new business areas created by the exploitation of scientific discoveries; the development of new products, where we provide a complete implementation programme from concept generation, 'fast-track' development, prototyping, and production engineering to manufacture. Product sectors include consumer, industrial, communications, office, financial services and healthcare. The design, manufacture and supply of advanced production machinery using our own equipment modules in both robotic and special-purpose applications. The Technology Partnership is majority-owned by its staff.

Contact Dr Christopher Graeme-Barber
Size over 100

Christopher Terrell Associates

24 Lancaster Road, Wimbledon, London SW19 5DD
Telephone 081-879 1986/946 5918

CTA has 16 years' track record for multidisciplined product innovation (some of these are now industry standards) with a Design Award for medical resuscitation equipment. Clients include Barbour Index, Daler Rowney, ICI Petrochemicals, Michrophax, Readers Digest, Surrey University, Drayton Controls, Inventalink and Glynwed International. Specials are injection moulded mechanisms. Production costs are estimated using computerised parts listing, materials contents, labour rates, machine rates and capital investment charges. Also intellectual property, patents, patent breaking and selling/licensing of inventions. Facilities: toolroom, CAD. Costs: computerised time sheets give client full details.

Contact Mr Christopher Terrell
Size 1-5
Affiliations SCD, ICE, BMA,

3T Ltd

7 Ladbroke Park, Millers Road, Warwick, Warwickshire CV34 5AE
Telephone (0926) 411422 Fax (0926) 492780

3T – The Art of Industry – Innovative support for commercial and manufacturing companies. 3T's objective is to ensure success in designing, developing, manufacturing and promoting products, processes and services. Whether a client requires new products, special machinery, manufacturing advice, corporate development or graphic design, 3T have the necessary skills. Embodying design management with an enthusiastic team of industrial designers, production engineers and graphic designers, 3T ensure that the best concepts are developed, achieving maximum product performance at least cost. 3T also assist to initiate and sustain successful and profitable manufacture.

Contact Mr Michael Beard
Size 11-20
Affiliations CSD, IMechE, RSA

TQC Ltd

Hooton Street, Carlton Road, Nottingham, Nottinghamshire NG3 2NJ
Telephone (0602) 503561 Fax (0602) 484642 Telex 377998

TQC is a well-established company with design expertise in mechanical, electrical, computer and software engineering. It specializes in the design of consumer and scientific products, together with automated equipment for production testing and materials handling. Company facilities include substantial investment in software development equipment as well as in-house workshops for both mechanical and electronic prototyping. The company operates in most engineering fields, including high volume component manufacture, medical and process control industries. Typical clients include BP, GEC, General Motors, Kodak, Prestcold, Lucas, and Black & Decker.

Contact Mr Michael Bolton
Size 21-50
Affiliations IEE, IMechE, IChemE

Trog Assoc Ltd

P O Box 243, South Croydon, Surrey CR2 6NZ
Telephone 081-686 3580/081-786 7094

Technology audits for BS5750 and AQUAP1 quality approvals. With training, manuals and procedures produced to your specification. O & M studies of product flows, from sourcing components to engineering the finished product. Hands-on engineering problem solving with 25 years of know-how being applied. Working German both spoken and written. (Spräcke und Schrift arbeit Deutsch).
Products: Highpride – thermal buffet mask; X-Ray manufacturing system. Sobatec – car accessory modules; head-up display. Trog Assoc – SGML software package; expert planning system.
Mobile phone no: 0831 372534.

Contact Mr Eric Sutherland
Size 1-5
Affiliations BCS, IEE, IOD, APm, SOA

Roland S Wagstaff BSc, CEng

8 Devonshire Drive, Duffield, Derby, Derbyshire DE6 4DD
Telephone (0332) 841162

Heat transfer, mechanical design and development of thermal processes are the main technical services offered. Ovens, heat exchangers, vapour condensers, gas scrubbers and coolers are examples of items for which design expertise is available. Problems of temperature control and uniformity, product quality and process efficiency are investigated using portable instruments. Design and development of equipment for improved quality, control and efficiency, including modifications to improve the performance of existing equipment, frequently result from the investigations. Prototype and test rig design, research and development, and project engineering services are also offered.

Contact Mr Roland Wagstaff
Size 1-5
Affiliations IMechE, InstE

Walkbury Ltd

1 Alfric Square, Woodston, Peterborough, Cambridgeshire PE2 0JA
Telephone (0733) 23507 Fax (0733) 238041

Walkbury is a private limited company formed in 1978, employing 20 people in modern premises on the Woodston Industrial Estate, Peterborough. The following services are being offered:
Microprocessor system design and development;
Electronic and engineering design;
Sub-contract assembly of production items.

Contact Mr John Nicholls
Size 11-20

Wessex Designdraft Ltd

42-44 Chipper Lane, Salisbury, Wiltshire SP1 1BG
Telephone (0722) 335112 Fax (0722) 412521

Innovation to design and manufacture by a 60-strong team of qualified engineers, draughtsmen and technicians best describes our activities. For over a decade we have responded quickly to the needs of a wide range of industries from agriculture to aerospace, designing anything from high-speed assembly machines to robotic investment casting mould cells and have established a long list of satisfied clients and friends.
Our design offices and manufacturing division operate under an approved quality assurance system to BS5750 Part 1 Design: ISO.9001 since1987, and AQAP 1 Ed.3. A brochure is available describing our skills and the projects we have undertaken.

Contact Mr Peter Pyke
Size 51-100
Affiliations EDC, EIA

Wolfson Unit for Marine Technology & Industrial Aerodynamics

University of Southampton, Southampton, Hampshire SO9 5NH
Telephone (0703) 585044 Fax (0703) 671532 Telex 47661 SOTON U

Consultancy in marine technology and industrial aerodynamics, including towing tank testing in calm water and waves of vessels of all types and wind tunnel testing of yachts, ships, hovercraft and racing cars and building developments. Development and sale of computer-aided design programs for the naval architect, including development of special programs. Design and build supervision of welded aluminium fabrications, especially yacht and boat hulls. Mechanical testing and failure analysis. Facilities include towing tanks, wind tunnels, mechanical test facilities and access to scanning electron microscope.

Contact Mr William Allday
Size 11-20
Affiliations Weldl, RINA, IMechE

Wulstan Designs & Controls Ltd

DESIGN
COUNCIL
REGISTERED

98c Blackpole Trading Estate West, Worcester, Worcestershire WR3 8TJ
Telephone (0905) 58555 Fax (0905) 54325

To meet clients' needs we offer a full range of skills and expertise in mechanical, electronic and electrical engineering. Our activities are generally as follows: mechanical and electronic design; mechanical and electronic feasibility studies; electrical design; mechanical and electronic drawing office service and mechanical and electronic manufacture; computer microprocessor applications, CNC retrofitting; PLC applications. Clients include: Apperley Honing (Cheltenham), British Steel, Brintons, Hymatic Engineering, Metal Box Engineering, MOD (Malvern), Stenner (Tiverton), Cosworth, Turbine Blading, Cookson Precision Castings, and Lapointe.

Contact Mr Bob Rose
Size 1-5
Affiliations IMechE, IProdE, IElecE

DIRECTORY OF **DES***ign*ERS 1991

Addison

60 Britton Street, London EC1M 5NA
Telephone 071-250 1887 Fax 071-251 3712

We are a worldwide design consultancy with over 200 specialists working from major cities in the Far East, USA and Europe. Our expertise covers architecture, ergonomics, graphics, leisure, office and retail, production design and transportion together with design research.
Our ergonomists work closely with designers on projects in all sectors, in addition to providing external ergonomics consultancy in transportation, workstation and product fields.

Contact Mr John Williamson
Size over 100
Affiliations CSD

AIT Ltd

16 Bell Street, Henley on Thames, Oxfordshire RG9 2BG
Telephone (0491) 579272 Fax (0491) 573903

Making computer systems easy to use is a design problem as well as a computing problem. User interface design from AIT enables you to bridge this gap and ensure that usability is built into your computer systems from the start. Working with us is an effective, cost-efficient way for you to profit from the most up-to-date expertise available in screen design, computer graphics, graphical user interface, icon languages, task analysis and user-centered development methods. Our application of visual design to the human-computer interface makes us unique in the computer industry.

Contact Mr Rupert Essinger
Size 11-20
Affiliations ACM, SIGCHI

CAMBIT, The User Interface

1 Rowan Close, Bottisham, Cambridge, Cambridgeshire CB5 9BN
Telephone (0223) 811487

Expertise: human-computer interaction; designing, prototyping and reviewing user interfaces, screen design, WIMPs; user-centred task analysis, user-error analysis; reviews of product usability, writing for publication.
Clients include: National Computing Centre, Hoseasons Holidays, Prime Computer R&D, Alper Systems, Training Agency (COIC), Delta-T devices, Cambridge Science Park companies, instrument designers and manufacturers.
Typical projects: designing user interfaces, especially system structure from the user's point of view; reviewing existing systems and recommending user interface improvements; investigating user errors and difficulties.

Contact Dr John Harris
Size 1-5
Affiliations BPsS, ES, BCS, HCI SG

Control Room Projects

13 Rosemont Road, London NW3 6NG
Telephone 071-433 3305/071-435 5659 Fax 071-435 9032

We design information technology interiors to support effective systems control. Our ergonomic and environmental design concepts are prototyped and proven for their response under all predicted conditions of operational use.
Clients who use our human factors and design skills include: BBC (World Service), Ewbank Preece, Bank of England, BP Research, SW Water Utilities, Home Office, Isle of Man Police, Castelli International, Swiss Banking Corporation International, Metropolitan Police, Devon & Cornwall Constabulary, Mercury Communications, Philips Communications, Thames Water Utilities, States of Guernsey Electricity Board, Ericsson Information Systems.

Contact Mr Barry Drake
Size 6-10
Affiliations RCA, CSD, RIBA, Human Fac Soc

Crombie Anderson

16 Comely Park, Dunfermline, Fife, Scotland KY12 7HU
Telephone (0383) 620247 Fax (0383) 620357

Crombie Anderson is a multidisciplinary consultancy with particular skills in computer interaction design (ie the human factors aspects of computer software) and the design of user-friendly control and display interfaces. Crombie Anderson has an in-house capability for software development coupled with industrial design and production engineering skills necessary to ensure optimum user acceptance of modern consumer and capital goods. Crombie Anderson has direct experience of 'user feature' versus 'product cost' analysis for volume applications.

Contact Mr Douglas Anderson
Size 21-50
Affiliations BIM, IMC

Davis Associates

39a High Street, Baldock, Hertfordshire SG7 6BG
Telephone (0462) 490262 Fax (0462) 895722

Recent examples of our work include the design and evaluation of: control rooms (for the modernized Central Line), seating, transportation (eg the cab of the Manchester Metrolink tram), information (the design of all interior signs for Docklands Light Railway), industrial workplaces and software dialogues and screen formats.
Davis Associates analyses the users' needs and creates appropriate solutions. We regularly test prototypes of rooms, products and software, and successfully work alongside our clients' own in-house design, engineering and marketing teams.

Contact Mr Martin Bontoft
Size 6-10
Affiliations ES, Human Factors Soc of USA, CSD

Design For Change Ltd

Unit 5, 1st Floor, Panther House, 38 Mount Pleasant, London WC1X 0AP
Telephone 071-837 2109 Fax 071-833 1211

Since 1986 Design For Change have been offering clients a full range of services. Design: magazines, leaflets, posters, programmes etc. Typesetting: 980 fonts, artwork, photography and illustration.
Clients include: HelpAge International, NCH, Terence Higgins Trust, Amnesty International, Camden Council, NALGO, Black Theatre Forum.
If you think we can help – call. NGA recognized.

Contact Ms Sue Grant
Size 1-5

The HCI Service

PO Box 31, Loughborough, Leicestershire LE11 1QU
Telephone (0509) 264083 Fax (0509) 234651

The HCI Service provides access to the widest range of services and technical expertise in human-computer interaction available in Europe. In particular, it offers the services of experts in disciplines such as ergonomics, computer science, psychology, linguistics and phonetics. This broad range of expertise forms the basis of the UK's most comprehensive HCI design service.
The following advice and consultancy services are available from the HCI Service: design audits, human interface design, rapid prototyping, usability evaluations, regulation conformance evaluation and HILITES – the HCI Information and Literature Enquiry Service.

Contact Dr Peter Reid
Size 51-100

ICE Ergonomics

75 Swingbridge Road, Loughborough, Leicestershire LE11 0JB
Telephone (0509) 236161 Fax (0509) 610725

ICE Ergonomics is an established and internationally recognized company of ergonomists, psychologists, biologists and engineers. It offers ergonomics consultancy and research services to manufacturers and designers of industrial, commercial and domestic products, facilities and environments, vehicles and transport facilities. In addition to designing for usability, we are particularly experienced in health and safety issues in the home, on the road and at work.

Contact Mr Ian Galer
Size 21-50
Affiliations ES, Human Fac Soc, RSS, IOSH

Loughborough Consultants Ltd

University of Technology, Loughborough, Leicestershire LE11 3TF
Telephone (0509) 222597 Fax (0509) 231983 Telex 34319

This company markets the expertise and technical facilities of Loughborough University of Technology. We have considerable expertise available in the human factors aspect of design through the Institute for Consumer Ergonomics and the HUSAT (Human Sciences and Advanced Technology) Research Centre, and the Department of Computer Studies. ICE and HUSAT have extensive experience in the man-machine and organization-system interfaces and have combined with the computing specialists in the Human-Computer Research Centre (LUTCHI) offering skills in computer graphics, speech recognition, picture interpretation, robotics and co-operative interface management systems.

Contact Dr Tony Ward
Size 21-50

Moggridge Associates

7/8 Jeffreys Place, Jeffreys Street, London NW1 9PP
Telephone 071-485 1170 Fax 071-482 3970

Moggridge Associates offer integrated product design development services with the user in mind. Human Factors specialists draw upon knowledge from various disciplines: anthropometry, biomechanics, engineering, psychology, physiology, sociology, statistics. Our specialist skills in interaction design extend from computer interfaces to people's use of systems/products. We have developed a design research method exploiting human factors observation techniques. Research is undertaken in stages to 'understand, observe and predict' before visualizing and testing out a potential product with hard models or software mock-ups. Clients: Claris (Apple), Dancall, Hewlett-Packard, Microsoft, Steelcase, Xerox.

Contact Mrs Ingelise Nielsen
Size 21-50
Affiliations RDI, RSA, CSD, HFS, DBA, IOD, IMechE, IED, IDSA, VDID

Robinson Associates

Red Lion House, St Mary's Street, Painswick, Gloucestershire GL6 6QR
Telephone (0452) 813699 Fax (0452) 812912

Robinson Associates specialize in designing products which contain computers and software. Our emphasis is on designing from the user's point of view so that the resulting product can evolve to match the market requirements. Past projects have included a wide spectrum of applications, from designing an intuitive graphics interface for machine tools to a more reliable system for cancer screening. Recent projects have involved energy management systems and interactive databases. Most clients are large well established companies who either need a fresh eye to improve their designs or who just need additional support with specialist expertise.

Contact Mr Brian Kirk
Size 6-10
Affiliations BCS

Satherley Design

The Old School, Exton Street, London SE1 8UE
Telephone 071-928 9377 Fax 071-928 5642 Telex 28604G ATT: SATHERLEY

Analysis and ergonomic design of:
Product hardware (control areas, information displays, anthropometry, usability); Control room and workstation design (mimic diagrams, seating, design standards); Software (screen layouts, help facilities, interaction with hardware); Information presentation (displays, manuals, forms); Environment (lighting, heating, ventilation, space planning); Evaluation (mock-ups, usability, questionnaire).
Specialist service available both to complement our existing resource (product design, engineering, modelmaking) and independently for specific project work.
Client base includes blue-chip, high technology, nationalized industry and product manufacturers (detailed under Product Design).

Contact Mr Alastair Prickett
Size 21-50
Affiliations CSD, BIM, IOD, ES

System Applied Technology Ltd

Sheffield Science Park, Howard Street, Sheffield, South Yorkshire S1 2LX
Telephone (0742) 768682 Fax (0742) 727990

System Applied Technology, an established creator of consumer/business software and technology-based training, has a reputation for producing technically demanding, highly graphical and innovative human-computer interfaces for a wide range of microcomputers. SAT's expertise spans varied technologies: touch screen, mouse, keyboard, touch pad. The most appropriate are chosen to suit the subject matter and user profile.
Clients include ICI, Dixons Stores Group, Club 24, TWS, Grand Metropolitan, Marsden BS, Training Agency and cover applications such as public information on unmanned computers, learning environments for children, industrial training and adult literacy.

Contact Mr Keith Shaw
Size 21-50
Affiliations RSC, BCS

System Concepts Ltd

Museum House, Museum Street, London WC1A 1JT
Telephone 071-636 5912 Fax 071-580 5069

SCL is an independent systems consultancy. In addition to conventional systems analysis skills, we offer human factors expertise in: analysing users and tasks; developing and running usability tests; prototyping; design user interfaces and support through; help screens, documentation; job design and organization development; devising office layouts; auditing existing systems; ergonomics training through the Ergonomics Training Centre. Our facilities include computing, video, laboratory and training rooms.
Clients include: government departments (DTI), product suppliers (Project), system and service suppliers (British Telecom, Access), users (Marks and Spencer) and international bodies (European Commission).

Contact Mr Tom Stewart
Size 1-5
Affiliations ES, BPsS, BCS, ACM

DIRECTORY OF DESIGNERS 1991

Haydon Williams International Ltd

121 Mortlake High Street, Mortlake, London SW14 8SN
Telephone 081-392 1444/5/6/7 Fax 081-876 9661 Telex 936268 COLOUR G

Consultants in design, colour and style: embracing automotive industry, textiles, carpets, plastics, consumer products, white goods. Specialists in product development opposite the volume market. Involvement also in sporting goods market and luggage.
International involvements in: Japan/Australia/New Zealand/USA/Europe/UK. Expertise in market development and presentation, and colour for the consumer and contract markets.

Contact Mr Haydon Williams
Size 6-10
Affiliations DBA

Loughborough Consultants Ltd

University of Technology, Loughborough, Leicestershire LE11 3TF
Telephone (0509) 222597 Fax (0509) 231983 Telex 34319

This company markets the expertise and technical facilities of Loughborough University of Technology. We have available specialists in all aspects of materials, eg rubbers, plastics, metals, alloys, plating and corrosion from a large postgraduate Institute of Polymer Technology and Materials Engineering. The Surface Analysis Group has extensive expertise in surface technology using the SIMS, LIMA, GDMS, Auger and ESCA techniques and the Carbon Research Group is expert in the technology of carbons and graphites including composites. The Vacuum Coatings Group of the Department of Physics is a centre for thin film technology.

Contact Dr Tony Ward
Size 21-50

Matsel Systems Ltd

6th Floor, Cunard Buildings, Water Street, Liverpool, Merseyside L3 1EG
Telephone 051-227 5080 Fax 051-236 1934 Telex 628052 SHARET G

Matsel Systems, a subsidiary of the international Elsevier group, are specialists in the field of computer aided engineering materials selection. Matsel sets new standards for materials selection software with the PERITUS system; the latest version, PERITUS 3, offers unequalled facilities for the handling of materials data. Matsel's combination of materials engineering and software expertise puts the company in a unique position to undertake consultancy/development of materials data systems, primarily for use by designers. Major contracts have been undertaken for industrial clients and for the Commission of the European Communities.

Contact Dr Arthur Fairfull
Size 1-5
Affiliations IM, ICorrST, PRI

PERA

Nottingham Road, Melton Mowbray, Leicestershire LE13 0PB
Telephone (0664) 501501 Fax (0664) 501264 Telex 34684 PERAMM G

PERA has in-depth experience of metals, metal matrix composites, surface engineering and treatments, electrically-conducting coatings, adhesives, plastics and reinforced polymers, advanced fibre composites and lightweight, high-strength materials, as well as volume production processing and on-line quality control systems. This experience of the design requirements and production techniques related to high performance materials is continually updated through extensive development work linked to UK/European materials and processing research programmes in collaboration with industrial companies, material suppliers and research institutes. See also PERA's entry under the Engineering Design and Product Design sections.

Contact Mr Alvin Wiggins
Size 51-100

Rubber Consultants

Brickendonbury, Hertford, Hertfordshire SG13 8NL
Telephone (0992) 554657 Fax (0992) 554837 Telex 817449 MRRDBL G

Rubber Consultants advises on design, development and production of rubber articles ranging from latex goods to off-shore engineering components. Backed by one of the world's largest rubber research organizations, recently given the PRI's Prince Philip Award for the successful development and implementation of rubber bearings for earthquake protection of buildings, Rubber Consultants offers a full design service for mechanical and civil engineering applications. Extensive facilities are available for physical testing of components and materials, analytical testing, and industrial trouble shooting. Information retrieval, bibliographic and market research facilities are also available.

Contact Dr Brian Tidd
Size over 100
Affiliations PRI, RSC, IOP

Salford University Business Services Ltd

Salford Tramways Building, PO Box 50, Frederick Road, Salford, Manchester M6 6BY
Telephone 061-736 8921 Fax 061-737 0880

Salford University Business Services is a commercial consultancy based within the University of Salford, employing the expertise of full-time in-house consultants supported by academic and industrial associates. As a university-based company, Business Services offers exceptional resources in the field of materials technology. The Product Design Group offers a wide range of experience in materials applications, testing and selection. Clients range in size from business start-ups to multinational companies such as ICI, British Aerospace and BICC.

Contact Mr Alan Postill
Size over 100
Affiliations IMechE, IProdE, IEEE, IEE, IED, IMet, RAeS, IOA, InstP

Sheffield University

Commercial & Industrial Development Bureau, 2 Palmerston Road, Sheffield, Yorkshire S10 2TE
Telephone (0742) 768555 Fax (0742) 725004 Telex 547216 UGSHEF G

Advice, training, research and development are all available from the largest centre in the UK for the teaching and research of materials. Two special service units, one in metals and the other in ceramics, glasses, polymers and composite materials, employ full-time staff to provide analysis, testing, problem solving, material characterisation and special fabrication of new materials and new structures. Extensive melting facilities exist (for glass and metals) and the services are supported by a full range of analytical and spectroscopic instruments including the latest techniques for surface investigation.

Contact Dr Robert Handscombe
Size over 100

GRAPHICS & PACKAGING

AD Creative Consultants Ltd

DESIGN COUNCIL REGISTERED

The Royal Victoria Patriotic Building, Trinity Road, London SW18 3SX
Telephone 081-870 8743 Fax 081-877 1151 Telex 299180 MONINT G

The company was formed in 1974 by Fred Barter, ex head of design at J Walter Thompson in London. The business has grown steadily and the client list now includes many major public companies, local authorities and institutions. Graphic design forms the major part of the business; but the company also has particular expertise in the design of retail sign systems.
In the same premises are architects, photographers, recording studios and quantity surveyors. This enables the company to provide a wide range of services as project managers for major design-related contracts.

Contact Mr Brian Mathews
Size 6-10
Affiliations STD, RCA, Mktg Soc

Addison

DESIGN COUNCIL REGISTERED

60 Britton Street, London EC1M 5NA
Telephone 071-250 1887 Fax 071-251 3712

We are a worldwide design consultancy with over 200 specialists working in the Far East, USA and Europe. Our expertise covers architecture, ergonomics, graphics, leisure, office and retail, product design and transportation together with design research.
Graphic design projects include corporate identity and communications, brand identity and packaging. Literature work ranges from report and accounts, marketing and employee literature to City documents. Our strength in problem solving is based on our experience focusing clients' needs, and providing a creative and relevant solution.

Contact Mr John Williamson
Size over 100
Affiliations CSD

The Advertising Design Partnership

DESIGN COUNCIL REGISTERED

Flemming House, Goldcroft, Yeovil, Somerset BA21 4DQ
Telephone (0935) 29093 Fax (0935) 71518

ADP is a versatile, experienced and multidiscipline graphic design practice based in Yeovil, Somerset. Although extremely well-equipped with Macintosh computers and many exciting software applications, the real strength of the company lies in its strong commitment to high standards of creativity, originality and professionalism. We provide coherent and relevant answers to a very wide range of communication problems encountered by our clients. These include work in copywriting, graphic design, artwork, exhibition design, brochure design, magazine/journal design and production (we have our own in-house typesetting service), packaging design, illustration, photography, corporate identity/housestyles, audio-visual slide programmes and OHP films, print management and purchase.

Contact Mr Gordon Barber
Size 6-10

AIT Ltd

16 Bell Street, Henley on Thames, Oxfordshire RG9 2BG
Telephone (0491) 579272 Fax (0491) 573903

Software and design consultancy AIT specializes in the development of interactive graphics applications. Working principally in point-of-sale, point-of-information, financial self- and assisted-service environments. AIT's systems are designed to be visually attractive, dynamic and with a zero learning curve. AIT can provide a total project service including the design of customer service terminals supporting literature and promotional items. Clients include Hertz, The Woolwich Building Society, Natwest and IBM.

Contact Mr Matthew Tidbury
Size 11-20
Affiliations ACM, SIGCHI

Diana Allen Associates

31 Great Percy Street, London WC1X 9RD
Telephone 071-837 1003 Fax 071-833 4207

Independent consultancy producing quality work in corporate identity and communications, marketing presentation, catalogue and book design and exhibitions.
Associates include specialist photographers, illustrators, product designers, architectural consultants.
Additional expertise in textile/fashion launch and promotion.
Clients include ICI Fibres, Courtaulds Textiles, Toray Textiles, Longmans, Royal Festival Hall, British Library, Kensington Chelsea & Westminster FHSA.

Contact Ms Diana Allen
Size 1-5

Nick Allen Design

The Old Convent, Beeches Green, Stroud, Gloucestershire GL5 4AD
Telephone (0453) 764436 Fax (0453) 763913

Design for all forms of communication, complete corporate identity programmes, company brochures, point-of-sale, packaging and exhibitions. Solutions that not only look good, but suit each client's marketing needs and budget.
A comprehensive service from concept and design through to production and print, with the highest standards being maintained throughout.

Contact Mr Nick Allen
Size 1-5

Associated Design Consultants Ltd

18 Danvers Street, Chelsea, London SW3 5AN
Telephone 071-823 3733 Fax 071-352 3926

With 21 years' experience in the design business we have the expertise to offer a consultancy service that relies on far more than just subjective, fashionable design solutions. Our work is based on relevant research, a well formulated brief, sound economic project management and professionalism. All this coupled with the flair and enthusiasm of our designers ensures that our creative solutions not only answer your brief, but truly sparkle! Experts in corporate identity, corporate and product literature, retail graphics, exhibitions, packaging, design research and design management.

Contact Ms Maxine-Jayne Horn
Size 11-20
Affiliations CSD, DBA

AVB Design

1 Clarence Street, Belfast, Co. Antrim, Northern Ireland BT2 8EH
Telephone (0232) 320663 Fax (0232) 235953

Not exactly your normal, average, everyday, run-of-the-mill, common or garden sort of design company . . .

Contact Mr Tony McIlwrath
Size 1-5
Affiliations IPA

Baddeley Associates

126-130 Tenison Road, Cambridge, Cambridgeshire CB1 2DP
Telephone (0223) 323351 Fax (0223) 323885

As information designers, we offer a range of creative and consultancy services. From the user's viewpoint, we design, write and provide guides for complex products and services. We've produced user guides and quick reference material for computer systems, telecommunications products, and professional services. We also design and write promotional material including corporate identities, product brandings, brochures, adverts and exhibition stands. Our services also include: advising on publishing strategies for internal and external corporate publications; and using human factor skills to design user interfaces for computer software and systems. Our clients include a wide range of blue-chip companies.

Contact Ms Caroline Webster
Size 21-50

Baillie Marshall Design

Balgray Building, Harrison Road, Dundee, Scotland DD2 3SN
Telephone (0382) 833855 Fax (0382) 810393

Why choose Baillie Marshall for your next design project?
As one of the top Scottish consultancies we can say with confidence that Baillie Marshall has the expertise to produce fully-integrated marketing strategies and design solutions which make a real contribution to the success of your business. That's because we have the high calibre of staff and the unique level of in-house support to maintain efficient project control and to create exciting, relevant design that works. Specialist areas of expertise include corporate identity, packaging design, direct mail and sales literature.
Send for our brochure or give us a call and we'll tell you more.

Contact Mr Peter Baillie
Size 21-50

Banks & Miles

1 Tranquil Vale, Blackheath, London SE3 0BU
Telephone 081-318 1131 Fax 081-318 2792

Over 30 years' experience in graphic design and typography, with the proven capacity to provide successful solutions to design problems from the very large corporate identity to the minute detail of a bank note. Studios in Hamburg and Brussels.
Corporate identity: Royal Mail, British Telecom, ImechE, HMSO, Mott Macdonald, Oxford Instruments, several universities.
Annual reports: Pearson, WH Smith, Consumers' Association and others.
Signposting: BAA, Lancaster University, QMW (London University), London and Whipsnade Zoos.
General graphics: CUP English Course, Government Environmental White Paper, Gardening Which?, the Phonebook typeface (which received several awards).

Contact Mr Colin Banks
Size 11-20
Affiliations CSD, STD

Barron Hatchet Design

65 Bridge Street, Manchester M3 3BQ
Telephone 061-834 2926 Fax 061-834 6821

Established in 1967 we have since grown to offer our own brand of carefully considered design not only to local businesses, but also to many national and international organizations. Recent work ranges from large corporate design projects for clients such as Manchester Airport, BBC North West and the Tootal Group, to smaller – but no less important – promotional activities (sometimes on shoestring budgets) for individuals, businesses and institutions.
Two decades experience has shown us that our sound appreciation of marketing is the foundation of all our successful work.

Contact Mr Geoff Royle
Size 6-10
Affiliations CIM, CSD

Barrow Parkhill Associates Ltd

1k Montague Mews North, London W1H 1AJ
Telephone 071-487 5706 Fax 071-935 0413

If it is important to you that your graphic design consultants should have experience of your industry or project, welcome. With over 20 years' experience, we have handled most types of design or marketing problem.
If, on the other hand, you want minds that are totally new to the situation, good. We're usually quick to grasp the essentials. Clients using our expertise include Baring Securities, BP, Bluebird Toys, Caledonian Paper, Dalgety, Kleinwort Benson, Lloyds Bank, Mattel, National Commercial and many other national and international organizations.
Ask for our brochure.

Contact Mr Robert Parkhill
Size 21-50
Affiliations DBA, IAA

Benson Design Ltd

DESIGN COUNCIL REGISTERED

123 Blythswood Street, Glasgow, Scotland G2 4EN
Telephone 041-226 5365 Fax 041-221 3896 Telex 779417

Benson Design offers a professional design service covering all aspects of corporate and business communication, packaging, and exhibition design. Our team of experienced designers particularly enjoys working for clients who demand the best. Our client list includes: manufacturing companies engaged in engineering, electronics and the food and drink industries; government agencies, local authorities and tourist boards; commercial concerns engaged in property development, transport and distribution; universities and the professions. To support our creative team and widen our range of client services, we have installed Scotland's only Aesthedes graphic computer system, and three mini-computers for slide production.

Contact Mr Willi Hamilton
Size 11-20

Bentley Woolston Ltd

DESIGN COUNCIL REGISTERED

12/13 The Forum, Rockingham Drive, Linford Wood, Milton Keynes, Buckinghamshire MK14 6LY
Telephone (0908) 670798 Fax (0908) 604837 Telex 82304 FORUM G

Bentley Woolston is a design consultancy providing a high quality, multidisciplinary creative resource. We specialize in corporate and brand identities, literature and direct marketing campaigns. Our clients range from blue-chip international companies to small independent businesses. As a mixed discipline team we are committed to ensuring that the work we produce is effective both in design and in performance. We aim to achieve the highest possible standards of creativity within the constraints of agreed corporate and marketing objectives.
We call this approach 'design in context'.

Contact Mr Richard Bentley
Size 6-10
Affiliations DBA

DESIGN AND COMMUNICATIONS CONSULTANTS

Bottom Line Design

DESIGN COUNCIL REGISTERED

100 The Street, Wickham Bishops, Witham, Essex CM8 3NN
Telephone (0621) 891844 Fax (0621) 892815

Designers Chris Liddiard and Harvey Shortt have worked together since the early '70s. Andy Greenhalgh joined them in 1987 and Alison Rayner in 1989.
They have produced brochures and sales material for many leading financial services companies and in 1990 completed four substantial corporate identity programmes including one for Murphy, the construction group.
Their brochure, Life at the Bottom, showing twenty years of work, is available on request.

Contact Mr Chris Liddiard
Size 1-5

GRAPHICS & PACKAGING

Bowes Darby Design Associates

Magdalen House, 136 Tooley Street, London SE1 2TU
Telephone 071-378 0637 Fax 071-378 0692

Design is a powerful business tool. Used effectively it can achieve significant benefits. We aim to provide the very best creative solution relevant to specific business objectives. We are specialists in the field of corporate communication.
Clients include: British Airport Authority, British Rail, British Telecom, Citibank, Grant Thornton, ICI Dulux, International Wool Secretariat, The Littlewoods Organisation, Royal Bank of Scotland.
A top 30 UK consultancy with offices in London and Manchester. For further information on the proven benefits of effective creative design, contact our marketing department.

Contact Mr P Kelly
Size 21-50

Brauer Associates

20 Dock Street, London E1 8JP
Telephone 071-481 2184 Fax 071-481 3368

Brauer Associates, founded in 1976, are architects specializing in the design, development and marketing of building products. Services include market research, product innovation, design, development and promotion involving product literature, exhibitions and advertising. The practice works with UK and foreign clients, and technical documentation has been prepared for use in the USA, Japan, and the European Community. Current clients include MK Electric, Escol, Norwood Partitions, Ergonom and Quelfire. Products include ceilings, trunking, floors, screens, ironmongery, building fixings, partitions, timber structures, external cladding, roofing, lighting and fire stopping materials.

Contact Mr Irving Brauer
Size 6-10
Affiliations RIBA, CSD

Brend Thomsen Shepherd

16 Ingestre Place, London W1R 3LP
Telephone 071-287 7000 Fax 071-494 0532

Brend Thomsen Shepherd is a well established, highly professional graphic design consultancy whose commitment to excellence has been rewarded by the enhancement of both its own and its clients' business achievements. Since its establishment in the 1970s the company has expanded to offer a total design service including advertising and video production. Our current client list includes; Arlington Securities, Anglia Television, EMI Music, Prudential, Tarmac, Richard Ellis, Legal & General, Consultants in Environmental Sciences, MEPC, Wimpey Waste Management and Kalon Technology Consultants.

Contact Ms Margaret Shepherd
Size 21-50
Affiliations CSD, RSA, DIA

BREND
—
Thomsen
—
Shepherd
—

Jennie Burns Design

19a Westbourne Park Road, London W2 5PX
Telephone 071-229 0603 Fax 071-229 3297

Design expertise linked to a comprehensive knowledge of the client's marketing needs is the hallmark of the approach to work by this small but professional practice. An essential element is the continuity established with clients throughout the life of a job, from concept through production, ensuring the most creative solution is soundly based. Jennie Burns Design has experience in several areas: retail environment, packaging, new product development, annual reports, corporate identity, stationery and promotional literature. Clients include Boots, Fortnum & Mason, Harrods, Safeway, The Guinness Group, Venice-Simplon-Orient Express, Hanbury Manor, Gateway, Charnos, Champneys, Spadel, Queens Moat Houses.

Contact Ms Jennie Burns
Size 1-5

GRAPHICS & PACKAGING

Business Design Group

24 St John Street, London EC1M 4AY
Telephone 071-490 1144 Fax 071-250 3005

Business Design Group is a multidisciplinary design consultancy that offers all aspects of graphic design and corporate communications. Its designers have experience in corporate identity, annual reports, signage, newspaper and magazine design, brochures and employee communications. They work independently or integrate with Business Design Group's space planning and interior design studios, providing strategic solutions to problems associated with company name changes, mergers, takeovers, rationalizations and relocation. Business Design Group employs over 140 staff in six locations: Bristol, Dublin, Frankfurt, London, Reading and Swindon.

Contact Mr Stephen Hitchins
Size over 100
Affiliations CSD, DBA

Buxton Wall McPeake Ltd

Cavendish House, 30 Pall Mall, Manchester M2 1JY
Telephone 061-835 1553 Fax 061-832 1902

We have helped many businesses to accurately project the appropriate company or brand identity for their particular markets. We have communicated their services in a creative, practical and cost-effective way, through literature, packaging, exhibitions and computer generated slides. At Buxton Wall McPeake our multidisciplinary approach provides you with a totally integrated design service that will help your company communicate more effectively.

Contact Mrs Lynne McPeake
Size 11-20

Cairnes Design Associates Ltd

1 Smiths Yard, Summerley Street, London SW18 4HR
Telephone 081-879 1233 Fax 081-947 1072

Graphic design forms the major part of our activities and includes corporate literature, sales and technical brochures, annual and employee reports, catalogues and calendars.
We have many blue-chip clients, but we enjoy working for small organizations as well as large corporations. Whatever their size, we help them to achieve their business objectives through creative, intelligent and cost-effective design.
We retain their loyalty by maintaining a close working relationship, acquiring a thorough knowledge of their areas of operation and providing a consistently friendly, personal and efficient service.

Contact Mr Denis Cairnes
Size 11-20
Affiliations CSD, DBA

Carrods Design and Communication

Belmont House, 129 High Street, Linton, Cambridge, Cambridgeshire CB1 6JT
Telephone (0223) 893677 Fax (0223) 894144

Carrods provides a design service with an emphasis on sound creative solutions to clients' promotional problems. Our expertise is clear and concise visual communication, be it a photograph, illustration, diagram or the written word, and although our designs have flair they are always dictated by logic.
Our main area of activity is business-to-business technical sales literature and corporate identities for the hi-tech electronic, scientific, chemical and engineering industries. Our experience spans many years, working in London, Europe and the United States.
Please ask for our brochure.

Contact Mr John Carrod
Size 6-10

Carrods

GRAPHICS & PACKAGING

Carroll Dempsey & Thirkell Ltd

21 Brownlow Mews, London WC1N 2LA
Telephone 071-242 0992 Fax 071-242 1174

Established 11 years. Specialists in design for print. Experience covers: packaging; corporate identity; corporate brochures; annual reports; magazine and editorial design; postage stamp design; film/TV promotion and credit sequences; newspaper design. Clients include: Abbot Mead Vickers, R & A Baileys, Boots, BBC, BP Chemicals, Central Television, Design Museum, The English Tourist Board, Gilbeys of Ireland, Granada Film Productions, International Distillers & Vintners, London Chamber Orchestra, Macmillan Press, Marks & Spencer, Norton Rose, The Observer, Phillips & Drew, The Post Office, The Scotsman, Smirnoff, Smiths Industries, The Sunday Independent, Victoria & Albert Museum, Virgin, Willis Group.

Contact Mr Nicholas Thirkell
Size 11-20
Affiliations CSD

Chameleon Group Two

1 Manor Yard, Stowey, Bishop Sutton, Bristol, Avon BS18 4TH
Telephone (0272) 333111 Fax (0272) 332479

Areas of experience: corporate identity, sales/technical/public relations literature, livery, signage, exhibition, display and advertisement design.
Client base: building, computers, engineering, fine art, furniture, horticulture, insurance, laboratories, professional practices, relocation and trade associations.

Contact Mr Tony Baldaro
Size 1-5
Affiliations CSD

Chrissie Charlton and Company

The Old School House, 66 Leonard Street, London EC2A 4QX
Telephone 071-739 0540 Fax 071-729 5075

Chrissie Charlton and Company is a graphic design consultancy specializing in design for print, corporate identities and exhibition graphics. We work as a small, committed team with close partner involvement in each project, and aim to produce original work of the highest standard.
Our clients range from large corporate companies to small individual businesses and include the V&A, Queensberry Hunt, MMEC, Arts Council, RIBA and Next.

Contact Ms Chrissie Charlton
Size 1-5
Affiliations CSD, RCA

Checkland Kindleysides Design

Fowke Street, Rothley, Leicester, Leicestershire LE7 7PJ
Telephone (0533) 374282 Fax (0533) 374649

Established in 1979, Checkland Kindleysides has a reputation for highly creative work, matched with a mature ability for project management. Our approach puts total emphasis on the understanding of our clients' business aims and ambitions, enabling us to produce authoritative creative solutions that encompass many design disciplines including retail and interiors, graphics, corporate, literature, packaging, furniture and product. Our clients include: Levi Strauss (UK), Olympus Sport, Toyota GB, Dupont, Alfred Dunhill, Ballantyne Cashmere, Alexon and Lexus.

Contact Ms Marie Cooke
Size 21-50

Colin Cheetham Design Partnership

The Maltings, Brewery Road, Hoddesdon, Hertfordshire EN11 8HF
Telephone (0992) 464542 Fax (0992) 446086

Design, an analytical and creative exercise, not art; includes research, costing, copywriting, photographic directing, production specification and checking. Accent on value, technical accuracy, effectiveness, long term relationship.
Thirty years a company designing corporate identities, brochures, instruction manuals, quality awareness campaigns, mail order catalogues, packaging, posters, sign systems, point-of-sale, vehicle liveries. Large premises near M25, prototype workshop, computer DTP, communicative pleasant staff, complementary design skills (industrial design, exhibitions, interiors).
Clients: Aaronson, British Geological Survey, Cossor, Costain, Dexion, Fairchild, Merck Sharp & Dohme, Optrex, Wandsworth Electrical. Ask for our book.

Contact Mrs Sandy Chilton
Size 6-10 **Affiliations** CSD, RSA

Kim Church Associates Ltd

19 Short's Gardens, Covent Garden, London WC2H 9AT
Telephone 071-240 9731 Fax 071-836 8137

KCA are active in every area of graphic design including corporate identity, stationery, reports, literature, product development, direct marketing through to advertising.
We specialize in working in partnership with clients, to examine and understand the potential of communication through effective design.
In addition to our skill in concept development and design execution, KCA is experienced in project management and production. We are always pleased to discuss projects with prospective clients and ready to welcome any new challenge. KCA even boasts its own printing facility ensuring quality control and prompt delivery.

Contact Kim Church
Size 6-10

Citigate Design Ltd

7 Birchin Lane, London EC3V 9BY
Telephone 071-623 2737 Fax 071-623 1434

Citigate Design specializes in the design, production and strategic marketing of annual reports, corporate and marketing literature and corporate identity programmes.
We perceive design as a means to an end and not an end in itself. We approach every project from the perspective of the needs of the client and their audience groups to produce effectively targeted communications that maximize investment in design.
Clients come from many market sectors and include Cable & Wireless, Lloyds of London, The International Stock Exchange, The Royal Opera House, Granada Group and Abbey National.

Contact Ms Margaret Roberts
Size 21-50
Affiliations AP & PB, CSA, STD, CSD, Inst of Mktg

Roger Clinton-Smith Ltd

84 Haverstock Hill, Haampstead, London NW3 2BD
Telephone 071-267 7727 Fax 071-482 3862

Clinton Smith is an established independent design consultancy, specializing in packaging, corporate graphics and interiors. Our approach is pragmatic and commercially effective. It is tested every day on the shelves of food stores up and down the country, in the UK's main air and sea teminals and in every item of corporate graphics we produce. We insist on high creative standards. Our experienced designers work directly with clients ensuring that we understand their requirements, allowing us to produce well-designed solutions with realistic budgets and time schedules.

Contact Mr Roger Clinton-Smith
Size 6-10

92

Coley Porter Bell

4 Flitcroft Street, London WC2H 8DJ
Telephone 071-379 4355 Fax 071-379 5164

Coley Porter Bell specializes in building identities for companies and brands. Whether working to a corporate or marketing brief, our expertise is establishing and communicating, clearly and innovatively, what makes companies, products and services different from, and better than, their competitors. Our UK and international clients include United Biscuits, Lego, Smith Kline Beecham, A&P, Chase Manhattan, Wissoll, British Telecom and ICI.

Contact Ms Jan Hall
Size 51-100
Affiliations CSD, DBA, IOD, BPS

Communication Design Partnership

10 Cynthia Street, London N1 9JF
Telephone 071-833 3481 Fax 071-837 0952

We understand the importance of the balance between impact and content and are used to applying our guiding principles of informative clarity and innovative visual flair to the design, writing and production of promotional and technical literature.
Strong relationships with our clients and therefore understanding of their products and services enable us to produce clear, logical and well designed literature of all types within such areas as construction, computing, oil, interior design and finance.

Contact Mr Peter Hughes
Size 11-20
Affiliations CSD, RIBA

Communication by Design

6 The Courthouse, 38 Kingsland Road, London E2 8DD
Telephone 071-729 4000 Fax 071-739 5728

Communication by Design was established in 1978. As a multidiscipline consultancy the company specializes in corporate graphics, technical literature, guide books, signage programmes and exhibition graphics. Our resources include computer generated graphics, copywriting, photography, illustrators, artwork through to print buying, which provides our clients with a total service. Our clients include: Lloyds Register, British Aerospace, Mobil Shipping, British Gas, BBC, BP Chemicals, Metropolitan Police, Hampton Court Palace amongst others.

Contact Mr David Angus
Size 11-20
Affiliations CSD, DBA

Corporate Culture Ltd

BEC, Brunswick Business Park, Sefton Street, Liverpool, Merseyside L3 4BD
Telephone 051-708 5999 Fax 051-708 5832

Our complete in-house service combines management, marketing and design skills to provide commercially viable and relevant solutions.
Working closely with our clients, from a wide range of blue-chip companies to medium and smaller-sized organizations, throughout all stages of development, we apply design to give unity and purpose, strengthening the image of the whole organization.
Services include a complete appraisal of existing communications, design management, corporate identity, public relations, company newspapers, manuals, annual reports, sales presentations, exhibitions, brochures, new company packages, interiors, product development, company functions and acquisitions.

Contact Mr Timothy Leyland
Size 11-20

CORPORATE CULTURE

Creative Input Design Ltd

Stratfield House, 53 Wellington Road, Hampton Hill, Middlesex TW12 1JY
Telephone 081-943 5435 Fax 081-977 9647

A highly experienced design group specializing in corporate identity, corporate and product brochures, packaging, point-of-sale/merchandising and exhibition designs. Fully computer aided with all output facilities. Our strengths: attention to detail and ability to produce innovative design solutions allied to the practical application of sales and marketing ideas – within agreed budgetary constraints; each project being controlled by one of our senior partners, from initial brief through to final print production. Clients include: Beechams, BUPA, Canon, Coca-Cola, Coverdale, DTI, DHL, Express Foods, Financial Training, Gallaher International, Gillette UK, Henkel, Item Group, Kallo Foods, Kentucky Fried Chicken, Pizza Hut, Thames Water, The Wellcome Foundation, Wella.

Contact Mr Rash Nagar
Size 11-20
Affiliations CSD

Crombie Anderson

16 Comely Park, Dunfermline, Fife, Scotland KY12 7HU
Telephone (0383) 620247 Fax (0383) 620357

Crombie Anderson's Graphics Division provides complete design services addressing a broad range of communication needs. Our creative contribution begins with planning support and the formulation of clear communications strategies. It is on this that we build innovative solutions to particular marketing problems. Our work embraces corporate identity, profile and service support literature, product identity and branding, product literature and exhibition graphics.
Our portfolio covers: manufacturing, the professions, property development and retail sectors.

Contact Mr John Whyte
Size 21-50
Affiliations BIM, IMC

Daglish Hurst Ltd

100 Hermitage Road, Hitchin, Hertfordshire SG5 1DG
Telephone (0462) 421203 Fax (0462) 420775

Daglish Hurst is an experienced design agency involved in packaging design, brand imagery and new product development.
We offer a specialist integrated design service including: redesign, new pack design, repositioning of brands, range development, planning, new product development, 3D mock-ups, research, artwork studio.
Clients include Cadburys, Gateway Foodmarkets, Butterkist, Devenish Brewery, MFI, Winsor & Newton, Charles Wells Brewery, Ahsbury Confectionary, Lyons Bakeries and Lyons Patisserie.

Contact Mr Bill Hurst
Size 6-10
Affiliations DBA, D&AD

Davies Hall Ltd

The Forum, 74-80 Camden Street, London NW1 0EG
Telephone 071-387 7112 Fax 071-387 7112

Davies Hall is a small graphic design consultancy specializing in packaging, literature and corporate identity. Our approach is to work closely with our clients analysing each project and developing effective design solutions.
Clients include: Dewe Rogerson, Oasis (fashion retailer), Safeway, Sainsbury's, Tesco, Hoppers Farmhouse Bakeries, Sotheran's Antiquarian Books, Marks & Spencer, Lever Design, Continental Can Europe, Hampstead Theatre, Abbey National, Bass.

Contact Ms Nicky Burgin
Size 6-10
Affiliations DBA, D&AD

Brian Delaney Design Associates

10 Whitehorse Mews, Westminster Bridge Road, London SE1 7QD
Telephone 071-620 0820 Fax 071-620 1088

We are an established graphic design consultancy who firmly believe in producing work which is both creative and sensitive to clients' needs while still meeting their financial and marketing guidelines.
Our clients range from city firms to start-up companies and from well-known high street retailers to specialist organisations.
They include: Midland Bank, Marks & Spencer, John Lewis Partnership, The Post Office, Logica, Jaycare, Dulwich Picture Gallery and The Natural History Museum.

Contact Mr Brian Delaney
Size 6-10
Affiliations CSD

The Design Board

The Cottage, 28A High Street, Wombourne, Wolverhampton, West Midlands WV5 9DN
Telephone (0902) 324499 Fax (0902) 324520

The Design Board, formed in 1987, has carried out a variety of communications projects for international, national and local businesses. As a young progressive design consultancy, our alternative direct approach has had much to do with our success. We work in many fields of industry such as construction, property, brewing, retail, engineering, transport, leisure and professional organizations. Our designers work closely with clients so that solutions are not created in isolation, whether it is for corporate identity, advertising, packaging, brochures, exhibitions, or other associated communication assignments.

Contact Mr John Eaves
Size 1-5
Affiliations CSD

The Design Bridge UK Ltd

8-16 Cromer Street, London WC1H 8LX
Telephone 071-833 1311 Fax 071-837 3084 Telex 263459 BRIDGE G

The company is founded on a high level of experience in packaging design and corporate identity work. Clients include many leading names such as Sharwood's, RHM Foods, Lever Bros, Premier Brands, James Burroughs Distillers, Heinz, Nabisco, as well as international banks, industrial and detergent and drinks companies on the corporate side. These are balanced by a number of smaller clients who need a more comprehensive service. Our company offers a balance of real marketing with design and a detailed knowledge of many foreign markets. The results speak for themselves.

Contact Mr Philip Lawder
Size 21-50
Affiliations DBA

THE DESIGN BRIDGE

The Design Department Ltd

7 Imperial Road, London SW6 2AG
Telephone 071-731 4900 Fax 071-731 6550

We are specialists in the design and production of annual reports, corporate, financial and marketing literature and corporate identities.
We are dedicated to achieving the highest creative standards to help our clients communicate as effectively as possible with their target audiences and thus achieve their commercial objectives. Input from the principals on every project and attention to detail are hallmarks of our service.
Clients include AMI Healthcare, British Rail Property Board, Blue Circle, Brown & Root, Burston-Marsteller, Milk Marketing Board, Reckitt & Colman and Tiphook. Brochure available on request.

Contact Mr Mike Werkmeister
Size 6-10
Affiliations DBA, D&AD

Design House Consultants Ltd

120 Parkway, Camden Town, London NW1 7AN
Telephone 071-482 2815 Fax 071-267 7587

Design House has two decades' experience of working with clients to build brands and identities, and has an outstanding reputation for innovative design backed by sound marketing analysis and technical proficiency. We specialize in brand development, effective packaging, packaging technology and corporate identity. We also provide expert services in the design and production of annual reports and corporate and sales literature.
Design House currently holds the DBA Design Effectiveness Award for the Rabone Chesterman packaging range. Our portfolio of major brands includes: Lowenbrau, Persil, St Ivel Gold, Teacher's Whisky and Tetley Tea. Corporate communications clients include: Allied Lyons, Royal Trust Bank, Thomson Travel Group and Goldcrest Films.

Contact Ms Jessica Stevens
Size 6-10

Design Research Unit (DRU)

94 Lower Marsh, London SE1 7AB
Telephone 071-633 9711 Fax 071-261 0333

DRU works in all areas of graphic, communication and exhibition design. We have designed logotypes, corporate identities, brochures, annual reports, promotional literature, POS displays, packaging and signing systems for major corporations, retailers, manufacturers, banks, transport authorities and many others ranging from multinational organizations to local enterprises. Our knowledge of the exhibition business and display techniques enables us to achieve maximum promotional benefits for our clients. We have designed temporary and permanent exhibitions for local, national and multinational clients as well as governments and international organizations.

Contact Ms Clare Hulley
Size 21-50
Affiliations CSD, RIBA, BCB, DIA

The Design Revolution

10A Saint George's Place, Brighton, East Sussex BN1 4GB
Telephone (0273) 676151 Fax (0273) 670363

An established consultancy with fresh and innovative ideas, The Design Revolution provides a full graphic design service to both national and regional clients. From corporate identity and brochures to packaging and promotional literature, the company enjoys a reputation for high quality and professionalism. With clients as diverse as Rank Xerox, Lever Brothers and The Penguin Group, The Design Revolution develops relationships built on personal committment and inventive flair – whatever the brief.
The Design Revolution – turning design into action.

Contact Mr Richard Wheatley
Size 1-5

Dickson Huggins Associates Ltd

234 West Regent Street, Glasgow, Scotland G2 4DQ
Telephone 041-226 3555 Fax 041-204 1454

We are a fast growing, highly motivated design company with a prestigious client list and a wealth of experience in all aspects of graphic design. We are committed to a professional and commercial approach and our wide range of expertise enables us to work with each client to produce a highly individual and effective solution. We know we are judged by the high standards of the companies who are our clients and who continue to use our services. We welcome the opportunity to discuss design with you and to present our work.

Contact Mr Ian Dick
Size 11-20

Dowry Design Associates

28 Alma Vale Road, Clifton, Bristol, Avon BS8 2HY
Telephone (0272) 237995 Fax (0272) 238001

Dowry Design Associates are a multidisciplinary design partnership combining original, creative talent with down-to-earth experience. A compact team from many backgrounds with collective experience on national accounts, able to offer senior designer involvement at every stage.
We offer full graphic design facilities covering packaging for new product development, corporate identity and promotional literature, exhibitions and advertising. We are currently working for: Black Horse Agencies, Cockburns, Chesterton International, DRG Medical Packaging, Harveys of Bristol, Pearce Developments, The Taunton Cider Company.

Contact Mr Nicholas Bassett
Size 11-20
Affiliations CAM

Drawing Board

The Design Centre, 44 Canal Street, Manchester M1 3WD
Telephone 061-236 5500 Fax 061-236 3386

Drawing Board is an independent design group based in Manchester, with associate offices in Paris, Barcelona and New York. Our company objective is to design high quality corporate identity, publicity and packaging. Because of our blend of creative, marketing and production skills we have a proven track record of working successfully with a wide and varied client base. Multidisciplinary skills and involvement in our client's marketing strategy means that we often become involved in other areas of activity such as trade advertising, interiors and promotional concepts.

Contact Mr Richard Pemberton
Size 11-20
Affiliations CSD

The Drawing Room

1 Trinity Mews, Priory Road, Warwick, Warwickshire CV34 4NA
Telephone (0926) 495066 Fax (0926) 410168

The Drawing Room, formed in 1976 and currently occupying purpose-built studio space in historic Warwick, offers a service which covers all aspects of graphic design and print. The clients for whom we work regularly span a wide range of commercial interests from pharmaceuticals and engineering to the arts and leisure.
3M Healthcare, ICI Thoro, Lucas, International Wool Secretariat and The Royal Shakespeare Company are just a few examples from our client list, companies with whom we have developed an on-going creative relationship.

Contact Mr Richard Marshall-Hardy
Size 6-10
Affiliations CSD, DBA

Earl & Thompson Marketing

1 Hucclecote Road, Barnwood, Gloucester, Gloucestershire GL3 3TH
Telephone (0452) 372000 Fax (0452) 371344

Earl & Thompson Marketing was formed ten years ago to provide a 'whole service' design-led consultancy. The organisation, which has a team of ten full-time graphic designers, has a high reputation for corporate and product identities, brochures and support literature, together with packaging, annual reports and point-of-sale material. The team comprises four visualizers, two illustrators, and two finished artists. Additional skills within the team include typography, airbrush and technical illustration. The consultancy has three writers and is supported by an independently run press and public relations unit.

Contact Mr Robin Thompson
Size 21-50
Affiliations IPR, NS, PRCA, CSD, CIM

'Eleventh Hour' WZM Ltd

4 Lowndes Court, Carnaby Street, London W1V 1PP
Telephone 071-434 1348 Fax 071-734 3212

The successful application of creative solutions to marketing problems through design and copywriting for packaging, promotional material and advertising campaigns. A strategic thinking creative service with a broad spectrum of experience in consumer and commercial products, from FMCGs to company corporate images.
Working mainly with clients in food and drink, computers, financial, household and pharmaceutical, oil and petroleum and their advertising agencies.

Contact Mr Ziggy Zdziebko
Size 1-5

Epps Ransom Associates

Studio 24, Ransome's Dock, 35-37 Parkgate Road, London SW11 4NP
Telephone 071-228 8858 Fax 071-350 2389

We enjoy working with a wide range of clients whose activities present us with a variety of interesting problems to solve, from corporate identities through design for print, to exhibition design and build. Dealing with many disciplines has given us a thorough knowledge of production possibilities, thus enabling us to reach powerful creative solutions within budgetary constraints.

Contact Mr Tim Epps
Size 1-5

Eyedea Creative Consultancy Ltd

Newton House, 457 Sauchiehall Street, Glasgow, Scotland G2 3LG
Telephone 041-332 5454 Fax 041-331 1618

Design concepts for all forms of communication, including complete corporate identity programmes, company brochures and annual reports, point-of-sale and packaging, poster and exhibition work. Our approach to design is based upon solid marketing foundations and every product or company in totally researched prior to the initial design group meeting. Our client list is select and includes IBM, Montagu Evans, General Accident, GMI, SCOTVEC and Bass Export.
Our creative teams consist of highly experienced individuals who know the real meaning of client and target audience communication – in short, total professionalism.

Contact Mr Bill Alexander
Size 11-20

Fielding Rowinski

11 Princeton Court, 55 Felsham Road, Putney, London SW15 1AZ
Telephone 081-780 1309 Fax 081-780 1310

Fielding Rowinski has developed a reputation for providing stylish and original creative solutions that have received numerous design awards. All projects are efficiently and professionally managed with a particular emphasis on attention to detail.
We work across a wide range of business sectors including publishing, commercial property development, financial services and public relations and specialize in the following areas of activity: corporate identity, company literature (including annual reports), book design and packaging.

Contact Mr Paul Fielding
Size 6-10
Affiliations CSD, D&AD

Matthew Finch Design Consultants Ltd

17 High Street, Swanley, Kent BR8 8AE
Telephone (0322) 69333 Fax (0322) 614157

Established 1968, MFDC is an independent consultancy specializing in creative design for communication and marketing. Activities encompass corporate literature, brochures, packaging and retail design including new concepts for new companies, new products and services; also visual indentity management for established organizations.
MFDC is rated as one of the most efficient and effective design companies of its size in the UK.
MFDC is a founder member of Design International Resource Ltd and has affiliate offices in Chicago, Rome, Paris, Amsterdam, Dublin and Brussels.

Contact Mr John Hickinbottom
Size 21-50
Affiliations CSD, CIM, IOD, DBA

Fir Tree Design Company Ltd

46 Newport Road, Woolstones, Milton Keynes, Buckinghamshire MK15 0AA
Telephone (0908) 661100 Fax (0908) 670055 Telex 825908

Fir Tree are a specialist design consultancy, established in 1978 and based in central Milton Keynes.
We maintain a reputation for quality and creativity of work on corporate identities, corporate literature, packaging and product design. We have direct experience in many industries and are recognized for our ability to assess and address complex graphic problems.
Design, production and project management along with close involvement by the client combine to ensure a continuity of quality and approach.

Contact Ms Caroline Knight
Size 11-20

Fitch RS Design Consultants

4 Crinan Street, London N1 9UE
Telephone 071-278 7200 Fax 071-833 1014 Telex 22826

At Fitch we have built our graphics reputation on our ability to understand and respond to the business issues facing our clients and on specializiation. Our particular stengths are in corporate and brand identity, information design and simplification, marketing and corporate print, retail graphics and environmental graphics. Many of our projects involve blending graphics with the skills of our product and environmental design groups. The internationalism of Fitch RS is a particular benefit to clients in the US and mainland Europe; we are presently working in 19 countries.

Contact Mr David Rivett
Size over 100

FMO Design Consultants

67 George Row, London SE16 4UH
Telephone 071-237 8037 Fax 071-237 7386

FMO designs and produces printed material – corporate booklets, financial reports, brochures, exhibitions and press advertising. Specialist areas: financial services and pharmaceutical. Working knowledge of French and experience in producing Arabic publications. Clients include: Minet Holdings, Willis Corroon, Crawley Warren Group, British Telecom, Dubai Aluminum Company, Lipha Pharmaceuticals and Kimball Europe. The company is in its eighth year of trading.

Contact Mr Ken Osborn
Size 1-5

GRAPHICS & PACKAGING

Folio Graphics

7 Spelter Site, Maesteg, Mid-Glamorgan, Wales CF34 0TW
Telephone (0656) 730277 Fax (0656) 737937

Folio Graphics provides a comprehensive range of graphic design services including corporate identity design, packaging, promotional literature, brochures, company reports, point of sale and exhibition design. Our Creative Director is Canadian with a broad base experience in Canadian, American and British design and advertising. Clients range from manufacturing industries varying from engineering to cosmetics, retail outlets, also tourism attractions, service industries and public service sector.

Contact Mr Dennis Cassidy
Size 6-10

Forman Peacock Advertising Ltd

Thornfield House, Delamer Road, Altrincham, Cheshire WA14 2NG
Telephone 061-928 2224 Fax 061-926 8799

As an expanding advertising and design agency with our own art studio and dark room, our expertise involves all areas of graphic design, artwork and marketing, including corporate ID, sales literature, training manuals, exhibition/point-of-sale materials, property development, technical reports, packaging and press advertising (campaign scheduling and space booking).
Clients include: Thorn EMI Electronics, Soya Health Foods (UK and New Zealand), James Robertson & Son, Mopa Breweries (Nigeria), Plasticall (Europe), Hassall Homes (Cheshire), Hassall Homes (Cumbria), and NWS Bank.

Contact Mr Richard Forman
Size 11-20

Fosbueary Hamblin Design Associates

Unit 6E, 101 Farm Lane, Fulham, London SW6 1QJ
Telephone 071-385 1266 Fax 071-385 5493

Our strategy has been that of achieving effective creative solutions specifically targeted to our clients' requirements across a wide range of business environments. Our design pedigree, management skills and commitment to quality have assured a successful transition into marketing services in order to provide a complete client support role.
The key to this success lies in our having full in-house facilities and a company structure which ensures the active participation of the senior partners on all projects – guaranteeing a high degree of creativity and personal attention at all times.
Current clients include: British Tourist Authority, Comet, Burwood House Group, Dun & Bradstreet, Fyffes Group, Granada, National Dairy Council and Whitbread.

Contact Mr Ray Edwards
Size 21-50

The Four Hundred Ltd

6a New Concordia Wharf, St Saviours Dock, Mill Street, London SE1 2BA
Telephone 071-237 0587 Fax 071-231 6064

The Four Hundred is a well established design practice who until this year was known as H&P Design. We specialize in marketing communications planning combined with the highest level of design creativity. This unique combination of talents has enabled us to effectively handle corporate image programmes, brochures and technical publications and we are now listed, by Design magazine, in the top 50 award winning consultancies and No 8 for editorial/book design.

Contact Ms Win Rogers
Size 6-10
Affiliations CSD

Fox + Partners

The Old Forge, Norton St Philip, Bath, Avon BA3 6LW
Telephone (037 387) 271 Fax (037 387) 756 Telex 9312110903 FP G

We are a well established consultancy working on a wide range of projects (including corporate identity, promotional publications, packaging, annual reports, books, exhibitions) for an equally wide range of clients (including Ernst & Young, Consumers' Association, Herman Miller, Jordans, Macmillan Education). We're creative, committed and conscientious. But we're also extraordinarily flexible, and possess some unusual resources: we have our own editorial staff, to oversee complete publications or add professional polish to clients' copy, and we have wholeheartedly adopted computers as aids to page design, typography and illustration. Our rural location means that our overheads are low and our charges competitive.

Contact Ms Val Fox
Size 11-20
Affiliations CSD, STD

Freestone Design Consultants Ltd

30 The Forum, Rockingham Drive, Linford Wood, Milton Keynes, Buckinghamshire MK14 6LY
Telephone (0908) 676200 Fax (0908) 667181

Freestone Design Consultants provide a high calibre of design consultancy services. Our specific areas of expertise include corporate identity through sales and promotional literature, exhibition graphics, packaging and new brand development. Our clients range from local, small, dynamic companies to large multinational companies, including Laing Homes, Mercedes Benz, NEC, Argos and Next Directory. The two senior designers are also directors and enjoy a close working relationship with their clients. They have the experience to identify and to respond to a wide range of design needs and are able to call upon an impressive list and range of freelance services to customise the creative input needed on each design job.

Contact Mr Stuart Freestone
Size 6-10

Furneaux Stewart

24 Beaumont Mews, London W1N 3LN
Telephone 071-935 5724 Fax 071-486 0304

Our special quality as a company is the fertile combination of pure graphics and three-dimensional design to create realistic but lateral-view interpretations of client needs. Our field of activity includes exhibitions and special events, product launches and conferences, corporate communications, museum, leisure and heritage sites and commercial interiors. The wide range of our client list reflects the diversity of our projects: BET, British Marine Industries, British Telecom, City of Westminster, English Heritage, Hewlett-Packard, ICL, Natural History Museum, Nuclear Electric, Porsche Cars, STC, Sultanate of Oman.

Contact Ms Laurie Stewart
Size 6-10
Affiliations CSD, IOD, DBA

Gannon Design & Advertising

23/28 Penn Street, Islington, London N1 5DL
Telephone 071-729 4094 Fax 071-729 3793

The company prides itself on its ability to take on a wide variety of multidisciplinary work on behalf of clients in the service, retail, business-to-business, financial and commercial areas of activity. In particular, our knowledge of corporate identity applies and relates to all areas of the marketing mix, providing an integral co-ordination of activities through one source to give clients a total solution. Clients include: Rosentiel's Fine Art, Gulf International Bank, London Underground.

Contact Mr Paul Gannon
Size 6-10

GANNON

Genesis Advertising & Design Consultants

49 Hugh Street, London SW1V 1QJ
Telephone 071-630 0633 Fax 071-630 5202

'Unless an organization decides for itself the image it wants to project, other people will decide for it.'
(Dorothy Drake, former Director of Information, CBI). Good design is a vital element of good marketing –
it starts with the corporate image and encompasses packaging, advertising, direct mail, POS and so on – all
areas of Genesis expertise, a consultancy with 17 years' experience in creating appropriate and cost-
effective design. Our client list includes British Tourist Authority, English Tourist Board, Hamptons
International, Heinz, National Westminster Bank, P&O Containers, Parfums Stern, Premier Foods, Reed
Information Services and Videotron Cable TV.

Contact Mr Lional O'Hara
Size 6-10
Affiliations D&AD, AADC, ADM Creativity, GPMU

The Grand Design

217 Davidson Road, Croydon, Surrey CR0 6DP
Telephone 081-656 2045 Fax 081-656 0192

The Grand Design is a company with a reputation for creativity, an understanding of marketing and superb
client service. We are committed to accurate problem analysis and inventive, suitable solutions.
We produce promotional literature, annual reports, technical literature, exhibition display and corporate
identities; working closely with our clients who come back to us again and again.
Our high level of creativity is backed up by excellent copywriting and photography, and our in-house
typesetting, artwork and Apple Mackintosh facilities give us tight control over quality, deadlines and
budgets.

Contact Ms Charlotte Desorgher
Size 6-10

Grandfield Rork Collins

Prestige House, 14-18 Holborn, London EC1N 2LE
Telephone 071-242 2002 Fax 071-430 0952

Our objective is to fulfil the requirements of our clients by providing excellent visual communication to
their specific audiences. As part of a corporate and financial communications agency, our skills can be
enhanced by incorporating specialists from public relations, investor relations, employee relations and
consumer finance marketing, thus adding value to a company's marketing programme. Clients include:
Alsop Wilkinson, H Clarkson, Eurotunnel, Laing & Cruickshank, Midlands Electricity, Morgan Grenfell Asset
Management, SD-Scicon and Wiggins Teape Appleton.

Contact Mr Cameron Carruthers
Size 6-10
Affiliations D&AD

Graphex Design Consultancy

David Mews, 11a Greenwich South Street, Greenwich, London SE10 8NW
Telephone 081-853 3028 Fax 081-858 2128

Established in 1966, Graphex design has developed an experienced and skilled team offering services that
combine a high level of creativity with an understanding of client needs. An ability to create designs with
longevity and impact has given us a reputation as a 'thinking' design company.
Our clients didn't give us their work without agreeing the same. An ability to work with them as a team
was also a deciding factor.
As well as providing clients with the full thought process, we also provide a complete technical back up.

Contact Ms Rachel Hayward
Size 11-20
Affiliations CSD, CIM, IOD

Graphic Partners

Gladstone Court, 179 Canongate, Edinburgh, Scotland EH8 8BN
Telephone 031-557 3558 Fax 031-558 1430

Graphic Partners is one of Britain's leading graphic design consultancies. Winner of five Clio Awards and nominations in 1989 and 1990, the consultancy works at an international level. Specialists in creative design for the successful marketing of products and services – principally in corporate literature, brand packaging and corporate identity.
Clients include Invergordon Distillers, BP Exploration, Courtaulds, Dunedin Fund Managers, Marine Harvest, Northern Telecom, Marks & Spencer, Premier Brands, Allied Distillers, Scottish Widows, Tyne and Wear Development Corporation,Vaux Brewery, Edinburgh Marketing, United Biscuits, Crown Perfumery and W A Baxter.

Contact Mr Graham Duffy
Size 21-50
Affiliations CSD, IOD, DBA

The Green House

64 High Street, Harrow-on-the-Hill, Middlesex HA1 3LL
Telephone 081-422 6178 Fax 081-864 8370

The Green House specializes in packaging design and new product development. We pride ourselves in producing effective design which promotes and sells our clients' products. This is only achieved through a thorough understanding of the needs of our clients and their consumers, and of course the ability to produce highly creative design. Our team of experienced designers is supported by experienced marketing professionals with access to all types of market research. Our clients include: Brooke Bond Foods, Eden Vale, Hasbro, Lever Brothers, Lipton (Export), McCormicks, Nestlé, Premier Foods, Safeway.

Contact Mr Hugh Lee
Size 11-20
Affiliations DBA

Grey Matter Design Consultants plc

28 Scrutton Street, London EC2A 4RJ
Telephone 071-247 1887 Fax 071-377 9909

Grey Matter is an independent, multidisciplinary, award-winning design team specializing in graphic design and industrial design. The graphics portfolio includes annual reports, corporate brochures and promotional material, corporate identity programmes, editorial design and product packaging.
The designers' in-depth expertise includes strong technical skills, print buying and full production management. Our client list is broad, ranging from small start-up companies through to multinationals.

Contact Mr Mark Gandy
Size 11-20
Affiliations RSA, DBA, D&AD

Grundy & Northedge Designers

Thames Wharf Studios, Rainville Road, London W6 9HA
Telephone 071-385 3344 Fax 071-381 6217

The aim of Grundy & Northedge is to remain a small close-knit group so the partners can remain directly involved with the design process at all stages from conception to print. For the past ten years we have employed our own distinctive typographic, illustrative and design skills over a wide variety of projects to create visually exciting and individual solutions. Our clients cover a broad span from government departments and public institutions to publishers, businesses and other design groups and creative practices.

Contact Ms Tilly Northedge
Size 1-5
Affiliations DBA, D&AD

Timothy Guy Design

Moresk Road, Truro, Cornwall TR1 1DG
Telephone (0872) 75444 Fax (0872) 70388

For 20 years, the studio has provided creative solutions for diverse projects in graphics, corporate identity, interiors, exhibition and enviromental design, serving the world's top companies – ICI, GE (USA), Thorn EMI and local Cornish business, achieving a reputation for the highest standards in design and print. The studio's new premises (opened late '90) demonstrate the designers' skills in architecture, shop fitting and display.

Contact Mr Timothy Guy
Size 6-10
Affiliations CSD, RSA

GWA Design Consultants Ltd

79 Long Acre, Covent Garden, London WC2E 9NG
Telephone 071-379 7972 Fax 071-240 7793

GWA is a long established, medium-sized company offering design services in all areas of graphic design, principally corporate print work and corporate identity.
Our intelligent, functional approach to design problems has led to a successful relationship with the professions. In-house production services, including extensive DTP facilities, enable GWA to provide a varied, full and cost-conscious service to a wide client base.
Other areas of expertise include information design, from statistical product area/industrial reviews to annual reports and publishing, both for commercial clients and publishing houses.

Contact Mr Graeme Wilson
Size 6-10
Affiliations DBA

HALLRichards

94 Leonard Street, London EC2A 4RH
Telephone 071-729 1880 Fax 071-739 1862

Working throughout Europe, in America and the Middle East, HALLRichards gives a comprehensive service in products, graphics, packaging, furniture, lighting, interiors and exhibitions. Market orientated, innovative concepts are taken through detail design, development, prototyping and testing, utilizing our CAD sysytem and fully equipped workshops. We are experienced in sourcing sub-contractors and supervising production. Design of literature, packaging, corporate and brand identity completes the service. Clients include American Express, AGB, British Rail, Courtaulds, Exxon, National Bank of Kuwait, Next, Philips and TSB.

Contact Ms Stella Gilleberg
Size 11-20
Affiliations CSD, IEE

Halpen Graphic Communication Ltd

Victoria House, Gertrude Street, Chelsea, London SW10 0JN
Telephone 071-351 5577 Fax 071-352 7418

Good design sells.
Our business is to provide our clients with well designed brochures and literature that will help sell their products and services. Halpen is an established graphic design company with a well equipped modern studio. We can create artwork for any type of job, however complex, and manage all stages of production through to printing. For the companies that have their own desk-top publishing systems we also provide a bureau service enabling them to output their work on our typesetting equipment.

Contact Mr Philip Sweny
Size 11-20
Affiliations IM

GRAPHICS & PACKAGING

John Harris Design Consultants Ltd

151a Gloucester Road, South Kensington, London SW7 4TH
Telephone 071-370 4191 Fax 071-370 0956

John Harris Design Consultants is a small specialist consultancy founded in 1968 by the current chairman, John Harris.
The company offers four areas of expertise: corporate identity consultancy, brand identity, packaging and corporate literature.
In order to preserve high creative standards, emphasis is placed on a combination of analytical and design skills and the flexibility to meet each client's individual needs.
Clients include: Allied Lyons, United Distillers, Safeway, British Shoe Corporation, Wessex Water, Peter Black, Avis and Mobil Oil.

Contact Mrs Emmeline Winterbotham
Size 11-20
Affiliations CSD, DBA

The Harrison Greenwell Partnership Ltd

No 3 Lionel Street, Birmingham, West Midlands B3 1AQ
Telephone 021-233 4404 Fax 021-200 1594

Now established as a leading design consultancy, specializing in corporate identity, brochures, promotional literature, point-of-sale, packaging and exhibitions.
Design solutions are always creative and intelligent, carefully researched and targeted, from concept to implementation.
The companies we have worked with during the last five years include Cadburys, Delta, Horizon Holidays, The National Trust, The Nature Conservancy Council, Polycell, Qualcast Garden Products, Swish, TSB Bank, Williams Holdings

Contact Ms Denise Harrison
Size 11-20

Harrison/Zulver (Design & Marketing Consultants)

21-27 Seagrave Road, Fulham, London SW6 1RP
Telephone 071-381 4258 Fax 071-385 8726

Our well established company has been commissioned by national and international clients, in the service and manufacturing industries, for corporate identity, corporate, sales and technical literature, product image and packaging, including the complete marketing and research requirements in establishing distribution system networks for the introduction of European speciality foods into North American supermarket groups. Clients include: Courtaulds, The George Wimpey Group, The International Tennis Federation, Lazard Brothers, Legal & General, Shamrock Foods, A & P of Canada, Thornycroft, Vickers Shipbuilding & Engineering and Woolworths. Brochures available.

Contact Mr John Harrison
Size 11-20

Henrion, Ludlow & Schmidt

12 Hobart Place, London SW1W 0HH
Telephone 071-235 5466 Fax 071-235 8637

Henrion, Ludlow & Schmidt is one of the leading international corporate identity consultancies in Europe, working for major clients worldwide in a variety of key business areas. We specialize in corporate, brand and retail identity as well as in corporate print and promotion. Clients include Coopers & Lybrand (Worldwide), London Underground, Mitsubishi Motors (Tokyo), J P Morgan (New York), KLM Royal Dutch Airlines and British Midland Airways. Our extensive knowledge of world markets is partnered by acknowledged creativity and design excellence.

Contact Mr Chris Ludlow
Size 21-50
Affiliations CSD

John Herbert Partnership

8 Berkley Road, Primrose Hill, London NW1 8YR
Telephone 071-722 3932 Fax 071-586 7048

The John Herbert Partnership is a multidisciplinary design consultancy of graphic, interior and product designers. We specialize in corporate identity, strategic planning, new concept development and building refurbishment, for retail, leisure, financial services, offices and restaurants. We are committed to creative and cost-effective design and professional service for our clients. These include: Selfridges, British Airports Authority, British Shoe Corporation, Marks & Spencer, British Rail, Capital & Counties, Norwich Union, National Trust. Award-winning projects for Sears Holdings, Coventry Building Society and British Gas.

Contact Ms Patricia Herbert
Size 21-50
Affiliations CSD, RICS, BCSC, RSA, DBA

Herron Oakley Design

Thorpe House, 17 Dormer Place, Leamington Spa, Warwickshire CV32 5AA
Telephone (0926) 451750 Fax (0926) 833650

Herron Oakley Design is a graphic design consultancy specializing in corporate identities and high quality print literature including brochures and annual reports. Clients include Vauxhall Master Leasing, LINK Recruitment, Leamington Spa Building Society, City of Westminster Insurance plus many smaller companies.
Started in 1984, Herron Oakley has grown steadily and is conveniently located in Leamington Spa. We offer a comprehensive service which includes not just design but copywriting, photography and print supervision. In fact, everything necessary to achieve a first class result, efficiently and to a previously agreed budget.

Contact Ms Linda Herron Oakley
Size 6-10
Affiliations CSD

Barry Hill Design

34 Harwood Road, Fulham, London SW6 4PH
Telephone 071-384 2280 Fax 071-386 8194

Barry Hill Design is a small London based consultancy, formed in 1981, providing creative design solutions for clients ranging from small businesses to international companies. Our work includes annual reports, corporate identities, packaging, posters and calendars.
We also work in conjunction with the Paris based design group BTH. Clients: Otis, John Lewis Partnership, Kodak, BSN, Marketing Improvements, Crisp & Wilson.

Contact Ms Mary Hurley
Size 1-5

Glenn Hilling

Unit 19, 10-11 Archer Street, London W1V 7HG
Telephone 071-439 0397 Fax 071-734 8771

Recent work includes: the complete visual presentation for a major London charity exhibition; devising and applying a logo to promote a new marketing image at the Royal Opera House; new product design for the Royal Academy of Arts shop; an extensive range of promotional material for the Royal Institute of Public Administration as well as corporate development programmes for several new companies.

Contact Mr Glen Hilling
Size 1-5

GRAPHICS & PACKAGING

Hi-Tech Video

6 Baird Close, Stephenson, Washington, Tyne & Wear NE37 3HL
Telephone 091-417 7266 Fax 091-416 3914

With years of experience in all areas of audio and visual communications, Hi-Tech Video can offer a complete service to companies of all sizes. Whether the brief is for a simple corporate video or complete project design, our clients benefit from our comprehensive in-house production facilities, encompassing the latest technology available.
Hi-Tech Video is much more than just a video production company as clients such as Thorn EMI, Barratt Developments, Tilcon and British Gas are finding out.

Contact Mr Malcolm Hall
Size 1-5

Nick Holland Design Group Ltd

The Bank, 10 Mount Stuart Square, Cardiff, South Glamorgan, Wales CF1 6EE
Telephone (0222) 490293 Fax (0222) 471225

A high-quality multidisciplinary design group, internationally recognized for contemporary design in consumer and industrial markets.
We provide comprehensive services in graphic, product and surface design, backed up by marketing and market research consultancy. Our services in graphic design include corporate identity, packaging, promotional and technical literature, print, point-of-sale and exhibitions.
Clients include a broad spectrum of international blue-chip companies and small businesses throughout the UK and overseas.

Contact Mr Nick Holland
Size 11-20
Affiliations CSD, DBA, RSA, IM

Sarah Holland

52 Wilberforce Road, London N4 2SR
Telephone 071-226 2862

I have been working as a freelance graphic designer for the past six years, before which I was employed by several major design consultancies. My work covers the broad range of graphic disciplines, such as: annual reports, brochures, exhibition catalogues, corporate identities and packaging.
Clients have included: the Crafts Council, Pentos, Heinz, Athena Art Awards, Planters, Heal's & Sons, the Arts Council, Habitat, Bridgewater Ceramics, Harvey Nichols, the Multiple Sclerosis Society, British Telecom and British Rail.

Contact Ms Sarah Holland
Size 1-5
Affiliations CSD

Holmes Linnette

3-5 Bleeding Heart Yard, Off Greville Street, Hatton Garden, London EC1N 8SJ
Telephone 071-242 2131 Fax 071-404 5700 Telex Modem 071-430 9852

Holmes Linette is an amalgamation of the Holmes Design Consultancy and Linnette Design and Advertising, and as such supplies a wide range of clients with a complete deisgn and marketing service. From product development and corporate design through to production, every aspect of each project is closely monitored by the directors (all working designers) ensuring that clients obtain creative business solutions at an affordable price.

Contact Mr David Holmes
Size 6-10

Susan Holton Design Consultancy

London House, 42 Upper Richmond Road West, London SW14 8DD
Telephone 081-876 0102 Fax 081-878 2070

The firm specializes in corporate image, annual report and brochure design. We seek to present our clients' business, personality and style effectively, appropriately and with impact – doing more than simply presenting information. Our deliberately small size allows large and small projects to be approached creatively and cost-effectively, with high standards of service and attention. We offer a full consultancy service from initial planning through design to preparation for reproduction, print, etc and we are equally happy to tackle small or one-off projects. Our experience includes work for finance, industry, commerce and leisure.

Contact Ms Susan Holton
Size 1-5
Affiliations CSD

Martin Hopkins Partnership

31 The Parade, Cardiff, South Glamorgan, Wales CF2 3AD
Telephone (0222) 461233 Fax (0222) 497208

We are a high quality graphic design consultancy specializing in corporate identity projects, the design and production of annual reports, company brochures, all forms of promotional and informative literature, packaging and exhibitions. Our clients include government agencies, local authorities, tourist boards, food manufacturers, consumer services. Projects have included interior store designs and displays for a chain of national stores. We aim for high quality in both creativity and typography, and personally project manage all our work.

Contact Mr Robert Martin
Size 6-10
Affiliations CSD

HRO'C Design Ltd

HRO'C House, 53 Church Road, Edgbaston, Birmingham, West Midlands B15 3SJ
Telephone 021-454 9707 Fax 021-454 8011

HRO'C concentrates upon marketing-based brand, product and corporate design, development and communication. The company is managed by designers with extensive hands-on experience of corporate communications, packaging and literature design. The client base is broad, ranging from fashion to building products, high technology to earth moving.

Contact Mr Ian West
Size 11-20
Affiliations CIM, Mktg Soc, IOP, NPA, PPA, IOD

Hutton Staniford

5 Apollo Studios, Charlton Kings Road, London NW5 2SB
Telephone 071-482 2140 Fax 071-485 6068

We believe in working closely with organisations – partner to client – with no intermediaries blurring communications at any stage of a project. The solutions we propose are as individual as our clients. Whatever the size of the project, the same principles apply: close partner involvement, attention to detail and strict devotion to the highest standards of finish. Clients include: Boots, Channel 4, Coopers & Lybrand, Deloitte, Letraset, Midland Montagu and Tesco. Packaging for Tesco won us an international Clio award last year.

Contact Mr Steve Hutton
Size 6-10
Affiliations D&AD

GRAPHICS & PACKAGING

The Idea Works

6-7 Trim Street, Bath, Avon BA1 1HB
Telephone (0225) 338366 Fax (0225) 319719

The Idea Works covers all the usual areas of packaging, literature, direct mail, corporate identity and promotions, but it does it in an unusual way with what we call a Total Communication Package, allowing one strong, carefully evaluated theme to permeate through every aspect of a company's output. We are very unlikely to produce a single item in isolation, but rather create the whole marketing and visual platform. This we do for clients, both national and local, who share the same philosophy: to understand that 'creativity' isn't just pretty pictures, but a whole way of thinking – and the best way to earn a return from their efforts.

Contact Mr Paul Barrett
Size 21-50

Illsley Wilson Baylis Ltd

Beaver House, Victoria Road, Swindon, Wiltshire SN1 3AU
Telephone (0793) 486922 Fax (0793) 619252 Telex 449703

Accomplished design group with a 20 year track record in packaging, design for print, POS and corporate work. Around 30 designers and visualizers, illustrators, finished artists and computer operators provide flexible and highly creative in-house capability and fast and cost-effective production facility.
Major clients include: St Ivel, Dowty Group, Radio Rentals, London Transport, Marks & Spencer, Scott, Benckiser, Castrol, Science Research Council, Bayer, Racal, Daler Rowney, Rank Hovis, Post Office, NEM Insurance. Office also in central London. Brochure on request.

Contact Mr Marc Adams
Size 21-50

IMA Design Consultants

346 Old Street, London EC1V 9NQ
Telephone 071-729 4473 Fax 071-729 6214

Established in 1987, four years have produced many exciting and successful projects within diverse business arenas for clients such as: Association for the Monetary Union of Europe, Avatar, Bovis Construction Group, Digital, the Enterprise International Development Company, Euro Disneyland, Kumagai Gumi, Le Manoir aux Quat' Saisons, Letraset International, Marlin Lighting, MEPC, Merlin International Properties, Midland Bank Group Treasury, Midland Bank Trust Corporation (Jersey), Midland Montagu, Olympia & York, Open-Plan, Reed Business Publishing Group, Regalian Properties, Shimizu Corporation, TSB (South Wales), Young & Co.
IMA is presently working with a variety of UK based clients and is involved with projects in Europe and Japan.

Contact Mr Ian Hatton
Size 11-20
Affiliations DBA, CSD, STD

Imagination Ltd

25 Store Street, South Crescent, London WC1E 7BL
Telephone 071-323 3300 Fax 071-323 5801 Telex 291788

Imagination has been producing high quality design and setting the standards for effective 'live' communications for twelve years. Today it is Europe's most innovative design and communication company with major clients in the industrial, consumer, retail and public sectors, and a New York office. Based in an award-winning building in the heart of the West End, designed by in-house architects Herron Associates, Imagination have a strong design capability with specialist consultants in corporate print, brand development, retail and exhibitions and packaging.

Contact Ms Krystina Hunter-Coddington
Size over 100
Affiliations RIBA

GRAPHICS & PACKAGING

The Indigo Design Company

Studio 18, 43 Carol Street, London NW1 0HT
Telephone 071-284 1413 Fax 071-267 8118

The Indigo Design Company provides an integrated resource for the complete process of creating and managing corporate identity and corporate image, covering communications analysis, visual and facilities audit, identity design, design of corporate applications and implementation.
The company enjoys a reputation amongst its current clients for high quality work and a commitment to budgetary control and timescale management.

Contact Mr Nick Herbert
Size 6-10
Affiliations CSD

Liz James Design Associates Ltd

18 Pindock Mews, Maida Vale, London W9 2PY
Telephone 071-286 5188 Fax 071-286 5121

We specialize in corporate and financial communications, corporate identities, brochures, sales/technical publications and associated areas of design. The consultancy has a long-standing reputation for the creative and enduring qualities of the design solutions it produces and aims for excellence in all aspects of its design work. Liz James Design Associates provides lasting solutions to a design brief which look beyond the obvious influences of changing fashionable taste.
Clients include: Barclays Premier Card, British Olivetti, Gardiner & Theobald, The Sainsbury Family, Michael Samuelson Lighting, Sun Life Assurance Society.

Contact Ms Liz James
Size 1-5
Affiliations CSD, DBA

Marion James Design Consultants

19 Church Street, Warwick, Warwickshire CV34 4AB
Telephone (0926) 496886 Fax (0926) 410096

'To consult is to seek another's approval of a course already decided upon.' – Ambrose Bierce

(Those who believe this would be wise to consult a design group other than Marion James.)

Contact Mr James Boulter
Size 6-10

Jarvis White Design

The Old Mill, Mill Lane, Avening, Near Tetbury, Gloucestershire GL8 8PD
Telephone 045-383 5516 Fax 045-383 5561

One of the country's top three brand identity consultancies in the 1989 Design Effectiveness Awards and internationally judged in the 1990 Clio Awards in New York as finalists in two categories.
Our listening approach with our clients produces solutions, on brief, on time and to budget.
We specialize in corporate image, brand identity, packaging design and sales support design material. Our client base is as varied as the blue-chips – from McVitie's Group, Ranks Hovis McDougall, Kraft General Foods and the Department of Transport, to award-winning solutions for Design Council/ Initiative exercises.

Contact Mr Terry White
Size 11-20

Sally Jeffery

The Old Exchange, Cockfield, Bury St Edmunds, Suffolk IP30 0LY
Telephone (0284) 828933 Fax (0284) 827064

Publications design: a long-established specialist in typography for stuctures information. Clients include publishers, information and training consultants, software developers, design engineers, arts organizations, galleries and museums. Our concern is to produce clear, appropriate designs which we take right though production to ensure successful results. Editing and composition is done in-house on a Macintosh system, with text transfer via disc or modem: this integrated design process allows complex projects to be accurately visualized and responsively developed.

Contact Ms Sally Jeffery
Size 1-5
Affiliations CSD

Jones & Co Design Ltd

DESIGN
COUNCIL
REGISTERED

Greenland Studio, Greenland Street, Camden, London NW1 0ND
Telephone 071-482 4324 Fax 071-482 0089

Jones & Co Design is a creative team offering an in-depth consultancy service specializing in packaging design, brand identity, product development, point-of-sale, brochures and corporate identity.
Our client list is impressive – from small businesses to large multiples. To see our presentation, contact Jack Jones.

Contact Mr Jack Jones
Size 11-20

KB Design

DESIGN
COUNCIL
REGISTERED

18 Pindock Mews, Maida Vale, London W9 2PY
Telephone 071-286 5188 Fax 071-286 5121

We aim to provide unique design solutions which are refreshingly attractive, communicate effectively and which are efficiently managed and implemented. We are committed to the preservation of the environment and the way we process our design solutions reflects this.
The sectors we work in are: corporate identity, corporate literature, packaging, signage and retail environments. The geographical locations where we actively service clients are London, the Home Counties and, being Danish, I also act for clients in Scandinavia.

Contact Ms Karen Blincoe
Size 1-5
Affiliations IDD, CSD

Keeble & Hall

DESIGN
COUNCIL
REGISTERED

Holy Innocents Church, Paddenswick Road, Hammersmith, London W6 0UB
Telephone 081-563 0299 Fax 081-563 0301

Origins – Keeble & Hall is a small well established design consultancy.
Working together – the best work results from close consultation with our clients. Small and large projects produce equally innovative solutions.
Clients and consumers – our principles, central to the consultancy from the start, have been based on the clients' objectives and the versatility to adapt to different consumer requirements.
Experience – the wealth of our experience comes from packaging and promotional material for clients that include: WH Smith, Fisons, Saxbys, Adnams Brewery, Dole Fresh Fruit, King & Barnes Brewery.

Contact Mr Chris Keeble
Size 1-5
Affiliations RSA, CSD

Kilvingtons Design Consultants

The Bank Gallery, The High Street, Kenilworth, Warwickshire CV8 ILY
Telephone (0926) 50347 Fax (0926) 53844

Kilvingtons is a broad based graphic design practice specializing in corporate identity, brand identity and literature. The company has developed and implemented several major international corporate identity schemes including commissions for Massey Ferguson, Norton Rose M5 and Triumph Motorcycles. Whilst being respected for its award winning creativity the company is also recognized for a strong, stategic marketing-led approach to design, being both innovative and accountable.

Contact Mr Paul Kilvington
Size 11-20
Affiliations D&AD, DBA, CSD. RCA

Kirk Design Studio Ltd

17 Leazes Crescent, Newcastle-upon-Tyne, Tyne & Wear NEI 4LW
Telephone 091-222 1060 Fax 091-221 0185

Kirk Design Studio is a small, professional company offering a complete design service from concept through artwork to print.
We have a reputation for producing imaginative and successful solutions tailored to a client's particular needs. Our careful, personal approach has attracted a loyal client base which ranges from individuals running their own businesses to large, international companies. Our strengths include corporate identity and packaging, promotional literature and direct mail.

Contact Ms Judi Kirk
Size 1-5

John Kirk Design Ltd

Hayhill Industrial Estate, Sileby Road, Barrow Upon Soar, Leicestershire LE12 8LD
Telephone (0509) 813408 Fax (0509) 816098

Formed in 1975, John Kirk Design has grown in reputation as one of the leading design consultancies based in the Midlands. Our talents and expertise covers design for retail, leisure, commercial, museum, exhibition and graphic design, encompassing corporate identities, brochures, packaging and point-of-sale.
JKD offers a comprehensive service from concept and design to production, with the same high standards of creativity, service and commitment being maintained throughout.
Principal clients: British American Tobacco, British Shoe Corporation, Dixons, Trusthouse Forte, Wade Potteries and C P Rice Mills.

Contact Mr John Kirk
Size 21-50
Affiliations BECA, GDIM, DBA

Kubiak & Grange Design Associates

I Waterloo Street, Ironbridge, Telford, Shropshire TF8 7AA
Telephone (0952) 433566 Fax (0952) 433566

Consultants in advertising, information and publicity design – with good connections.

Contact Mr Anthony Kubiak
Size 1-5

Lackie Newton Ltd

DESIGN
COUNCIL
REGISTERED

13/15 Circus Lane, Edinburgh, Midlothian, Scotland EH3 6SU
Telephone 031-220 4141 Fax 031-220 4004

We are committed to making companies, products and services more visible through innovative design solutions. We make a point of understanding a company, its strengths and weaknesses, its personality, before starting the design process. We understand that design is all about selling and will work as a team with clients to achieve all these goals.
Clients include: Cambridge Computers, Scottish Provident, Ivory & Sime, The Royal Bank of Scotland, Scottish Widows, The Scottish Development Agency, Dawson International, Scottish Television, Spider Systems, Standard Life, Stewart Ivory and the WM Company.

Contact Ms Kate Lackie
Size 11-20
Affiliations IOD, CSD, D&AD

Lane Design

Henrietta House, 17/18 Henrietta Street, Covent Garden, London WC2 8QX
Telephone 071-836 9991 Fax 071-497 2633 Telex 265354

We are an award winning consultancy experienced in working internationally with large multinationals as well as small concerns. We provide expertise in the areas of corporate identity, literature, brochures and packaging. We speak English, German, French and Italian and have designed multilingual promotional material and annual reports.

Contact Lars Townsen
Size 6-10
Affiliations OIF

Lane
Design

Lawton Design Studio

2 The Firs, Pinfold Lane, Wheaton Aston, Stafford, Staffordshire ST19 9PD
Telephone (0785) 840283

A practising graphic designer and illustrator for 23 years and with the following principles of paramount importance during that period: approaching the client and his products with full understanding of the marketing area; producing a high standard of work in the firm belief that good design and print sells; flexibility – to think there is only one way is unprofessional; creating design and artwork that can be produced economically; building a good-working relationship with photographer, repro house and printer. Clients have included: PRD, Ironbridge Gorge Museum, The Griflex Group, Gibbons Locks, Dartec, Bell Metals, PDSA, Wrekin Tourist Board.

Contact Mr Robert Cox
Size 1-5

Lawton Hawthorne Advertising Ltd

DESIGN
COUNCIL
REGISTERED

Derby House, 12 Winckley Square, Preston, Lancashire PR1 3JJ
Telephone (0772) 556324 Fax (0772) 57059

The agency provides specialist design services for consumer goods packaging, from food products to duvets, with wide-ranging expertise in corporate identity work, literature and below-the-line promotions. We combine strong design, sound marketing knowledge and creative writing: elements vital to producing successful solutions. The importance we apply to these specialist skills is reflected in our recruitment of the highest calibre staff and our list of clients operating in Europe, the UK and North and South America

Contact Mr Peter Lawton
Size 21-50

Lewis and Medzavorian Design Consultants Ltd

1/7 Harbour Yard, Chelsea Harbour, London SW10 0XD
Telephone 071-351 7132 Fax 071-351 4804

A highly skilled consultancy with a defined philosophy, dedicated to imaginative clearly targeted design solutions. We provide full project management and specialize in corporate identity, product and service branding, communications literature, packaging, POS, promotions and exhibitions. Our work has been implemented cost-effectively within the marketing strategies of clients such as Rediffusion Films, Wimpey Homes, Lever Industrial, International Wool Secretariat, Linfood, Rombouts Coffee and Toshiba Photocopiers. Should you wish to see how we can benefit your company, please contact Chris Lewis.

Contact Mr Christopher Lewis
Size 1-5

Lewis Moberly

33 Gresse Street, London W1P 1PN
Telephone 071-580 9252 Fax 071-255 1671

Lewis Moberly specializes in brand identity, packaging and corporate identity design. We have a reputation for award winning design working hard in the market place. Our team of strategic planners and designers ensures that we communicate, not decorate. Clients include: Boots, Birds Eye Wall's, Eagle Star, Bennett Waller-Bridge Wilson & Associates, Hallmark, H J Heinz, Johnson & Johnson, Lever, Shipton Mill, Yves Rocher.
Services include: market research, strategic planning, design management, graphic design, structural design, packaging, environmental audits, implementation.

Contact Ms Fiona Gilmore
Size 21-50
Affiliations CSD, D&AD, Assoc Illrs

Light & Coley Ltd

20 Fulham Broadway, London SW6 1AH
Telephone 071-381 6644 Fax 071-381 2833

We have been producing successful graphic design for packaging, literature and corporate image since 1982. We believe that we continue to be an asset to our clients because we have clearly identified what is required to develop our people into a company that not only understands business objectives, produces quality and is committed to service, but is also a happy one.
Our clients include: The Economist, Jones Lang Wootton, McVities and Wilkinson Sword.

Contact Mr Nigel Morris
Size 21-50
Affiliations DBA

Lloyd Northover Ltd

8 Smart's Place, London WC2B 5LW
Telephone 071-430 1100 Fax 071-430 1490

Status: a world class, independent specialist consultancy in identity, corporate communications and design. Activities: corporate identity and brand management; brand identity and packaging; environments – retail outlets, offices, business environments; literature – annual reports, corporate literature. Our aim: to provide the most effective identity and design consultancy service for the world's most significant companies, organizations and entrepreneurs – a service which contributes tangibly to their long-term future success. Our method: teamwork, sound strategic thinking, exceptional creative innovation.
In Europe: Shining/Lloyd Northover, Paris office, 26 rue Benard, 75014 Paris, France. Tel: 010 331 40 44 9327. Fax 010 331 40 44 9347.

Contact Ms Philippa Emery
Size 21-50
Affiliations CSD, DBA, CBI, D&AD, RSA, Design Museum

David Lock Design Ltd

12 Peterborough Mews, London SW6 3BL
Telephone 071-731 4495 Fax 071-731 4533

We specialize in expressing company culture, both externally and internally. Any company can only deliver its external promise if its message is understood, committed to and implemented by its employees. Externally this belief has led us to carry out corporate positioning and identity programmes, annual reports and corporate communications. Internally we have a unique track record in internal marketing including recruitment, Total Quality Management, customer care and best practices programmes. We have 20 years' multinational experience working for such companies as Barclays Bank, Dow Europe, IBM Europe, SD-Scicon and Visa EMEA.

Contact Mr David Lock
Size 1-5
Affiliations ABC, CSD, D&AD

The Ian Logan Design Company

42 Charterhouse Square, London EC1M 6EU
Telephone 071-606 1803 Fax 071-726 6419

Established for 20 years in graphics and packaging, we are an experienced and creative design company working for many top clients: Boots, W H Smith, Waitrose, Harrods, Perrier, Heinz (Italy), London Transport and The Post Office.
Our aim has always been to increase sales for our clients while pushing creative design, within the framework of the brief, to the limit.

Contact Mr Ian Logan
Size 11-20
Affiliations RSA, CSD

Ruth Lowe Advertising & Graphic Design

Observation Court, 84 Princes Street, Ipswich, Suffolk IP1 1RY
Telephone (0473) 217118 Fax (0473) 231294

Our company, started in 1984, consists of five employees – a team of creative designers, finished artists and administrative staff. All members of the company have had many years' experience in advertising and design. The company specialises in designing for print, in areas ranging from a complete corporate image or company brochure, to packaging and exhibition displays. Advertising, direct mail, merchandising and marketing complete our service, from the initial creative concept through to the final finished product. Our clients include GRE, Thompson & Morgan, Fisons, London Anglia Developments and Pauls Agriculture.

Contact Ms Ruth Lowe
Size 1-5

Magee & Company

12 Port House, Square Rigger Row, Plantation Wharf, Battersea, London SW11 3TY
Telephone 071-924 3244 Fax 071-223 8254

Magee & Company specialize in creative design for the successful marketing of products, services and information. We research, manage, and execute projects, to the highest level, working principally in the areas of corporate identity, annual reports, promotional and marketing literature.
Clients include Royal Mail, Psion, Paisner and Co Solicitors, amongst others.

Contact Mr David Magee
Size 1-5
Affiliations D&AD, IM

Magus Advertising

Northfield House, 51 Staplegrove Road, Taunton, Somerset TA1 1DG
Telephone (0823) 259366 Fax (0823) 252214

Magus is a marketing and design company, wholly committed to intelligent marketing, originality of thought, arresting graphics, pleasing presentation and informative reading.
Established for ten years in the centre of the West Country, our client base includes regional and national companies, with national and international markets. Work includes corporate identity, sales literature, direct marketing material, packaging and exhibition design.

Contact Mr Michael Lanigan
Size 11-20
Affiliations SIAD, IOM, IPR

Marketplace Design Partnership Ltd

Pulpit House, One The Square, Abingdon, Oxfordshire OX14 5SZ
Telephone (0235) 554499 Fax (0235) 532878

Marketplace Design Partnership is a multidisciplined consultancy, founded on the principle that design must produce profitable results which can be achieved only if set within a strategic context. We believe the real effectiveness of design depends on developing a successful relationship between client and consultancy. Our appointment to designing and implementing an increasing number of assignments, both large and small, is testimony to our unique combination of graphics and interior skills. Our work includes: corporate identity and print communication, retail identity and store design, design for leisure environments, office design, packaging and product development.

Contact Mr Bryan Brown
Size 21-50
Affiliations CSD, DBA, CBI, RSA, D&AD

Marshall North Griffiths

170 New Bond Street, London W1Y 9PB
Telephone 071-491 9266 Fax 071-491 9277

First formed in 1984, Marshall North Griffiths is a multidisciplined design consultancy with a strong emphasis on creative solutions. We handle a large variety of clients from multinationals to sole traders, bringing together expert teams tailored to the requirements of each project.
Our work includes corporate identities and literature, packaging, exhibitions, brochures and periodicals. Clients include Volkswagen UK and Jones Lang Wootton amongst others.

Contact Mr Giles North
Size 1-5

The Paul Martin Design Company Ltd

32 Dragon Street, Petersfield, Hampshire GU31 4JJ
Telephone (0730) 65814 Fax (0730) 63014

We specialize in distinctive design solutions, primarily in the areas of packaging, promotional literature, point-of-sale and corporate identity. Our highly experienced team has a firm commitment to creativity, quality and service, coupled with a clear appreciation and understanding of marketing objectives.
A selection of work from our extensive portfolio may be seen in our current brochure.

Contact Ms Jenny Ryan
Size 11-20
Affiliations CSD, D&AD

GRAPHICS & PACKAGING

The McCadden Design Group

2-4 Cromwell Road, Belfast, Co. Down, Northern Ireland BT7 1JW
Telephone (0232) 234603 Fax (0232) 330693

Established in 1983, The McCadden Design Group specializes in corporate identity, design for print and packaging design. In 1989, we added to our expertise by incorporating interior design into the practice, thereby providing a more comprehensive service to many of our clients. We strive for excellence in our design and aim to provide effective design solutions which prove to be profitable for our clients as well as ourselves.

Contact Mr Colin McCadden
Size 6-10
Affiliations CSD

McCombie/Skinner Ltd

1-5 Beehive Place, London SW9 7QR
Telephone 071-274 2244 Fax 071-326 1055

McCombie/Skinner is a creative graphic design and advertising consultancy, offering a comprehensive service covering all aspects of corporate identity, information, sales and marketing graphics, exhibition and display. General and recruitment advertising. Clients include: Adel Rootstein Group, Amoco (Europe), BAT Industries, BP Chemicals, English Heritage, Lombard NatWest, Security Pacific Investment Group. McCombie/Skinner has experience, creative skills and resources for the production and management of all the projects it undertakes, ensuring solutions that are successful, on time and within budget.

Contact Ms Sarah Jones
Size 6-10
Affiliations CSD, DBA, NPA, NS, PPA

Method Design Consultants

The Old Chapel, Thearne, near Beverley, North Humberside HU17 0SF
Telephone (0482) 869672 Fax (0482) 869672

Method Design Consultants' studio is a converted Primitive Methodist chapel built in 1867 and renovated for a new lease of life in 1970. Activities cover the fields of graphic design, illustration, technical illustration, photo-retouching, advertising, exhibitions and corporate identity programmes. The company serves a wide variety of industries providing a professional design service and the necessary back-up facilities to support a specific marketing plan.

Contact Mr Trevor Clarke
Size 1-5
Affiliations CSD, CIM

Metropolis 88

1-3 Sedley Place, Woodstock Street, London W1R 1HH
Telephone 071-493 6969 Fax 071-495 2605

Metropolis 88 works for a variety of clients. Our work is punctual and unique, reflecting our clients' individual markets, products and corporate strategies. Rather than impose 'house style', we pursue tight quality control to achieve outstanding design solutions. Metroplis 88 have worked with the following organizations in the implementation of corporate and brand identity systems, corporate literature, environmental design, packaging and new product launches: The Body Shop, Boots, Hunter & Partners, John Heyer Paper/Zanders, Nationwide Anglia Building Society, Rowntree Mackintosh, J Sainsbury, Tesco, Trebor Bassett, Waterstone and Company and Winsor & Newton.

Contact Mr Steve Kitsberg
Size 11-20

GRAPHICS & PACKAGING

John Michael Design Ltd

Albion House, 20 Queen Elizabeth Street, London SE1 2LS
Telephone 071-357 6002 Fax 071-403 9938

For 25 years, JMD has been at the forefront of the design industry. Our heritage is based on creative innovation, complemented by a professional level of service.
Specializations include: communication audits, corporate identity, brochures and reports, promotional and environmental graphics.
Our personalized approach offers the same care and attention to small and large companies for small and large projects.
JMD has its own in-house CAD system with typesetting facility, full artwork studio and computerized cost controls, ensuring projects are to budget and on time.

Contact Mr Louis Naudi
Size 21-50
Affiliations CSD

Millaer Seale

10 Tib Lane, Manchester M2 4JB
Telephone 061-832 0701 Fax 061-832 4082

Millaer Seale Design is a marketing lead design consultancy, producing effective targeted design solutions for all our clients' promotional needs. Every project is approached using a careful process of analysis, planning, creativity and control.
We work closely with our clients, and repeat business is frequent due to the professional friendly service and tangible success they receive. We offer a full service from concept through to final print.
Clients: AMEC Properties, Empire Stores, Makro, Boots Opticians, Pilkington, Lamborghini.
Services: design management, DTP.

Contact Ms Annie Millar
Size 6-10
Affiliations CIM, CSD, NUJ, STD

Minale Tattersfield & Partners Ltd

The Courtyard, 37 Sheen Road, Richmond, London TW9 1AJ
Telephone 081-948 7999 Fax 081-948 2435

Established in 1964, international design consultants Minale Tattersfield specialize in corporate identity/corporate image making, packaging, and product, environmental and interior design. Their design work has received numerous awards and has been the subject of many prestigious exhibitions worldwide. Recent clients include National Westminster Bank, BP, Toyota, Boehringer, Royal Academy, BAA, Gucci, Giorgio Armani, Garden Company, Cadbury Schweppes, House of Fraser, Irish Distillers, Johnnie Walker, Spontex, Parkway, Fendi, Kansai Paint, Tesco, Valentino, Elida Gibbs, Thorntons, Coutts, Manchester Olympic Committee, The Post Office and Harrods. Minale Tattersfield also has design studios in Australia, Brussels and Paris and offices in Milan, New York, Hong Kong, Osaka, Barcelona, Casablanca, Cologne and Madrid. Brochures available.

Minale, Tattersfield & Partners Limited

Contact Ms Liza Honey
Size over 100
Affiliations CSD, DBA, JIDA, CA, RIA, RAIA

MJL Ltd

DESIGN COUNCIL REGISTERED

2 Walsworth Road, Hitchin, Hertfordshire SG4 9SP
Telephone (0462) 431477 Fax (0462) 433030

MJL has a simple business philosophy: to gain an intelligent understanding of a client's marketing objectives so that we can produce effective, well-crafted, creative solutions. We apply the same care and thoroughness to all projects, both large and small, across a whole range of material, such as company literature, brochures, advertising, corporate identities, publications, packaging and exhibitions. In-house services include copywriting, design, artwork and typesetting.

Contact Mr John Heaps
Size 11-20

M & M Design Associates

3 Palm Street, New Basford, Nottingham, Nottinghamshire NG7 7HS
Telephone (0602) 708950 Fax (0602) 780366

To gain and maintain a competitive advantage in the market place, there is a need for serious attention to every facet of the way companies present themselves and their products.
M & M Design Associates specialize in corporate and product communications. In-house support services include computer graphics (including Matisse Paintbox), DTP, typesetting and pre-print facilities.
Client portfolio: Boots, Bostik, British Shoe Corporation, Center Parcs, Crayola, Department of Trade and Industry, Derbyshire County Council, East Midlands International Airport, Fisons Pharmaceuticals, Morphy Richards, Nottingham Polytechnic, Nottingham University, Owen Brown, Pedigree Petfoods, Powergen, Pretty Polly, Roche, Saxone, Speedo, Waterman Fine Arts, Wrangler.

Contact Ms Kim Munro
Size 21-50
Affiliations DBA, ISP, CIM

Helen Morris Graphics

Pillar & Lucy House, Merchants Road, Gloucester, Gloucestershire GL1 5RG
Telephone (0452) 300553 Fax (0452) 309729

Established in 1981, the practice has a reputation for professional project management and client satisfaction. Each design brief is developed with care. The design development is managed with attention to detail and quality. A rare combination of fresh creative thinking, typographic skills and electronic page makeup, unite the highly committed team in their pursuit of excellence.
We specialize in the design and production of high quality literature, manuals and corporate identity.
Recent clients include: SKF, Leeds Permanent Building Society, Thorn EMI, Lucas, MAN Volkswagen.

Contact Mr Christopher Morris
Size 1-5
Affiliations CSD, IQA

Mustard Design Ltd

Mayors Road, Altrincham, Cheshire WA15 9RP
Telephone 061-941 1538 Fax 061-927 7466

Mustard Design, established in 1975, is a graphic design-led marketing services company offering clients throughout the UK a proven creative ability, backed by wide experience and a complete production service. We solve problems in corporate and brand identity; we design and produce all forms of brochures and literature; and we design packaging, including new product development. In addition, we create and administer complete promotional packages, trade advertising and exhibition stands. Our clients range from multinationals and household names to small, specialized companies. We believe design is a vital marketing tool.

Contact Mr Ron Stephens
Size 11-20

John Nash & Friends Ltd

10 New Concordia Wharf, Mill Street, London SE1 2BA
Telephone 071-231 9161 Fax 071-237 3719

The company, established in 1969, offers a wide range of skills relating to all aspects of graphic design. At the beginning of 1984, we purchased and moved to a new purpose-designed studio on the river by Tower Bridge. A versatile team of designers is led by John Nash FCSD. Typical projects undertaken include promotional and technical literature, corporate identity programmes, annual reports, packaging, stationery and form design, fixing instructions, point-of-sale and promotional material. We offer a complete service from initial design concept through to writing, illustration, artwork and supervision of print production.
Projects completed for Alcan, Bovis, BP Chemicals, BUPA, Design Council, Greycoat, Hamleys, IWS, Mitsuig, Morgan Grenfell, Phillips & Drew, Rosehaugh, Rothschild, Thorn.

Contact Mr John Nash
Size 6-10
Affiliations CSD, DBA, DIA, IOD

GRAPHICS & PACKAGING

Benjamin Nazroo Associates

Meadows House, Well Street, Buckingham, Buckinghamshire MK18 1EW
Telephone (0280) 823322 Fax (0280) 822246

Established in 1982, design group BNA has built up a broad base of national and international clients. We offer every client the same high standard of creativity, service and commitment, regardless of size. Each member of the team contributes a creative input and maintains direct communication with you, the client. We see this as a crucial factor in understanding marketing problems and responding to your design brief by producing successful creative solutions promptly and cost-effectively. Our clients include: Booker, Scania (GB), Tate & Lyle, Volkswagen Audi (UK), Yamaha Kemble.

Contact Ms Helen Brook
Size 6-10

N & N Ltd

7 Atlas Mews, Ramsgate Street, London E8 2NA
Telephone 071-254 0166 Fax 071-249 4056

N & N has a substantial track record, embracing corporate identification, print design, vehicle and aircraft liveries, packaging and corporate brochures. We offer a comprehensive service from analysis through creative design to cost-effective implementation. We have been responsible for some of the best-known corporate identities in the world: Laing, The Rank Organisation and Vickers/Rolls-Royce Motors. Other clients include British Gas, British Airways, English Heritage, National & Provincial Building Society, National Maritime Museum, Northern Dairies, the University of Birmingham, Academy of St Martin in the Fields, Aynsley China and Waterford/Wedgwood Group.

Contact Mr Romanus Odiwe
Size 6-10
Affiliations CSD, STD, RSA

Oak Design Consultancy Ltd

Charles House, Low Lane, Horsforth, Leeds, Yorkshire LS18 5DE
Telephone (0532) 587880 Fax (0532) 582608

Oak Design Consultancy has over the past 15 years established an enviable reputation for designing quality work for national clients. Our success is the result of producing well thought out creative solutions to marketing briefs. Oak works in the areas of corporate identity, design for print, both retail and financial POS, packaging, exhibition and advertising design.
Our client list speaks for us: ASDA, Halifax Building Society, K Shoes, Perstorp Warerite, National Breakdown, Ohmeda, Burton Group, British Coal, Total Oil.
London address: 33 Corsham Street, N1 6DR. Tel: 071-490 2969.

Contact Mr Peter Heward
Size 21-50
Affiliations CAM

Vernon Oakley Design Ltd

97 White Lion Street, London N1 9PF
Telephone 071-837 4898 Fax 071-837 4902

VOD are multidisciplined design and marketing consultants. Established in 1974, we have worked on almost every facet of design for clients in insurance, banking, automobiles, electronics, leisure and tourism, local authorities and transportation. We produce corporate identities and corporate communications, sales literature, direct mail, financial and annual reports, magazines, video, promotional and incentive material, point-of-sale, exhibition and packaging for clients who include: Sun Alliance, Citroën, English Tourist Board, Ross Electronics, BACS, Virgin Atlantic, BUPA, Sun Life, National Mutual, Thomas Cook and many others.

Contact Mr Tony Searle
Size 11-20
Affiliations CSD, DBA

GRAPHICS & PACKAGING

Patrick O'Callaghan Graphic Design

10 Barley Mow Passage, Chiswick, London W4 4PH
Telephone 081-994 6477 Fax 081-995 6228 Telex 8811418 SPACES G

In practice since 1975 and working to the highest professional standards, Patrick O'Callaghan Graphic Design offers a comprehensive design service for company brochures, leaflets, catalogues, stationery, logos, company corporate styling, magazines, travel brochures, book design and all print related design.
A personal service is offered to clients and the aim is to give imaginative, cost effective design solutions of measurable benefit to the client.
Please call to see examples from our portfolio.

Contact Mr Patrick O'Callaghan
Size 1-5
Affiliations CSD

Oliver and Company Ltd

1 Charlotte Square, Newcastle-upon-Tyne, Tyne & Wear NE1 4XF
Telephone 091-261 5842 Fax 091-232 9845

A specialist company advising solely on the design and production of annual reports. The results achieve a balance of creative excellence by producing interesting and effective reports, the end product being designed to be an up-to-date marketing tool and a document of record.
Major clients: Cala, Ivory & Sime, Jarvis Porter, Mansfield Brewery, John Menzies, Northern Electric, Northern Foods, Northern Investors, Westbury.
Scottish office: Gardiner Oliver, The Old Kirk, Carrington, Midlothian EH23 4LR.

Contact Mr Howard Oliver
Size 6-10
Affiliations CA, BIM, DBA

Omega

Olympus House, Staniland Way, Peterborough, Cambridgeshire PE4 6NA
Telephone (0733) 78988 Fax (0733) 73604

Working across a wide range of creative disciplines, our expertise covers a broad spectrum of business activity including consumer, industrial, businesss-to-business, hi-tech and financial services markets.
Our commitment to creative excellence is matched by a belief in providing the highest standards of client service, based on a sound knowledge of marketing principles. From the initial brief right through the design and production process we ensure that effective, creative solutions are achieved whilst budgets and deadlines are strictly adhered to.

Contact Mr Carl Brodie
Size 11-20
Affiliations IM

Origin Studios (S-o-T) Ltd

67 Bournes Bank, Burslem, Stoke-on-Trent, Staffordshire ST6 3DP
Telephone (0782) 817966 Fax (0782) 575229

Origin Studios is a small company offering a freelance consultancy service in the following areas: ceramic design (shape design, modelling etc); surface pattern design and artwork; graphics (house style, corporate identity, brochures, packaging etc); and illustration.
Clients include Dunoon Ceramics (coffee mugs, kitchenware), The New Victoria Theatre (posters, programmes etc), Remploy (general print design), H & R Johnson Tiles (tile designs), Qualcast (sanitaryware), Royal Worcester (giftware, tableware).
We have also undertaken projects for many nationally known pottery manufacturers.

Contact Mr Jack Dadd
Size 1-5
Affiliations CSD

Packaging Innovation Ltd

1-5 Colville Mews, Lonsdale Road, London W11 2AR
Telephone 071-727 3226 Fax 071-727 4831 Telex 946240

We specialize in designing packaging, with emphasis on creativity and market awareness. We start by creating new concepts and end with finished artwork – all in-house. We work for big brands and small new ones, creating entire concepts including naming and branding. Investment in computer technology enables us to work fast on projects. Our graphic, product and technical expertise combine to create integrated and entirely innovative packaging (see Product Design).
Clients include: Procter & Gamble, Nestlé, Glaxo, Conoco, Heinz, Monsanto, Total Chimie, RHM, Wellcome Foundation, Rowntrees.

Contact Ms Sheila Clark
Size 21-50
Affiliations CSD, DBA, D&AD, IoP, Mktg Soc, RSA

PACKAGING INNOVATION

The Pack Design Company

75 Leonard Street, London EC2A 4QS
Telephone 071-739 7436 Fax 071-739 7806

Small, well-established in the branded area. Clients have included Benson & Hedges, British Gas, Burlington International Group, Colgate-Palmolive, Danepak, Dreamland, Dunhill, Ferguson, Fidelity, Glenfarclas, ICI Garden Products, Parker Pens, Rawplug, Robinsons Fruit Drinks and Baby Food, Saccone & Speed, Terrys of York.

Contact Ms Hana Reynolds
Size 1-5
Affiliations CSD

Panel Design

22/23 Star Road, Partridge Green, West Sussex RH13 8RA
Telephone (0403) 711445 Fax (0403) 711437

Established in 1986, specializing in packaging design from three dimensional and graphic design to technical and material specification and development, Panel Design has built its reputation on highly creative design solutions and innovations incorporating high levels of marketing and production, expertise and understanding. Specialist packaging knowledge offers the latest technologies and materials as well as assuming a trouble free transition of ideas and design into production.
Clients include Laura Ashley, Swarovski, Ciba Geigy, Makro, Vesutor, Smith Kline Beecham, British Gas, Wedgwood.
North West contact: (0270) 841167.

Contact Mr Neal Bryant
Size 6-10
Affiliations IOP

Paris/Kerr Ltd

89a Quicks Road, Wimbledon, London SW19 1EX
Telephone 081-540 9884 Fax 081-540 9889

Specializing in the design of packaging, point-of-sale, product development, graphics and interiors, Paris/Kerr, formerly Peter Kerr Design Associates, boasts a highly creative and progressive design team, responding with a high degree of success to often very strict marketing briefs. The combination of design and photographic studios within the same building permits the total control of the image-making process and offers an economical alternative to high art direction costs. Clients: Asda, Liberty's, Colgate Palmolive, Beecham, Timex, Chase Manhattan Bank, British Airways, International Wool Secretariat, Spillers, General Trading Company, Lever Brothers.

Contact Mr Peter Kerr
Size 6-10
Affiliations DBA, CSD

GRAPHICS & PACKAGING

Parker Stratton Design

6 Rossetti Studios, 72 Flood Street, London SW3 5TF
Telephone 071-376 5215 Fax 071-352 7551

A brand development and design consultancy concerned with all aspects of consumer brands including NPD, packaging, three-dimensional design and retail design for a variety of client companies.
We are a team of 12 designers and writers, supplemented as necessary by associate specialists in marketing and research.
We believe good design should be effective design and we have the success stories to prove it.
Clients include: Aquascutum, Bass, Coca-Cola Schweppes, Geemarc, Guinness, Halifax Building Society, Harvey Nichols, Holsten, Napolina, RHM, Ritz Paris, Smiths Foods, Unilever NV, Valentino.

Contact Mr Terry Stratton
Size 11-20
Affiliations CSD, IM, D&AD, DBA

The Partners

Albion Courtyard, Greenhill Rents, Smithfield, London EC1M 6BN
Telephone 071-608 0051 Fax 071-250 0473

Since our formation in 1983, we have established a formidable reputation as one of the largest and best pure graphic design consultancies in the United Kingdom. We believe success is due to the unusually high degree of principals' input into every project the practice takes on. We are able to do this by the sharing of management responsibilities between the six partners. The firm believes that clients are entitled to enjoy the efforts and special dedication of the principals rather than a team of more junior staff, however talented they may be.

Contact Mr David Stuart
Size 21-50
Affiliations CSD, DBA, STD, RCA

Pauffley & Company

Baird House, 15-17 St Cross Street, London EC1N 8UN
Telephone 071-405 1854 Fax 071-405 5285 Telex 23744 PCO G

Pauffley & Co is a design consultancy specializing in corporate and financial communications. Our aim is to employ sound design to achieve well-defined and hard-working results. Our skills include the design and writing of corporate literature, financial product marketing material, annual reports, corporate identities and financial documentation. We aim to produce work that is not only effective, but also highly cost-efficient, while ensuring adherence to the highest production standards.
Clients include: BOC, BAT Industries, Cadbury Schweppes, Gulf International Bank, Pilkington, Tate & Lyle, Glaxo, Thorn EMI.

Contact Mr Reg Pauffley
Size 21-50

Malcolm Payne Design Group Ltd

37-38 Hatton Garden, London EC1N 8EB
Telephone 071-242 7328 Fax 071-831 9569

We are a multidisciplinary group, providing the essential skills in graphics and exhibitions, architecture and interiors. Our graphics studio gives clients professional guidance on the development of their corporate identity and its application to the design of letterhead, publicity material and packaging. Our other disciplines carry the style through in their approach to signage, display, exhibitions and interiors.
Midlands Office at 212-213 Broad Street, Birmingham B15 1AY, telephone: 021-643 3159, fax: 021-631 3348.

Contact Mr Malcolm Payne
Size 21-50
Affiliations CSD, RIBA

GRAPHICS & PACKAGING

Pentagram Design Ltd

11 Needham Road, London W11 2RP
Telephone 071-229 3477 Fax 071-727 9932 Telex 8952000 PENTA G

Pentagram has a unique international reputation. It is a multidisciplinary practice offering graphics, architecture, exhibition, interior, and product design, with individual partners (directors) responsible for each.

Pentagram's six graphic partners undertake a diverse range of commissions from complete management and corporate communications systems to small company graphics. They have international experience in magazine, newspaper and book design, packaging, environmental graphics and corporate identity programmes. Clients include Boots, British Waterways, The Guardian, IBM, Lloyd's of London, Polaroid, Reuters and Scandinavian Airways

Contact Ms Deborah Richardson
Size 51-100
Affiliations RDI, CSD, AGI, STD

Tor Pettersen & Partners Ltd

56 Greek Street, London W1V 5LR
Telephone 071-439 6463 Fax 071-434 1299

Design is only as effective as the quality of the thinking behind it, so at Tor Pettersen & Partners we insist on starting each project with a clear understanding of the particular market involved. Our aim is always to provide a solution that is not only creative but also highly relevant. For over 20 years, we have worked with clients such as Lucas Industries, BP, RMC, BTR, BT, DEC, Enterprise Oil, Fisons, Arabian Bulk Trade, Inchcape and RTZ. We specialize in corporate identity, annual reports, corporate and marketing literature, name generation, new product and business development and packaging design.

Contact Mr Tor Pettersen
Size 21-50
Affiliations D&AD, IABC, IM

PFB Designers and Print Consultants Ltd

4 & 8 Slaid Hill Court, Shadwell, Leeds, Yorkshire LS17 8TJ
Telephone (0532) 661625 Fax (0533) 662002

Inspiration, perspiration, dedication and finely tuned commercial awareness. This is what PFB believe makes the difference between a good design and a great one. Whether it's design for a brochure, company report, corporate identity, sales aid, exhibition stand, advertisement or packaging, PFB have the people with the specialist skills to create a design that really works.

Designers, typesetters, finished artists and print buyers work in close harmony to ensure quality control is exercised at every stage and that the end product is produced to the highest standards.

Brochure available on request.

Contact Mr Dean Brewer
Size 21-50

The Picador Group

The Parsonage, Winford, Bristol, Avon BS18 8DW
Telephone (0275) 474704 Fax (0275) 472108

Effective communication through innovative design.

Established over 15 years ago, the Picador Group has built an impressive list of local, national and international clients.

Dedication in their approach to design, communication, quality and service is prominent throughout all of their work for small and large clients alike. Insurance and banking, hotel and leisure, travel, schools, property, retail and other clients each receive the same precise, exacting degree of service which is tailor-made to meet individual needs.

Contact Mr Richard Smith
Size 21-50

GRAPHICS & PACKAGING

Pira International

Randalls Road, Leatherhead, Surrey KT22 7RU
Telephone (0372) 376161 Fax (0372) 377526 Telex 929810

Pira International is an independent organization with the highest international reputation for providing research, consultancy, training and information services for the paper, printing and packaging industries. Its Design Unit, run by specialist designers backed by Pira's substantial research facilities, takes packaging through all phases of development from product evaluation through material and machinery selection to the finished package, including the distribution container. Using the CAD facilities of an Apple Mackintosh IIcx to undertake projects of any size, the unit sees the creative design as an integral part of the packaging function.

Contact Mr P Parsons
Size over 100

Pointsize Associates

48 West George Street, Glasgow, Scotland G2 1BP
Telephone 041-332 3939 Fax 041-332 2326

Our design consultancy produces work for local and national organizations, providing creative, practical and market-conscious solutions to a wide variety of design problems. Work includes corporate identity projects, brochures, posters, annual reports and books of all kinds (in highly demanding fields of art/museum publishing) as well as on major exhibitions and audiovisual presentations. Pointsize is a design studio run by designers. We believe that dealing direct with our clients means jointly arriving at a more accurate design brief which produces a smooth working relationship and creative solutions within agreed budgets.

Contact Mr Ken Cassidy
Size 11-20
Affiliations CSD, DBA, IOD

Portland Design Associates

90-92 Great Portland Street, London W1N 5PB
Telephone 071-436 5301 Fax 071-631 1242

Portland Design Associates, with offices in London and Glasgow, combines the considerable experience of its principals with the creative input of a young and enthusiastic design team to produce exceptional creative solutions to well researched and well understood client briefs. Our expertise in specific commercial categories such as retail stores, shopping centres, marine interiors and property development is well-established and recognized through a client list that includes Grosvenor Square Properties, Bredero, P&O European Ferries, Woolworth Cyprus, Land Securities, Meadowhall Centre and Thresher Wine Merchants.

Contact Mr Chris Cook
Size 21-50
Affiliations CSD, DBA, RIBA, BCSC

Precept Design Communications Consultants Ltd

Babylon Bridge, Waterside, Ely, Cambridgeshire CB7 4AU
Telephone (0353) 662959 Fax (0353) 667010

Employing 35 staff in 3 offices. Providing three autonomous divisions integrating when required to realize a full range of marketing support services. Communications: write, design and produce persuasive and informative commercial literature for major companies in all sectors of business and industry. Packaging: specialist team of designers creating surface graphics for retail sector. Services provided extend to market research and analysis. Management consultancy: provides industry and business with a range of skills to assist with development, implementation and training on computer and management information systems.

Contact Mr Cavan Bickell
Size 21-50

Proctor & Stevenson

12 Cave Street, Bristol, Avon BS2 8RU
Telephone (0272) 232282 Fax (0272) 241269

Proctor & Stevenson is a hard-working design consultancy where particular attention is paid to the function and effectiveness of design. Because we regard design as an integral part of broader strategic marketing issues, emphasis is placed on combining sharp analysis and research with adventurous and original creative work. At international, national and regional level we have provided co-ordinated design solutions for clients in high technology, financial services, the professions, retail, publishing, engineering, construction, film, brewing and medical services.

Contact Mr Roger Proctor
Size 6-10
Affiliations CSD, DBA

Pylon Design Consultants

45-47 Westow Hill, London SE19 1TS
Telephone 081-766 6605 Fax 081-766 6594

Pylon Design Consultants specialize in corporate identity, design for print, direct mail, architectural graphics, exhibitions and illustrations. Our aims are based on the intelligent use of design in order to provide clients with innovative as well as practical answers. We establish a close working relationship with clients, handling all projects from concept to production, however large or small they may be.
Clients: British Rail, Capital Marble, David Leon & Partners, the Design Council, Duke of Edinburgh's Award, First Impressions Flooring, Limehouse Board Mills, Sadlers Wells, Safeway and Wiggins Teape.

Contact Mr Andrew Fewster
Size 1-5
Affiliations CSD, STD

Vivienne Rawnsley Graphic Design

Old Bailey, 18/19 Lombard Street, Little London, Rawdon, Leeds, Yorkshire LS19 6BW
Telephone (0532) 505182 Fax (0532) 501156

A small, highly professional consultancy working in all areas of graphic communication. We specialize in corporate identities, brochures, packaging and sales and technical literature. Based in Yorkshire, we have a wide range of experience designing for national and local organizations.
Clients include: Silver Cross, Bowers International Holdings, Calder Book Company, The Public Relations Company, Solk Furniture, MBA Publishing, Cyprus Construction and Watson Batty Architects.

Contact Ms Vivienne Rawnsley
Size 1-5
Affiliations CSD

Regatta Design Consultants

The Manor House, Uttoxeter, Staffordshire ST14 7JQ
Telephone (0889) 567900 Fax (0889) 564030

We specialise in literature and brochure design, point-of-sale, report and accounts and corporate image. Our team of creative designers has a wide range of experience and is totally committed to producing innovative and effective design solutions.
Clients include Britannia Building Society, Brother, Amtico, Rolls-Royce and JCB. Contact Jacqui Yates or Gill Collins to arrange to see our portfolio.

Contact Ms Jacqui Yates
Size 6-10

REGATTA
DESIGN CONSULTANTS

Robson Design Associates Ltd

Dudmoor House, Kingsbury Episcopi, Martock, Somerset TA12 6AT
Telephone (0935) 822522 Fax (0935) 825350

Established in 1976, RDA is now a leading design consultancy with a well-earned reputation for individual, innovative and effective graphic design. Our thoughtful solutions are always accurately targeted on the marketing and strategic objectives of our clients. Every client receives individual service, each project is professionally managed with care and attention to detail at every stage, from concept through to implementation. Our expertise covers corporate identity, retail graphics, literature, annual reports and packaging.

Contact Mr Ian Robson
Size 6-10
Affiliations CSD, DBA, RSA, IOD

Roundel Design Group

7 Rosehart Mews, Westbourne Grove, London W11 3TY
Telephone 071-221 1951 Fax 071-221 1843

We give particularly careful consideration to our clients' problems and ensure that the work done on their behalf meets the highest creative standards as well as being appropriate to their product or service and its target audience. We specialize in most areas of graphic design, particularly corporate identity, design for print and packaging. We have close contacts with many of the country's top research companies, copywriters, illustrators and photographers. Our clients include British Rail, Express Foods Group, Financial & General Bank, ITN and London Underground.

Contact Mr Michael Denny
Size 11-20
Affiliations CSD, D&AD

Benjamin Rowntree Reports Ltd

153 Regent Street, London W1R 7FD
Telephone 071-437 9567 Fax 071-439 2052

Specialists in corporate and financial communications – especially annual reports, employee reports, corporate brochures and similar documents.
Clients include: Tarmac, British Rail, BBC, Schroders, Godfrey Davis, LEB, J Bibby and Sons and Moss Bros.
Last year we won the International Stock Exchange award for large companies' annual reports and the Print Buyer brochure award.
We have substantial experience in managing printing companies; in fact our knowledge of printing and understanding of accounts might be unique amongst design groups. Please ring for our brochure.

Contact Mr Benjamin Rowntree
Size 6-10
Affiliations BIM, IOD

Russell Design Associates Ltd

9 Newton Place, Glasgow, Scotland G3 7PR
Telephone 041-332 2311 Fax 041-332 7917

Russell Design Associates specialize in the design and production of high quality corporate communications, including annual reports, all forms of promotional literature, packaging and displays. The company has been in business since 1970 and has earned a reputation for creative design and first class service to clients. Our client list includes major national companies and organizations as well as smaller locally based businesses.

Contact Mr Glyn Price
Size 11-20
Affiliations CSD

GRAPHICS & PACKAGING

Sears Davies Ltd

Unit A, 25 Copperfield Street, London SE1 0EN
Telephone 071-633 0939 Fax 071-633 9953

As a multidisciplined design group with a proven capacity for innovation, Sears Davies has built a reputation for developing and delivering highly effective corporate communications. Our major areas of activity include financial literature, company brochures, annual reports, corporate identity, engineering brochures and promotional campaigns for fashion and theatre, from concept to print. Current clients include: The Burton Group, DTI, French Wools, Sir William Halcrow, Lawn Tennis Association, Lovel White Durrant, Olympus Sports, Pentos, Property Enterprise Trusts, Provident Mutual, Reedpack and Thomas Telford.
A company profile is available on request.

Contact Mr Richard Sears
Size 11-20

Sector Design

Golley Slater Group, 9-11 The Hayes, Cardiff, South Glamorgan, Wales CF1 1NU
Telephone (0222) 388621 Fax (0222) 238729

Sector Graphic Design offers a comprehensive service in the field of corporate communications, from producing high profile corporate identities to the smallest details of implementation. All creative work is supported by thorough market research, resulting in highly effective, targeted solutions. Major investment in advanced DTP systems allows rapid and accurate production of corporate literature, annual reports, packaging concepts and liveries. Additional services include product graphics and multimedia advertising. Please call for a copy of our brochure, or to arrange an initial meeting.

Contact Ms Jane Ellis
Size 11-20

Set Square Design Ltd

Parker Court, Knapp Lane, St James' Square, Cheltenham, Gloucestershire GL50 3QA
Telephone (0242) 573740 Fax (0242) 221782

Set Square comprises an enthusiastic team of professionals working together to produce innovative, commercially aware design, marketing and public relations. Since all our managers are professionally qualified with solid business experience, we feel we are in the unique position of being able to offer creative solutions – that work. From our Cheltenham base we undertake a wide and diverse range of projects for many respected clients including British Waterways, London City Airways, Avon Cosmetics, W H Smith and General Foods. Our key areas of activity include creative design, corporate identity, packaging, retail design, direct mail, sales promotion, product development, and offer a full marketing and public relations service all supported by extensive in-house production facilities.

Contact Mr Michael Rushby
Size 11-20
Affiliations IOP, CSD, IM, IPR

Shaw Design Marketing & Print Consultants Ltd

18 Albany Street, Edinburgh, Scotland EH1 3QB
Telephone 031-557 5663 Fax 031-556 7379

Shaw Design provides creative and marketing consultancy for a variety of clients. Most work is in graphic design, particularly flat print and packaging, although we also have expertise in promotions and exhibitions design. The areas of operation range from own brand packaging for the largest Scottish independent supermarket chain and new product development for national breweries to annual reports, brochures and promotional print, as well as highly specialized service in corporate identity – most notably for the Scottish Tourist Board and The Scottish Sports Council.

Contact Mr John Shaw
Size 11-20

Shearing and Partners

Firle Cottage, Firle, East Sussex BN8 6NS
Telephone 0273 858466/858501 Fax 0273 858453

Shearing and Partners offer a highly individual and experienced approach to communication and corporate design. Over the past year, as well as a number of corporate identity exercises, we have concentrated on 'conceptual' corporate and product brochures for, amongst others, a presentation and communication consultancy, a City law firm, a charter airline and one of the world's leading chemical companies.

Contact Mr Jeremy Shearing
Size 1-5
Affiliations CSD

Silk Pearce

57A Priory Street, Colchester, Essex CO1 2WE
Telephone (0206) 871001 Fax (0206) 871002

The award-winning work of the group covers a broad spectrum including: corporate identities, brochures, catalogues, packaging, retail design, sign systems and promotional literature.
Silk Pearce works for a wide variety of clients throughout the country, ranging from national organizations, such as the Post Office and Berol Pens, to local firms, such as architects and computer systems consultants. We also work for European clients and our proximity to Stansted makes us particularly well placed to service them.
Please phone for brochure.

Contact Mr Peter Silk
Size 11-20
Affiliations CSD, D&AD

Smith & Milton Ltd

Franklin House, 2 Milmans Street, King's Road, London SW10 0DA
Telephone 071-351 6755 Fax 071-352 3967 Telex 929062 SMIMILC

A highly creative consultancy specializing in brand identity and corporate communications. Winners of six international Clio Awards since 1988, and a Spicer & Oppenheim Award for financial communications, we believe in working to produce creative results that are always beneficial to enhancing the client's product. Clients include: ICI Dulux, Boots, Gillette in Europe, Texas, Unilever, Natwest, Girobank, Tate & Lyle, Rowntree.
We are in the business of character-building, which stems from our philosophy to think strategically and to always apply the total marketing mix disciplines to the design solution.

Contact Mr Juan Gallo
Size 21-50
Affiliations CSD, D&AD, DBA

Sphere Advertising & Communications Ltd

Temple Court, 27 Mathew Street, Liverpool, Merseyside L2 6RE
Telephone 051-236 5755 Fax 051-236 4322

Excellence in graphic design and a first class marketing service have established Sphere as a highly professional design consultancy. Market experience and creative expertise ensure effective design solutions, and comprehensive studio facilities provide a full service. We specialize in packaging design, illustration and photography; technical literature, illustration and drawing; corporate identity, product literature and stationery; consumer and trade advertising; promotional creation and production; exhibitions and conference presentations. In over 18 years of development, our clients have included market leaders, international organizations, local authorities and government agencies.

Contact Mr Ray Shaw
Size 11-20

GRAPHICS & PACKAGING

Spirit Associates

33 Leslie Hough Way, Salford University Business Park, Salford, Manchester M6 6AJ
Telephone 061-745 8246 Fax 061-745 8083

Spirit Associates is a small and efficient company specializing in all forms of graphic design. We provide a personal and comprehensive service from concept to print, offering a fixed price contract.
Now in our seventh year of practice our clients include British Waterways, English Tourist Board, National Power and Manchester University.

Contact Ms Carole Spirit
Size 1-5
Affiliations CSD, STD

Splash of Paint Ltd

Larch House, Sulhamstead, Near Theale, Reading, Berkshire RG7 4BB
Telephone (0734) 323566 Fax (0734) 323252

Splash of Paint is a design consultancy based on the outskirts of Reading. From here we are able to offer the quality of service normally only associated with London from our purpose-built studio complex in its rural location.
Services include design, packaging, corporate identity and advertising. We aim to provide design solutions positioned to be both appropriate and effective, and in order to do so it is essential to have clients with vision. The vision to realize the potential of design.

Contact Mr Malcolm Hatton
Size 11-20

Starling Corporate Design

58 Ayres Street, London SE1 1EU
Telephone 071-378 1678 Fax 071-407 5927

Starling Corporate Design is best known for creating visual identities and corporate literature. Our objective is to understand our clients' business and their needs and provide creative, effective, commercial solutions. We were responsible for creating the visual identities for Lloyds Bank, Boots, Dalgety, AMEC and The Institute of Chartered Accountants. We also work with clients such as Sears, Guinness, Fisons, Black Horse Agencies, Connell, Sheraton Securities, on items ranging from annual reports and corporate brochures to promotional newsletters, information manuals and design applications including stationery, vehicles and staff uniforms.

Contact Ms Lora Starling
Size 6-10
Affiliations CSD

Steel Designs

The Coach House, 127 Hampton Road, Redland, Bristol, Avon BS6 6JE
Telephone (0272) 237471 Fax (0272) 237507

The function of design is to provide a vehicle for successful communication. The market in which most companies operate has become increasingly competitive and distinguishing your services from your rivals is more vital than ever.

That's why you should come to Steel Designs in Bristol.

We set out to create strong, unified design solutions utilizing our own unique system of design management.

Contact Mr Simon Steel
Size 6-10
Affiliations IOD, CSD, RIBA

GRAPHICS & PACKAGING

Michael Stewart Design Ltd

Studio 21, Church Road, Poole, Dorset BH14 8UF
Telephone (0202) 715175 Fax (0202) 715130

International design and marketing consultancy with packaging, corporate identity, advertising and brochure/promotions design. Associate offices in Europe and USA offer research and design for internationals markets.
Our clients are medium, large and international companies in food, drink, toiletries, cosmetics, consumer goods, chemical processing and marine leisure. We have won many awards, but our greatest successes are the increases in our clients' profile or sales generated by intelligent design. Good design is not necessarily expensive. We believe in the strength of our designs, and offer performance-related fees.

Contact Mr Mike Thrasher
Size 6-10
Affiliations LSIA, IOP, ASIA

Stills Design Group

66 Lower Dock Street, Newport, Gwent, Wales NP9 1EF
Telephone (0633) 246149 Fax (0633) 841078

We are well known for our top quality design and our commitment to the highest standards of personal service to our clients. We have many years' experience of working closely with our expanding national and international client base.
Our main areas of expertise are in graphics, exhibitions, interiors, retail, marketing and urban renewal.

Contact Mr Chris Carpenter
Size 6-10
Affiliations CSD

Strata'Matrix Ltd

1 Talbot Street, Canton, Cardiff, South Glamorgan, Wales CF1 9BW
Telephone (0222) 231231 Fax (0222) 372798

With offices in Cardiff and Aberystwyth, Strata'Matrix is expert in the design and writing of product literature, advertising and corporate brochures and in the development of corporate identities. We also offer public relations services. Clients across the UK include Johnson & Johnson, Surgikos, Barclays Bank, HTV, BBC Radio Cymru, S4C, National Rivers Authority, Forestry Commission and Welsh Lamb Enterprise. We are adept at meeting deadlines, with additional flexibility provided by in-house typesetting and finished artwork.
Darperir gwasanaeth cyflawn yn Gymraeg ac yn Saesneg.

Contact Mr Brian Shields
Size 21-50
Affiliations D&AD, CBI

Studio 74 Ltd

Red Scar Works, Burnley Road, Burnley, Colne, Lancashire BB8 8LF
Telephone (0282) 869060 Fax (0282) 863958

Studio 74 is an established design studio operating conventional and electronic design departments.
The main areas of activity include: corporate identity, sales literature, POS, packaging design, direct mail, illustration, exhibition graphics.
A staff of seven full-time designers is complemented by an excellent dedicated typesetting team, utilizing full page make-up and over 1000 typefaces.
The design studios are also supported by their own in-house colour printing and origination companies.

Contact Mr Trevor Hind
Size 21-50
Affiliations InstM

GRAPHICS & PACKAGING

Studio M

7 Tyers Gate, London SE1 3HX
Telephone 071-403 8090 Fax 071-403 5424

The Studio specialises in fashion-related graphics: art direction and design of clients' corporate identity and image through advertising material, brochure design and package and presentation.
The Studio is guided by quality of work, not size of project. We also offer complete garment design services (see Fashion & Textiles section).
Clients: UK – Henri-Lloyd, International Wool Secretariat, Laurence J Smith, L'Uomo Menswear, Next Directory, Next Retail, Rocco L'Uomo; France – Harris Wilson; Japan – Kakiuchi, Ogorishoji.

Contact Miss Kenya Chapman
Size 6-10

Tatham Pearce Ltd

9 Hatton Street, London NW8 8PL
Telephone 071-706 4303 Fax 071-262 0486

Tatham Pearce has established a reputation for creative design work combined with mature strategic analysis for both corporate and consumer clients. We specialize in three main areas of graphic design: corporate identity, print (annual reports, brochures) and retail (packaging, point-of-sale, retail graphics). Clients include: Land Rover, Lloyds Bank, Ratners, LWT, TVS, Laser Sales, The ITVA, Country Gardens, MFI, J Sainsbury, Mobil, London International Group and Assuranceforeningen Gard.

Contact Ms Amanda Tatham
Size 11-20
Affiliations CSD, DBA, D&AD

Tayburn Design Ltd

15 Kittle Yards, Causewayside, Edinburgh, Scotland EH9 1PG
Telephone 031-662 0662

Graphic, exhibition and interior design group rated in the UK top 20.
Projects include corporate identity, packaging, corporate literature and annual reports, as well as bank, retail and leisure interiors, exhibition stands and museums. Staff number 60, turnover around £5 million.
Clients include: Bank of Scotland, Gleneagles, United Distillers, Standard Life, Coopers & Lybrand Deloitte, Wm Low, Ericsson, Scottish Enterprise.

Contact Mr Erick Davidson
Size 51-100
Affiliations CSD, INSTM

The Team

120 Putney Bridge Road, London SW15 2NQ
Telephone 081-877 0888 Fax 081-874 6994

The Team's strengths are concentrated in graphic design, both two- and three-dimensional. We offer creative, well managed business solutions for: corporate identity (OFFER – Office of Electricity Regulation), international retail identity (Levi Strauss), packaging (Sainsbury's), company and product literature (STC), financial and annual reports (EITB), exhibition and displays, point-of-sale (Boots No 7), conference theming and promotion (Volvo) and property marketing (Hillier Parker).
The Team has 20 members with design and production teams using CAD facilities for efficient, cost effective and creative solutions.

Contact Mr Jim Allen
Size 11-20
Affiliations D&AD, CSD, IM, DBA

132

Teviot Design Ltd

7 Dublin Street Lane South, Edinburgh, Scotland EH1 3PX
Telephone 031-557 3389 Fax 031-556 8771

Teviot Design Ltd are creative design consultants specializing in promotional literature, corporate identity and general graphics. Teviot offers a complete design and print management service. Our computerized studio is probably one of the most advanced available for the production of graphics and print. Over the years we have successfully applied creative solutions to meet our clients' commercial objectives. The consultancy's clients include insurance companies, banks, financial groups, building and shipping companies, defence contractors and retailers, for whom we design an extensive range of brochures, promotional literature, catalogues and reports.

Contact Mr Brian Hall
Size 11-20
Affiliations CSD, STD

Thomson Wright International

Number One, New Burlington Street, London WIX 1FD
Telephone 071-287 9088 Fax 071-439 9417

Thomson Wright International is a marketing-led design consultancy specializing in corporate identity and communications, with a reputation for creating original designs, tailored to meet the specific needs of companies in differing markets. TWI works hard to give its clients better quality, better service and better value, achieving effective communication through design. Since 1984 the company has produced creative design solutions for many leading names in business and industry – including the Advertising Standards Authority, Birds Eye Wall's, Channel 4, Crown Berger, Dunhill, Express Foods, Lever Brothers, Scott, Texaco and Wellcome.

Contact Mr Ross Thomson
Size 6-10
Affiliations CSD, DBA, CBI, IOD

Thumb Design Partnership Ltd

53 Corsica Street, Highbury Fields, London N5 1JT
Telephone 071-704 6000 Fax 071-226 6482 Telex 94017347 THMB G

Thumb is a consultancy with a reputation for providing creative solutions to complex graphic design problems. Thumb's clients range from some of the UK's largest financial, cultural and commercial institutions to professional practices and galleries. These include the Royal Academy of Arts, Abbey National, Business Design Centre and Balfour Beatty. With a network of computer aided design and image-setting support systems the consultancy undertakes projects including annual reports, corporate identities and company brochures, catalogues and promotional material. Please ask to see Thumb's brochure and portfolio.

Contact Mr Andrew Wakelin
Size 11-20
Affiliations CSD, STD, D&AD

Total Concept Design (UK) Ltd

No 1 Warrington Street, Ashton-under-Lyne, Manchester OL6 6XB
Telephone 061-339 5616 Fax 061-339 1740

Based in Manchester and specializing in the North West, Total Concept Design has 19 years' experience in graphic design-concept, design, artwork and print. Clients range from local commerce to national companies with products and services as diverse as lasers and strawberry jam.
Total Concept offers a complete service: a new house style and application, stationery, technical and sales brochures, packaging, exhibition displays, livery, etc.
Clients include: Plessey (electronics), ASD (steel), JSB (lighting), Bowater (liquids), Authorities (health; education), International Brands (food export).
Philosophy: client and designer working together.

Contact Mr Derek Baxter
Size 11-20

John Towersey Design Associates Ltd

52 Smith Street, Warwick, Warwickshire CV34 4HS
Telephone (0926) 494104 Fax (0926) 410198

Total in-house design facility for corporate, packaging, advertising, retail and exhibition design, providing a complete service based on a highly creative team.
A considerable amount of experience has been gained in franchising companies, employee communication, the holiday business and the motor industry.
Some recent projects include: Caterham Cars Motor Show exhibition stand. Magdalen College/Oxford Science Park property brochures, Horizon Holidays' brochures, Burnfield corporate design, County Bureau corporate design and advertising and solicitors' promotional material for the Lawnet Group.

Contact Mr John Towersey
Size 6-10

Trapeze Design Company

Rockley Studio, 44 Rockley Road, London W14 0BT
Telephone 071-603 1286 Fax 071-602 3442

Effective marketing literature, POS and packaging. Listed as a consultant under the DTI Design Initiative Scheme.
Our work includes: copywriting, art direction of room set/exterior set/location photography and print management.
Clients include: ICI Paints, Armstrong Floors, Embassy Hotels, Trusthouse Forte.
Of the Colour Dimensions work, John Banham, Director General of the CBI, commented, 'an excellent, proven piece of communication in a field where it is extraordinarily difficult to come up with new ideas'.

Contact Mrs Marilyn Sturgeon
Size 1-5
Affiliations CSD, STD, IOP, DBA

Triplicate Design Ltd

7 Linenhall Street, Belfast, Co Antrim, Northern Ireland BT2 8AA
Telephone (0232) 233296 Fax (0232) 249252

Triplicate Design specialize in the creation and implementation of marketing-led corporate design programmes embracing corporate identity, brand identity, packaging, promotional literature and exhibition design.
We also have a product and three dimensional design department. With an emphasis on results-based creativity, Triplicate offer a total service from concept to finished production.

Contact Mr Ian Bennington
Size 21-50
Affiliations CSD, DBA

Tristram Kent Associates

58 Stone Road, Broadstairs, Kent CT10 1DZ
Telephone (0843) 68889 Fax (0843) 860246

Tristram Kent Associates is a design-led communication arts partnership, providing a personal and comprehensive creative service for clients. We are equally experienced in devising integrated concept, design, copy and production solutions, as in individual design and corporate identity projects. Now in our seventh year of practice, we have successfully undertaken work for clients such as Peugeot Talbot and Rank Xerox, as well as new product promotions for Periscope Software, corporate retail graphics for the Marise Clare group, and numerous business-to-business commissions.

Contact Mr Tristram Branscombe-Kent
Size 1-5
Affiliations ISMM

GRAPHICS & PACKAGING

Ed Turnbull Design Associates

Brailsford House, Knapp Lane, St James Square, Cheltenham, Gloucestershire GL50 3QA
Telephone (0242) 231111 Fax (0242) 232030

With subsidiaries in Bristol, Plymouth and York, our design solutions have become recognizable assets for leading British and overseas companies in foods, horticulture, finance and leisure industries. We provide the most cost-effective design survey to your budget and the highest quality production service on new product development, packaging design, corporate design, brand creation and launch material. Our portfolio includes – Rowntree Mackintosh, Birds Eye Wall's, The Wrigley Company, Farley's Foods, Cadbury Schweppes (NZ), Television South West, Coutts & Co Investment Bank, Guiness Mahon Investments.

Contact Mr Ed Turnbull
Size 1-5

Via Design Ltd

10/12 Carlisle Street, London W1V 5RF
Telephone 071-287 0858 Fax 071-494 3718

Via Design specializes in packaging for major brands, own label and direct-selling companies (graphics and 3-D), and were one of the first consultancies to work with the Soviet Union in the post-Glasnost environment, producing a perfume bottle and carton concept.
Clients include: Unilever, Marks & Spencer, Sainsbury's, Jeyes, Peter Black, Kleeneze, Grand Metropolitan (Foods).
The key point of difference clients have benefited from is the experience its directors have in the field of design management and marketing, gained with international blue-chip companies.

Contact Mr Ken Jones
Size 11-20
Affiliations CSD

Vineyard Design Consultants

46a Rosebery Avenue, London EC1R 4RP
Telephone 071-833 5956 Fax 071-278 3549

Vineyard is a design-led consultancy specializing in packaging, and offers a full repertoire of design services needed by companies for whom the pack is the primary means of communication. Accordingly we are expert in name generation, identity design and new product development. Our list of clients includes: CTT (Irish Export Board), Destrooper Olivier, Elida Gibbs, J Sainsbury, Smithkline Beecham, Unilever Export, Wilkin & Sons (Tiptree), etc.

Contact Mr Nigel Bullivant
Size 1-5

VINEYARD

DESIGN CONSULTANTS

LONDON

Visible Means Ltd

56 Bernard Street, Leith, Edinburgh, Scotland EH6 6PR
Telephone 031-553 7817 Fax 031-555 0791 Telex 72165

Visible Means is a graphic design company using state-of-the-art computer technology to provide a creative design service for clients in the industrial, financial and public sectors. Our design for marketing service is geared towards helping businesses to promote their products or services as effectively as possible. We have all the necessary resources to handle complete design projects. Our resources include graphics, photography, illustration and copywriting as well as a full electronic page make-up system with on-screen illustration facility for the production of publications, pack designs etc.

Contact Mr John Franchetti
Size 6-10

Alan Wagstaff & Partners

Crown Reach, 147a Grosvenor Road, London SW1V 3JY
Telephone 071-834 0534 Fax 071-834 1810

An independent consultancy – dedicated to producing relevant solutions to diverse marketing opportunities on brief, on budget and on time. We combine a flexible and responsive approach to client handling to ensure the service we provide is second to none. A full in-house facility operating from purpose-built studios in central London supports our work on NPD packaging, print and corporate styling. With extensive experience of UK, European and Arabian markets, we enjoy a comprehensive client base within FMCG, leisure, stationery, property and financial sectors, ranging from multinationals to smaller companies with an eye for effective design.

Contact Mr James Wilkes
Size 21-50

Watermark Communications Group Ltd

71-79 Waterside, Chesham, Buckinghamshire HP5 1PE
Telephone (0494) 791911 Fax (0494) 791838

Fast establishing a reputation for imaginative and effective design, Watermark Communications believe in the tried and tested formula of exceptional creative talent and professional marketing expertise. Our team of designers are experienced in corporate identity, all forms of corporate communication, printed and promotional material, as well as exhibition and environmental graphics. The high standards we set at Watermark Communications have enabled us to help manufacturers, retailers and service companies in communicating efficiently with their clients, customers, employees and the general public.

Contact Mr Adrian Waddington
Size 1-5
Affiliations CSD, STD

Westpoint Design Consultants Ltd

3 Park Gate, Glasgow, Scotland G3 6DL
Telephone 041-333 9275 Fax 041-332 3545

Westpoint are specialized graphic designers. Based in Glasgow, our small professional design consultancy serves a wide variety of clients from major national companies to small start-up businesses.
For the past ten years we have created corporate identity schemes, company brochures, promotional literature, packaging, point-of-sale material, posters, calendars and books.
Our designers work closely with clients, building a trust and mutual understanding from which the ideal design solution evolves.
Our consistency, creativity, innovation and meticulous attention to detail are the basis of our success and our reputation.

Contact Ms Pat Halliburton
Size 11-20

Williams and Phoa Ltd

2a Pear Tree Court, London EC1R 0DS
Telephone 071-490 2029 Fax 071-253 9947

Williams and Phoa is a graphic design consultancy specializing in design for print and corporate identity. We work hard to provide original, individual and intelligent responses to our clients' needs. We believe that each piece of work we design is contemporary rather than merely fashionable.
Each results from a thorough understanding of the brief and from close partner involvement at all stages in the design process. Recent projects include the corporate identity and a series of brochures for Arup Associates, an annual review and accounts for Post Office Counters and a set of product brochures for Humber.

Contact Mr Clive Bidwell
Size 11-20

Wilmot & Partners Ltd

Charles House, 7 Leicester Place, London WC2H 7BP
Telephone 071-439 1178 Fax 071-437 0390

Specializing in design, corporate identities, graphics, advertising, marketing and public relations.

Contact Mr Richard Wilmot
Size 11-20

Windsor Jennings

Beech House, Church Lane, Godstone, Surrey RH9 8BW
Telephone (0883) 744322 Fax (0883) 744294

Windsor Jennings is a design consultancy specializing in all forms of graphic design and finished artwork, photography and illustrative work allied to sales promotion and packaging. Both partners have considerable experience working for design consultancies, advertising agencies and publishing houses. Recent design projects have been on behalf of Birds Eye Walls, Brooke Bond Foods, The Rank Organisation, Smith Kline Beecham, Trusthouse Forte, plus many medium sized companies and business start-ups.
Windsor Jennings' experience is wide ranging, and embraces cosmetics, pharmaceuticals, pet food, catering/food, hair products, wine, spirits and beers, cigarettes and tobacco, magazines and retail chains.

Contact Mr Jeff Windsor
Size 6-10
Affiliations CAM, CSD

Wings Design Consultants Ltd

7-10 Batemans Row, London EC2A 3HH
Telephone 071-739 7500 Fax 071-739 7573 Telex 888941 LCCI G Wings

Design consultancy working in the following business areas: brand packaging, corporate identity, corporate literature, exhibitions, marketing literature, print consultancy, product packaging, retail packaging, signing systems, technical literature. Special facilities include DTP.
Client companies include: BFRC, Briggs Amasco, Cape Boards, John Laing Developments, The Rawplug Co, Redland Bricks, Redland Roof Tiles, Richard Ellis, Sainsburys, Waitrose and Westminster Abbey.

Contact Mr Malcolm Park
Size 1-5
Affiliations CSD, DBA, D&AD

The Yellow Pencil Company Ltd

2 Cosser Street, London SE1 7BU
Telephone 071-928 7801 Fax 071-927 1419

Expertise in the management of image through observation and innovation: at The Yellow Pencil Company our discipline is the management of image. Essentially, it is about controlling the way your identity, image and hence reputation is perceived. To do this successfully we commit ourselves to careful observation of the problem and when that is complete we agree a reasoned assessment with our client. Only then do we embark on the process of innovation. It's a process that has proved itself by results.

Contact Mr Andy Ewan
Size 6-10

The Yellow Pencil Company
DESIGN CONSULTANTS

Andrew Younger & Associates

30 The Avenue, Bedford Park, Chiswick, London W4 1HT
Telephone 081-995 8787 Fax 081-747 8396

Design for marketing and communications.
More and more business decision-makers are finding it pays to consider the design factor from start to finish of every project. We go out of our way to acquire a detailed knowledge of each client's needs in terms of marketing, strategy, budgets, timescales and overall aims. This enables us to take a fresh yet realistic approach to each project. Our clients range from major international corporations to small companies and specialist organizations. We offer to them all the same well-organized creative and production skills, allied effectively to their corporate and marketing aims. Above all, we offer a friendly and personal service.

Contact Mr Andrew Younger
Size 1-5
Affiliations CSD

Zappia & Zappia Design Partnership

Hagley Hall Mews, Hagley, Stourbridge, West Midlands DY9 9LF
Telephone (0562) 886536 Fax (0562) 886540

Based within the grounds of stately Hagley Hall, three minutes from the M5 motorway, we are ideally located to service clients nationally and internationally. Our dedicated team have the proven ability to fulfil clients' needs through design and marketing solutions. The personal attention of a partner, and the back-up of an in-house Mac artwork studio ensure total control throughout each project. Since its inception Zappia & Zappia have helped: Cadbury Schweppes, Coloroll, Central TV, Horizon Holidays, The City of Birmingham, Struers, Glynwed, Royal Brierley Crystal, Billingham, Regal Blinds, MCC Foods.

Contact Ms Julijana Zappia
Size 11-20
Affiliations DBA, CSD

GRAPHICS & PACKAGING

DIRECTORY OF DESIGNERS 1991

INTERIORS & RETAIL

ACL & Partners

70 Mill Lane, London NW6 1NL
Telephone 071-433 3266 Fax 071-433 1972

ACL & Partners is a design practice specializing in retail design and as such working particularly with garden centres and other large retail outlets. ACL offers its clients full overall planning and design advisory service, retail and merchandise layout and planning as well as feasibility studies for all sizes of projects. ACL's expertise is backed by vast experience and thorough understanding of the retail business.
ACL also undertakes design work for clients from other retail sectors such as fashion, off-licences, bookshops, food stores etc.

Contact Mr Clifford Long
Size 1-5
Affiliations DSS

Addison

60 Britton Street, London EC1M 5NA
Telephone 071-250 1887 Fax 071-251 3712

We are a worldwide design consultancy with over 200 specialists working in the Far East, USA and Europe. Our expertise covers architecture, ergonomics, graphics, leisure, office and retail, product design and transportation together with design research. Our work covers all aspects of design including research, strategic development, concept design and implementation for both one-off and multinational companies. We place great emphasis on working closely with our clients to establish and plan project requirements, and balance creativity and innovation with sound commercial sense.

Contact Ms Kate Manasian
Size over 100
Affiliations CSD

The Anderlyn Consultancy plc

209 Harrow Road, London W2 5EG
Telephone 071-266 3779 Fax 071-266 3706

Established for 25 years, Anderlyn is a multidisciplinary design consultancy specializing in the office workplace and building interiors. We place particular emphasis on analysing our clients' business needs in relation to accommodation and providing creative, cost-effective solutions. We are able to provide a comprehensive package of professional services, as appropriate to the project, covering design, space planning, building services engineering, cost consultancy and project management. Our experience is wide, ranging from strategic accommodation planning for greenfield sites and relocation studies to refurbishment and fitting out of existing buildings.

Contact Mr Richard Beal
Size 1-5
Affiliations CSD, IAM, CIBSE, CIOB

Associated Design Managers Ltd (ADM)

15 Kensington Square, London W8 5HH
Telephone 071-938 2222 Fax 071-937 8335

ADM is concerned only with the office environment, the intelligent and economic use of space, staff comfort, and creating working conditions that aid fast communications and distribution of data. We provide high performance office interiors, embracing detailed space planning and corporate impact. We manage the total project from design concept through to completion of the total furnished and fitted interior. ADM only employs people who understand offices and how they operate. We are expert in digging deeply into company operational problems and providing the answers that influence the final and most efficient use of working space.

Contact Mr Michael Carson
Size 1-5
Affiliations CSD

Axis Design Europe

2 Cosser Street, London SE1 7BU
Telephone 071-633 9911 Fax 071-620 0238

Over the last decade we have experienced steady managed growth both in the size of our company and in the scale of the projects we have handled.
Effective design solutions require a balance between creativity, quality and cost efficiency. That balance is at the heart of our contract with the client. We provide creative solutions to a wide range of design needs including product design, furniture, interior architecture and space planning.

Contact Mr Jeremy Harvey
Size 11-20
Affiliations CSD

Bowyer Langlands Batchelor — Chartered Architects & Designers

Russell Chambers, The Piazza, Covent Garden, London WC2E 8RH
Telephone 071-836 1452 Fax 071-497 9581

The practice began with the 1951 Exhibition and since has specialized in exhibitions, museums, interior design and restoration. Recent projects include: the new Japanese Gallery and Prints and Drawings Collection at the British Museum, the Barry Rooms at the National Gallery, Cabinet War Rooms Museum, Gloucester Cathedral Treasury and National Portrait Gallery. Also branches of Barclays Bank, offices for IBM and London Borough of Southwark, special buildings for Shell Research and the mentally handicapped, restoration at the Royal Naval College Greenwich and Vanbrugh Castle. Current projects are more work at the Science Museum and at Windsor Castle.

Contact Ms Ursula Bowyer
Size 11-20
Affiliations RIBA, CSD, RSA

Brick Studio & Manufacturing Ltd

50 Kenilworth Drive, Oadby, Leicestershire LE2 5LG
Telephone (0533) 713301 Fax (0533) 718707

Brick Studio & Manufacturing provides a comprehensive professional design, technical development, manufacturing and contracting service to the retail and commercial industries. Centrally based in the UK at Oadby, Leicestershire, Brick's vast shopfitting experience and in-house expertise offer clients a complete one-stop facility including original concept design, point-of-sale, through to product development and specification, manufacture, installation and a full contract management service. Brochure available.

Contact Mr Nigel Lowe
Size 21-50
Affiliations IOS, IIM

Maurice Broughton Associates

38/39 South Molton Street, London W1Y 1HD
Telephone 071-493 0456 Fax 071-629 3856

Maurice Broughton Associates are concerned with the creation of modern high quality interiors. Each project is considered on a totally individual basis and is carefully detailed and controlled to produce a unique environment. Incorporating architecture, graphic and interior design disciplines, together with lighting, environmental engineering and project management, we provide the client with a complete design service.
Over the last 25 years, clients have included: Harrods, Simpson, Jaeger, BAA, Body Shop, C&A, Harvey Nichols, Knickerbox, Fenwick, Stockmann (Helsinki), Liberty, House of Commons, together with restaurants, offices and private apartments.

Contact Mr John Fung
Size 6-10
Affiliations CSD, RSA

Business Design Group

24 St John Street, London EC1M 4AY
Telephone 071-490 1144 Fax 071-250 3005

Business Design Group specializes in environmental design and visual communications, working with management to improve productivity in the workplace. Our wide range of expertise includes space analysis, graphic and interior design, project management, furniture supply, installation and customer support. By combining some or all of our services, we provide strategic solutions to problems associated with refurbishment, relocations and rationalizations. With over 140 staff in six locations (Bristol, Dublin, Frankfurt, London, Reading and Swindon), Business Design Group maintains a standard of service that is unique within the creative industries.

Contact Mr Keith Lawson
Size over 100
Affiliations CSD, DBA

The Chadwick Group

1a Birkenhead Street, Kings Cross, London WC1H 8NB
Telephone 071-278 5969 Fax 071-823 1621

The Chadwick Group comprises two separate but complementary divisions – Design and Space Management. Pfister Chadwick Design and Hulme Chadwick Architects offer an experienced architectural and interior design service with an international reputation for excellence, particularly in the field of office interiors.
The Space Management Division offers Organizational Modelling, a unique approach to space management which 'audits' business space to measure the efficiency of, and controls space use in, a property portfolio. The OM consultancy is available worldwide. Chadwick Computer Drafting offers a full range of CAD services, consultancy and training.

Contact Mr James Whitehouse
Size 21-50
Affiliations CSD, RIBA

Checkland Kindleysides Design

Fowke Street, Rothley, Leicester, Leicestershire LE7 7PJ
Telephone (0533) 374282 Fax (0533) 374649

Established in 1979, Checkland Kindleysides has a reputation for highly creative work, matched with a mature ability for project management. Our approach puts total emphasis on the understanding of our clients' business aims and ambitions, enabling us to produce authoritative creative solutions that encompass many design disciplines including retail and interiors, graphics, corporate literature, packaging, furniture and product.
Clients include: Levi Strauss (UK), Olympus Sport, Toyota GB, Dupont, Alfred Dunhill, Ballantyne Cashmere, Alexon and Lexus.

Contact Ms Marie Cooke
Size 21-50

David Clarke Associates

4 Tottenham Mews, London W1P 9PJ
Telephone 071-636 7172 Fax 071-436 3195

David Clarke Associates is a practice of architects, designers and energy consultants. The design work of the practice involves interior design and products related to building. Interior work completed includes shops, restaurants, design studios, offices and hotels; and product design work has included light fittings, a high quality mass-produced conservatory and a mass-produced garden building.
Past and present clients include: Bournville Village Trust, Department of Energy, European Commission, Monarch Aluminium, Newman Tonks, Property Services Agency, Til Leisure , Trusthouse Forte Catering and Way of Life.

Contact Mr David Clarke
Size 6-10
Affiliations RIBA

INTERIORS & RETAIL

Simon Conder Associates

The Old School House, 66a Leonard Street, London EC2A 4QX
Telephone 071-739 6492 Fax 071-729 5075

Simon Condor Associates are a multidisciplinary practice of architects, interior and product designers. Our work includes new buildings, conversions, the restoration of listed buildings, office, retail and residential interiors, as well as exhibition, product and furniture design.
Our clients range from individuals and small companies to major public companies and institutions such as First Leisure Corporation, Next, English Estates and the London Dockland Development Corporation. The practice has recently successfully completed retail projects in Germany, Japan and the USA for both UK and Japanese clients.

Contact Mr Simon Conder
Size 6-10
Affiliations ARCUK, RIBA, CSD

Czarska Designs Ltd

9-15 Neal Street, London WC2H 9PU
Telephone 071-836 6991 Fax 071-836 3979

Czarska is a multidisciplinary international design practice based in London. We are highly creative in our approach and understand that design is one amongst a number of business resources, the purpose of which is to successfully aid our client's business objectives. Our design expertise is extensive, including architectural and interior design, brand and identity development, product and industrial design, aircraft and airport interiors, graphics and signage and uniform design.
Our clients include Abercrombie & Kent, Air Europe, Annabels, Austin Reed, Barclays Bank, Birleys Sandwiches, British Caledonian Airways, British Midland Airways, Cathay Pacific Airways, General Motors, N M Rothschild & Sons, United Racecourses, Guinness Peat.

Contact Ms Isobel Czarska
Size 11-20

Dalziel & Pow

7/8 Greenland Place, Camden Town, London NW1 0AP
Telephone 071-482 4878 Fax 071-485 6026

Dalziel & Pow offers a comprehensive service in the disciplines of interior, retail, graphics, packaging and exhibition design.
We have established a reputation for creativity together with strong contract management, and since our formation in 1983 have strived to produce imaginative yet practical design solutions for a variety of clients. Clients include: C&A, Cobra Sports, Grand Metropolitan, Hintlesham Hall, House of Fraser, The Moorgate Group, Penneys Department Stores, River Island Clothing Company, Rydon Signs, J Sainsbury, Sir Owen Williams & Partners, Tiles International, Trusthouse Forte.

Contact Mr John Pow
Size 11-20
Affiliations CSD, RSA, IOD

Davies Design Ltd

25 Fouberts Place, London W1V 1HE
Telephone 071-287 8000 Fax 071-287 2120

At Davies Design, we place equal emphasis on creative design and its implementation, using a combination of interior, graphic design and project management skills.
Based in London and Edinburgh, we are active within the leisure, retail and office sectors and can offer specialist expertise in luxury transport interior design.
Current projects include restaurants, hotels, tourist attractions, cinemas, airport signage, office space planning, shopping centres and retail multiples for clients such as L & R Leisure, BAA, British Telecom, Heron Property Corporation, Oasis, Caroll and Adams Childrenswear.

Contact Ms Alyson Green
Size 6-10
Affiliations AA

Design House Consultants Ltd

120 Parkway, Camden Town, London NW1 7AN
Telephone 071-482 2815 Fax 071-267 7587

Design House specializes in creating stylish and effective design schemes for retail and leisure environments. As a leading interdisciplinary consultancy, we also provide skills in corporate identity, brand development, packaging and print design. Throughout all stages of a project, from concept to site management, we apply the same criteria: a realistic marketing perspective, rigorous attention to detail and a commitment to quality in the finished results.
Design House currently holds the DBA Design Effectiveness Award for retail design for the florists VASE. Other clients include: Allied Breweries, Midlands Electricity Board, Victoria Wine Company, Grand Metropolitan and the Portsmouth Building Society.

Contact Mr Tim May
Size 6-10

Design Research Unit (DRU)

94 Lower Marsh, London SE1 7AB
Telephone 071-633 9711 Fax 071-261 0333

DRU has over 40 years' experience both in the UK and overseas in interior, graphic and architectural design. We have particular expertise in all aspects of interior design from concept and space planning through to contract documentation, site supervision and the selection of furniture, furnishings and works of art. Our clients – who range from private individuals to multinational organizations – benefit from working environments tailored precisely to their needs and budget. Projects have included offices, hotels, ships, shops, banks, conference centres and transport facilities.

Contact Mr William Furbisher
Size 21-50
Affiliations CSD, RIBA, BCB, DIA

Dickson Huggins Associates Ltd

234 West Regent Street, Glasgow, Scotland G2 4DQ
Telephone 041-226 3555 Fax 041-204 1454

With staff expertise spanning various disciplines, from architecture to textile and graphic design, we can apply an appropriate blend of input in formulating our response to the design brief.
Recent projects include exhibition stands for the fashion and home textiles markets, domestic and office interiors, space planning and alterations to public buildings including civic offices, libraries, pubs, restaurants and themed decorative schemes for shopping malls.
We welcome the opportunity to discuss your projects and to present our work.

Contact Mr Brian Nicol
Size 11-20

Epic Interior Design Ltd

10a Royal Terrace, Glasgow, Scotland G3 7NT
Telephone 041-332 9382 Fax 041-332 7232

Epic interiors are specialists in the field of interior design, principally in the leisure industry. Established in 1975, Epic has vast experience in the production of design concepts for bars, hotels, clubs and discotheques. Increasingly we act as project managers taking a contract from the design stage through construction to completion of the finished article. We are acknowledged experts in converting good ideas into profitable ventures. Commercial projects, medical and dental surgeries now also benefit from Epic's design skills. DTI approved consultants.

Contact Mr Jim Dey
Size 6-10
Affiliations CSD, RSA

Fitch RS Design Consultants

4 Crinan Street, London N1 9UE
Telephone 071-278 7200 Fax 071-833 1014 Telex 22826

Fitch RS Design Consultants is one of the world's leading specialists in interior design for the retail and leisure industry. With offices in the USA, London and mainland Europe, we are able to offer our clients unique skills and experience. Our work ranges from repositioning of such department stores as Debenhams to small one-off projects such as the London Thai restaurant 'Singapura'. Projects are managed by dedicated teams of designers, retailing experts and marketing consultants. Clients include the Burton Group, Boots, Asda, De Bijenkorf, NMB Bank, Expo '92 and Jelmoli.

Contact Mr Rune Gustafson
Size over 100

Fletcher Design Ltd

Copland House, 130 Edmiston Drive, Ibrox, Glasgow, Strathclyde, Scotland G51 2YR
Telephone 041-427 5357 Fax 041-427 3356 Telex 778607

The company objective is to provide innovative designs with style and flair that are commercially relevant. The full design service includes design concepts including general arrangements, visuals and sample boards; design development using sectional elevations and submission of applications for planning and building control; design detailing including selection and specification of finishes, furniture, fittings and equipment. We offer to programme and co-ordinate all other professional consultants and offer full site supervision and project management of fit out.

Contact Mr Bill Henderson
Size 11-20
Affiliations CSD

The Four Hundred Ltd

6a New Concordia Wharf, St Saviours Dock, Mill Street, London SE1 2BA
Telephone 071-237 0587 Fax 071-231 6064

The Four Hundred is a well established design practice which until this year was known as H & P Design. Our new name has not changed our philosophy; we believe a company makes a statement about itself with everything it produces. Our combination of talents in both 2 and 3D enables us to develop an image and effectively apply it to all aspects of a project from corporate identity and printed matter through to exhibitions and interiors.

Contact Ms Win Rogers
Size 6-10
Affiliations CSD

THE *four* HUNDRED

Graham Frecknall Architecture and Design

9 Agincourt Street, Monmouth, Gwent, Wales NP5 3DZ
Telephone (0600) 6418 Fax (0600) 4507

The practice specializes in interior design, product design and architecture. Recent interior design projects range from work for major retailers through to hotel development, and many schemes result from their listing under the DTI Design Initiative. They are also an approved listed consultant with CADW for interior design work on listed buildings. Work on product and furniture design includes the initial design for Polycell double glazing systems, modular office furniture for G A Harvey and Abita window frame and window design. Offices also in Cirencester. Brochure available.

Contact Mr Graham Frecknall
Size 6-10
Affiliations RIBA, CIArb

INTERIORS & RETAIL

Gardiner and Torne Ltd

46 London Road, Reading, Berkshire RG1 5AP
Telephone (0734) 313700 Fax (0734) 310252 Telex 912881 GAD

Specialists in exhibition and corporate environmental design. Although noted for our expertise with telecommunication companies, we have substantial clients in the fields of chemicals, financial services, travel and electrical engineering. Our impressive client list includes BP Chemicals, Acro Chemicals, Extel Financial, Perpetual, Galileo UK, Austrian National Tourist Office, MK Electric and V & E Friedland – to name but a few. We have worldwide experience – handling projects in China, USA, Europe and Eastern Bloc countries. For more details of the company please send for a brochure.

Contact Mr Michael Torne
Size 6-10
Affiliations CSD, IOD

Glazebrook Interior Architects

25 Bar Street, Scarborough, North Yorkshire YO11 2HT
Telephone (0723) 375871 Fax (0723) 353920

GIA began 20 years ago as a one-man consultancy. Terry Glazebrook is proud that his first client – who commissioned a disco bar in 1970 with a budget of £500 – will in 1990/91 entrust GIA with various leisure projects with contract values approaching £5m. The team combines wide experience with professional expertise in architecture, interior design and project management, to provide corporate and private clients with a comprehensive service on time and within budget, in all leisure areas, particularly hotels/restaurants/swimming pools/pubs and clubs/holiday villages/sports facilities.

Contact Mr Terry Glazebrook
Size 11-20
Affiliations CSD, RIBA, RICS, CIOB

Haley Sharpe Associates

11-15 Guildhall Lane, Leicester, Leicestershire LE1 5FQ
Telephone (0533) 518555 Fax (0533) 519119

Haley Sharpe Associates is an interior, graphics and interpretive design consultancy specializing in three main areas: retail, museums and exhibitions. Retail experience is in the design, visualizing, development and project management of conversion areas within department stores, point-of-sale material and complete interior schemes. The museum specialities offered are feasibility studies and reports, research, design and development, visualizing, prototyping, modelmaking, illustration and project administration. Our clients include British Airports Authority, Allders International, William Grant and Sons, Estée Lauder, Sony, Mattel, Pedigree Petfoods, the Arts Council, Bass, Lego and Mars, amongst others.

Contact Mr Graham Brock
Size 21-50

Ivor Hall & Associates Ltd

34 Bisham Gardens, Highgate, London N6 6DD
Telephone 081-348 2338 Fax 081-348 8922

Office planning, shop and restaurant design – a full design management service provides clients with imaginative design solutions to the highest standards, within budget and to time. IHA's architect base ensures landlords' and all statutory authorities' requirements are properly incorporated and the project efficiently administered. Clients: Hard Rock Café, Liberty, Rover Group, British Shipbuilders.
Exhibition Design – 30 years' experience in the design/management of over 600 stands in 30 countries worldwide in Europe, Middle and Far East, Australasia, North and South America. Clients: British Telecom, British Shipbuilders, Lloyd's Register, McDonnell Douglas.

Contact Mr Ivor Hall
Size 1-5
Affiliations RIBA, AA, CSD

INTERIORS & RETAIL

John Herbert Partnership

8 Berkley Road, Primrose Hill, London NW1 8YR
Telephone 071-722 3932 Fax 071-586 7048

The John Herbert Partnership is a multidisciplinary design consultancy of graphic, interior and product designers. We specialize in corporate identity, strategic planning, design, new concept development and building refurbishment, for retail, leisure, financial services, offices and restaurants. We are committed to creative and cost-effective design and professional service for our clients. These include: Selfridges, British Airports Authority, British Shoe Corporation, Marks & Spencer, British Rail, Capital & Counties, Norwich Union, National Trust. Award-winning projects for Sears Holdings, Coventry Building Society and British Gas.

Contact Ms Patricia Herbert
Size 21-50
Affiliations CSD, RICS, BCSC, RSA, DBA

David & Miriam Howitt

33 Roehampton Gate, London SW15 5JR
Telephone 081-878 0520 Fax 081-878 0054

Architects/interior designers/product designers, specializing where these overlap: airports, hotel and catering facilities, showrooms and all types of refurbishment including domestic and for handicap. We designed the British Airways Shuttle and Executive Club Lounges, Heathrow; Whitewater Hotel, Cumbria; reception and offices for Arcontrol; showrooms for London Badge & Button Company; a prototype double-decker bus for Greater Manchester Transport; high technology check-in desks; light fittings using recent developments in light sources. We enjoy tackling any design problem and producing user-friendly solutions to suit our clients' particular needs. Brochure available.

Contact Mrs Miriam Howitt
Size 1-5
Affiliations CSD, RIBA

Interdec Design Group Ltd

Hunters Mill, Deanshanger, Milton Keynes, Buckinghamshire MK19 6HY
Telephone (0908) 562928 Fax (0908) 561684 Telex 826115 INTDEC G

Interdec works exclusively on commercial business interiors and has built up considerable experience in all aspects of interior developments. We believe that the correct balance between the building, its people and their technology needs is paramount to the success and business performance of the organization. Our services include: relocation consultancy, detailed facility planning, office space evaluation, commercial interior design, contract furnishing and fitting out, 3D interior and building modelling, facility management. Recent clients include: British Aerospace, Cadburys, VAG, Grants of St James's, Grant Thornton.

Contact Mrs Mary Crampton
Size 21-50
Affiliations CSD, IOD, CBI, ICMA

Katz Vaughan Meyer & Feltham

162 Ewell Road, Surbiton, Surrey KT6 6HG
Telephone 081-390 4658 Fax 081-399 8980

Katz Vaughan Meyer & Feltham practise as chartered architects and interior designers specializing in shopfitting and interior fitting contracts. Established in 1945, a number of original clients have been retained. Numerous hotel projects have been undertaken over the years ranging from small alteration works to large new hotels for major international groups. Involved also in the refitting of many departmental stores, ladies' fashion shops, bars and restuarants. Close attention is paid to detail and all design work is carried out under the personal supervision of the partners.

Contact Mr Peter Feltham
Size 6-10
Affiliations SIAD, RIBA

John Kirk Design Ltd

Hayhill Industrial Estate, Sileby Road, Barrow Upon Soar, Leicestershire LE12 8LD
Telephone (0509) 813408 Fax (0509) 816098

Formed in 1975, John Kirk Design has grown in reputation as one of the leading design consultancies in the Midlands.
We provide a full range of consultancy services in all areas of two- and three-dimensional design. Our specialities lie in the fields of leisure, retail, commercial, exhibition and graphic design. Project managers work closely with clients through planning, concept and design to production and delivery.
Principal clients: British American Tobacco, British Shoe Corporation, Dixons, Trusthouse Forte.

Contact Mr John Kirk
Size 21-50
Affiliations BECA, GDIM, DBA

Lees Associates

5 Dryden Street, Covent Garden, London WC2E 9NW
Telephone 071-829 8400 Fax 071-379 4280 Telex 299533 AST G

Through progression and expansion, Lees Associates have developed a team of architects and designers who dedicate themselves to clients who need projects delivered on time. Dealing in a changing world, Lees Associates provides solutions which respond to clients' aspirations and reach beyond their expectations. We like demanding clients, who include:
Financial: Salomon Brothers International, J P Morgan Bank, Chase Manhattan, Philipp Brothers, Phibro Energy, The Mortgage Corporation; Leisure: The Royal Horticultural Society, Trusthouse Forte, Swallow Hotels, Brent Walker, Ancaster Marina; Industrial: Courtaulds, Steinberg, Bairdwear; Retail: Browns, Alexon.

Contact Mr Jon Lees
Size 11-20
Affiliations RIBA, CSD

The David Leon Partnership

22 Greencoat Place, London SW1P 1EG
Telephone 071-834 7767 Fax 071-828 3874

Interior designers, space planners and architects. We work for a wide range of clients specializing in four sectors:
Science and technology: Fisons, Merck Sharp & Dohme, Johnson Matthey, Unilever, Roussel Laboratories, The Association for Consumer Research. Professional institutions and associations: Girl Guides Association, Institution of Structural Engineers, The Industrial Society, Institution of Mechanical Engineers. Financial world and professions: S G Warburg & Co, Alliance & Leicester Building Society, Cluttons, Gouldens, Levy Gee. Special projects: The Victoria and Albert Museum, British Rail, BMW, Nuffield Hospitals, Oxford University, Thomson Travel, The Royal Albert Hall.

Contact Ms Deborah West
Size 21-50
Affiliations CSD, RIBA

Peter Leonard Associates Ltd

535 King's Road, London SW10 0SZ
Telephone 071-352 1717 Fax 071-351 4307

Peter Leonard Associates are now regarded as one of the UK's leading design consultants. As a highly professional creative house we offer a comprehensive service which includes retail, commercial interiors, graphic design and project management. Whether we are working on a vast retail environment or a tiny reception area, we bring to each project the same combination of intelligent thought and creative flair.
Clients include: S4C (Welsh Channel 4), 3i, W H Smith, Ideal-Standard, House of Fraser, Virgin, Thorn-EMI, Science Museum, Oakland (Menswear) and the Charter Group.

Contact Mr James Stewart
Size 21-50
Affiliations CSD

Lloyd Northover Ltd

8 Smart's Place, London WC2B 5LW
Telephone 071-430 1100 Fax 071-430 1490

Status: a world-class, independent specialist consultancy in identity, corporate communications and design. Activities; corporate identity and brand management; brand identity and packaging; environments – retail outlets, offices, business environments; literature – annual reports, corporate literature. Our aim: to provide the most effective identity and design consultancy service for the world's most significant companies, organizations and entrepreneurs – a service which contributes tangibly to their long-term future success. Our method: teamwork, sound strategic thinking, exceptional creative innovation.
In Europe: Shining/Lloyd Northover, Paris office: 26 rue Benard, 75014 Paris, France. Tel: 010 331 40 44 9327. Fax: 010 331 40 44 9347.

Contact Ms Philippa Emery
Size 21-50
Affiliations CSD, DBA, CBI, D&AD, RSA, Design Museum

LLOYD NORTHOVER
The Identity Business

Marketplace Design Partnership Ltd

Pulpit House, One The Square, Abingdon, Oxfordshire OX14 5SZ
Telephone (0235) 554499 Fax (0235) 532878

Marketplace Design Partnership is a multidisciplined consultancy founded on the principle that design must produce profitable results which can be achieved only if set within a strategic context. We believe the real effectiveness of design depends on developing a successful relationship between client and consultancy. Our appointment to designing and implementing an increasing number of assignments, both large and small, is testimony to our unique combination of graphics and interior skills. Our work includes: corporate identity and print communication, retail identity and store design, design for leisure environments, office design, packaging and product development.

Contact Mr Bryan Brown
Size 21-50
Affiliations CSD, DBA, CBI, RSA, D&AD

McGown Snowden Designers

Broad Court, 43 Drury Lane, London WC2B 5RT
Telephone 071-240 0337 Fax 071-240 1157

McGown Snowden Designers was established in 1976, with the view to develop and express design attitudes and solutions – tuned to clients' specific problems and design needs. The practice has developed a range of skills and expertise which encompass environmental/office design from analysis of clients' problems, through to completion. Exhibition/graphic design work includes a number of marketing suites incorporating AV facilities. Retail design has been maintained with a number of our franchise sector clients. Recent clients include: Cowen, Holmen, International Clearing Services, Legal & General, J P Morgan, Nornews UK, Pierson Heldring & Pierson, Prontaprint, Prudential, Skipton Building Society, Speyhawk.

Contact Mr Robert McGown
Size 1-5
Affiliations CSD

John McNeece Ltd

2 Holford Yard, Cruikshank Street, London WC1X 9HD
Telephone 071-837 1225 Fax 071-837 1233

The creativity of interiors design and the technical skills of space planning are uniquely blended in our studios, providing creative solutions to work environment problems.
The core skills are supported by marketing, architectural, QS, and project management services and they each form part of our thorough but personalized service.
Currently we are working on products for Brent Walker, Ericsson, CAA, Touche Ross, Cunard and Chandris, where the design solutions created are in harmony with the cultural values of our client and the needs of the end user.

Contact Mr David Reed
Size 21-50
Affiliations CSD, DBA, RSA

John Michael Design Ltd

Albion House, 20 Queen Elizabeth Street, London SE1 2LS
Telephone 071-357 6002 Fax 071-403 9938

John Michael Design is a multidisciplinary design consultancy operating in the retail, leisure, graphics and corporate communication sectors. Our resources allow us to develop concepts and attach a graphic style through to project management, to ensure successful completion within predetermined budget and time guidelines. Our projects range from working with independents to major international organizations both in the UK and Europe.

Contact Ms Irene Maguire
Size 21-50
Affiliations CSD

Minale Tattersfield & Partners Ltd

The Courtyard, 37 Sheen Road, Richmond, London TW9 1AJ
Telephone 081-948 7999 Fax 081-948 2435

Established in 1964, international design consultants Minale Tattersfield specialize in corporate identity/corporate image making, packaging, and product, environmental and interior design. Their design work has received numerous awards and has been the subject of many prestigious exhibitions worldwide. Recent clients include National Westminster Bank, BP, Toyota, Boehringer, Royal Academy, BAA, Gucci, Giorgio Armani, Garden Company, Cadbury Schweppes, House of Fraser, Irish Distillers, Johnnie Walker, Spontex, Parkway, Fendi, Kansai Paint, Tesco, Valentino, Elida Gibbs, Thorntons, Coutts, Manchester Olympic Committee, The Post Office and Harrods. In addition to their London studios, Minale Tattersfield also has design studios in Australia, Brussels and Paris and offices in Milan, New York, Hong Kong, Osaka, Barcelona, Casablanca, Cologne and Madrid. Brochures available.

Minale, Tattersfield & Partners Limited

Contact Ms Liza Honey
Size over 100
Affiliations CSD, DBA, JIDA, CA, RIA, RAIA

MKW Design Partnership

3 Boroughloch Square, Edinburgh, Scotland EH8 9NJ
Telephone 031-662 0544 Fax 031-667 7271

Our service includes retail, commercial and leisure interiors, museum and exhibition design, environmental graphics and the design of building-related products.
Recent clients include: BAA, 3i, Scottish Development Department, TSB, Gateshead Garden Festival, Inverclyde District Council, British Rail, the Universities of Glasgow and Strathclyde and the Cumbernauld Development Corporation.

Contact Mr Bill Macpherson
Size 6-10

Robin Moore Ede Interior Designers

21 Bruton Place, London W1X 7AB
Telephone 071-629 6910 Fax 071-409 1742

Robin Moore Ede Interior Designers carries out work in three areas:
1 Corporate interiors: executive suites, dealer rooms, dining rooms, banking halls. Clients include Morgan Grenfell, John Swire & Sons, Cathay Pacific, TVS Entertainments, Prudential Bache Securities, ABN Bank, Chesterfield Properties, Christie's International.
2 Specialist retail interiors: art galleries, specialist shops/showrooms. Clients include Noble Jones, Holland and Holland, Findlater Mackie & Todd.
3 Private interiors: complete refurbishment of buildings including custom made furniture, furnishings and fittings; client list on request.

Contact Mr Robin Moore Ede
Size 6-10
Affiliations RSA, CSD

Murdoch Associates Ltd

2-10 Magdalen Street, London SE1 2EQ
Telephone 071-962 1122 Fax 071-962 1125

We specialize in offering a complete design and architectural service. This means we can deal with the full range of design and marketing considerations – interface with professional teams, complete building projects, planning issues, concept development and research, design and tender action, also site supervision. Murdoch's with their considerable experience from 20 years in practice can bring to bear an international perspective on each project. It is important that each job is assessed in relation to the relevant 'state of the art' in the field concerned.
Our clients include: Allied Lyons, Calmic (Wellcome), Fenwicks, Espree Leisure, ITL, THF, VAG, Pepsico, Wembley, Whitbread.

Contact Mr Peter Murdoch
Size 11-20

Northwest Design Associates Ltd

Old Coach Road, Kelsall, near Tarporley, Cheshire CW6 0QJ
Telephone (0829) 51555 Fax (0829) 52366

Established in 1974 as architectural and interior design consultants. Expertise includes: retail, office, restaurant and public house design; space planning, furniture and lighting design; domestic and industrial building design, both new and refurbishment. Measured building surveys, on-site project management. Projects include: over 140 shops for Laura Ashley, Aquascutum in Regent Street, new workshop and head offices for Industor AB in Chester, Pannell Kerr Forster's offices in Liverpool, public houses for Tetley Walker, Stanfords map shop in Covent Garden, members' rooms at the Royal Liverpool Golf Club. Also at Tri-Hen, Tre-Mostyn, Clwyd, Wales.

Contact Mr John Law
Size 11-20
Affiliations CSD, DBA

Jack Notman

34 Belmont Street, Glasgow, Scotland G12 8EY
Telephone 041-339 7276 Fax 041-334 4413

Our architectural and design practice, established in 1954, has consistently been directed towards excellence in design, suitability for purpose and style, particularly in the restoration/reinterpretation of existing buildings. Commissions have included projects for Scottish National Orchestra, Scottish Opera, The National Trust for Scotland, Clyde Shipping Company, Scottish Metropolitan Property, the Design Council, The University of Strathclyde, Bute Fabrics, Cumbrae Estates, many Clydesdale Bank branches, including the Clydesdale Bank's head office refurbishment, offices, restaurants and houses for private clients – resulting in Civic Trust and GIA Awards and continuing commissions from our existing clients. We welcome new challenges.

Contact Mr Jack Notman
Size 1-5
Affiliations RIBA, RIAS, CSD, RSA

Malcolm Payne Design Group Ltd

212-213 Broad Street, Birmingham, West Midlands B15 1AY
Telephone 021-643 3159 Fax 021-631 3348

We are a multidisciplinary group providing the essential skills in architecture and interiors, graphics and exhibitions. Our interiors studio is concerned with the provision of high standards in visual and functional design in offices, retail and leisure environments. We space-plan and reinforce corporate style in offices and shops. We provide new concepts for hotels, restaurants and pubs and we implement them using our technical and managerial skills.
Also at 37-38 Hatton Garden, London EC1N 8EB, telephone 071-242 7328, fax 071-831 9569.

Contact Mr John Seymour
Size 21-50
Affiliations CSD, RIBA

Pentagram Design Ltd

11 Needham Road, London W11 2RP
Telephone 071-229 3477 Fax 071-727 9932 Telex 8952000 PENTA G

Pentagram has a unique international reputation. It offers architecture, exhibition, interior, graphic and product design, with individual partners (directors) responsible for each.
Architecture and interior design are carried out by Theo Crosby, whose experience in a variety of public and commercial environments is considerable. Past projects include the adaptation of spaces for business, retail and public facilities, the restoration, conversion and refurbishment of buildings and the design of trade and cultural exhibitions.
Clients include the Barbican Centre, the International Shakespeare Globe Centre, ITM, Postbank NMB, Reuters and Unilever.

Contact Prof Theo Crosby
Size 51-100
Affiliations CSD, RIBA, RA

Mark Plumtree Design Associates

32 Hinton Close, Crowthorne, Berkshire RG11 6LA
Telephone (0344) 778583 Fax (0344) 778583

Founded in 1989, Mark Plumtree Design is dedicated to specialist top-quality interior design for hotel, pub, restaurant and leisure facilities. The firm believes in total co-ordination from concept to completion – offering creative yet practical cost-effective design solutions to any given brief and budget. Our experience is gained from many years spent in key positions held in the hospitality and leisure business.
Clients include: Brent Walker, Courage, Courtaulds, Lopex (Design in Action), Elders IXL, Everards.

Contact Mr Mark Plumtree
Size 1-5
Affiliations CSD

Portland Design Associates

90-92 Great Portland Street, London W1N 5PB
Telephone 071-436 5301 Fax 071-631 1242

Portland Design Associates, with offices in London and Glasgow, combines the considerable experience of its principals with the creative input of a young and enthusiastic design team to produce exceptional creative solutions to well researched and well understood client briefs. Our expertise in specific commercial categories such as retail stores, shopping centres, marine interiors and property development is well established and recognized through a client list that includes Grosvenor Square Properties, Bredero, P&O European Ferries, Woolworth Cyprus, Land Securities, Meadowhall Centre and Thresher Wine Merchants.

Contact Mr Chris Cook
Size 21-50
Affiliations CSD, DBA, RIBA, BCSC

Recording Architecture Ltd

21-23 Greenwich Market, Greenwich, London SE10 9HZ
Telephone 081-858 6883 Fax 081-305 0601

Acoustic, architectural and interior design of music recording studios and related building types; cost and project management (Roger D'Arcy – Hugh Flynn). Independent acoustic evaluation (TEF time delay spectrometry), design and monitor alignment (Nick Whitaker). Independent audio systems consultant. Installation design, specification and commissioning (Paul Ward).

Contact Mr Roger D'Arcy
Size 1-5
Affiliations RIBA, ES, PRS

INTERIORS & RETAIL

Rossetti Interiors Ltd

26 Grey Street, Newcastle upon Tyne, Tyne & Wear NE1 6AE
Telephone 091-261 4746 Fax 091-222 0877

Rossetti Interiors provides interior design space and planning and furniture design as separate services. It therefore provides continuity and consistency of approach to all aspects of design. Links with The Alan J Smith Partnership (Architects) provide Rossetti Interiors with extensive experience in contract preparation and project supervision, a service not normally provided by interior designers, so that large and complex interior commissions can be controlled from concept to completion.

Contact Mr Andrew Clark
Size 1-5
Affiliations CSD, RIBA

John Sermon & Associates

DESIGN COUNCIL REGISTERED

Hethe Design Workshop, Hethe, Bicester, Oxfordshire OX6 9HD
Telephone (0869) 278105 Fax (0869) 278337

John Sermon & Associates have been responsible for a wide variety of projects, varying from town centre developments (covering all facets from the housing, shopping, signing and the street furniture) to a small extension of a domestic house.
The practice also covers the design of interiors, exhibition stands, furniture design, industrial products, packaging and corporate identity. A store in Birmingham has been carried out as a fully integrated design study, considering the interior and exterior, its corporate image, the display techniques and the correct atmosphere for selling furniture and furnishings.

Contact Mr John Sermon
Size 6-10
Affiliations RSA, CSD

Stills Design Group

DESIGN COUNCIL REGISTERED

66 Lower Dock Street, Newport, Gwent, Wales NP9 1EF
Telephone (0633) 246149 Fax (0633) 841078

We are well known for our top quality design and our commitment to the highest standards of personal service to our clients. We have many years' experience of working closely with our expanding national and international client base.
Our main areas of expertise are in graphics, exhibitions, interiors, retail, marketing and urban renewal.

Contact Mr Chris Carpenter
Size 6-10
Affiliations CSD

Paul Sutton Design Group

DESIGN COUNCIL REGISTERED

798a Fulham Road, London SW6 5SL
Telephone 071-731 2859 Fax 071-731 5900 Telex 934524 0TM G

PSDG actually does offer every client a one-to-one service – at all levels. Specialists in health and leisure developments, including hydros, hotels, clubs and restaurants. Major office environments are created for airlines, banks, record companies, sound studios, travel headquarters, all with specialist requirements. Our designers are multilingual and we offer a full turnkey service including furniture design and supply.
Clients include, American Express, Autocue, Australian Airways, BET, Cougar Marine, De Fontes Television (Bermuda), Jet Set International Tours, Malaysian Airlines System, Mazda Hotels (India), Olympic Airways, Polyvideo, San Paolo Bank, SM Leisure, WEA Records (Warner Bros), Voice Shop.

Contact Mr Paul Sutton
Size 6-10
Affiliations CSD, RIBA

TACP Design

South Harrington Building, Brunswick Business Park, Sefton Street, Liverpool, Merseyside L3 4BQ
Telephone 051-708 7014 Fax 051-709 1503

TACP Design is a long-established, multidisciplinary practice with considerable experience and accumulated expertise in all its design fields. Within the broad categories of interior design and product design, particular specialities offered by TACP Design include: theatres, cinemas, auditoria, audiovisual installations, computer-controlled lighting systems, hotels, restaurants, licensed premises and retail shops, domestic products. Full architectural and town planning services are also provided, including specialities in space planning, conservation and restoration.

Contact Mr Joseph Parker
Size 11-20
Affiliations CSD, RIBA, ABTT

Tibbatts & Co Design Group Ltd

1 St Paul's Square, Birmingham, West Midlands B3 1QU
Telephone 021-233 2871 Fax 021-236 8705

Since its inception in 1979 Tibbatts & Co has developed a comprehensive and specialist knowledge of the leisure and hospitality market. Through a long-standing association with the leading operators in the leisure industry, Tibbatts has extensive experience of both their requirements and those of the consumer. The Group's disciplines include interior design, architecture, project management and contracting expertise. Projects range from new build to stand-alone units, to multiactivity leisure centres, Grade 1 listed buildings and two, three and four star hotels.
Clients include Bass Leisure, First Leisure, Granada, Themes International, Grand Metropolitan, Rank, Whitbread, Trust House Forte and Hilton.

Contact Mrs Pat Jones
Size 51-100
Affiliations CSD, DBA, RIBA

Tilney Lumsden Shane Ltd

5 Heathmans Road, London SW6 4TJ
Telephone 071-731 6946 Fax 071-736 3356

Established in 1980, Tilney Lumsden Shane have a reputation for high quality architectural, interior and graphic design solutions for the retail, financial, business and transportation sectors. Our combination of caring commitment, business understanding and innovative problem-solving sets us apart from our competitors and contributes to our clients' operational success. Each project, whatever the scale, is managed by one of the three design directors, to ensure that high standards of design and project mangement are maintained.

Contact Mrs Julie Thorne
Size 21-50
Affiliations CSD, RIBA, DBA

The Tooley & Foster Partership

Warwick House, Palmerston Road, Buckhurst Hill, Essex IG9 5LQ
Telephone 081-504 9711 Fax 081-506 1779

The Tooley & Foster Partnership is a multidisciplinary practice of architects, structural engineers and interior designers, with associated support disciplines. Established 1892, it provides a high quality, comprehensive design service to a wide range of private, commercial, institutional, public sector and educational clients. These include British Telecom, Capital & Counties, Clerical Medical Investment Group, Crown Estate Commissioners, Grosvenor Estates, Midland Bank, M&G Group, Monarch Airlines, P&O Properties and Royal Mail.
Practice brochure available.

Contact Mr Michael Foster
Size 21-50
Affiliations AA, RIBA, CSD, CIArb, IStructE, BIM

The Tooley & Foster Partnership
architects, engineers, designers

Townend Ryder Designers Ltd

13 Rosemont Road, London NW3 6NG
Telephone 071-794 3030 Fax 071-431 0386

T&R is a professional design company providing specialized working environments from initial concept to project completion. Our design expertise includes: information technology and operational interiors, space planning office environments, security design, applied ergonomics, special product design. We perceive clients' problems from real time, cost and quality viewpoints. Our clients realize that by using our services to assist in solving problems, they can save time and money in ways which provide them with value-added solutions. Full in-house Auto-Cad (AEC).
Also at: 146 London Road, Northwich, Cheshire. Telephone: (0606) 330136.

Contact Mr John Ryder
Size 6-10
Affiliations CSD, RIBA

20/20 Design and Strategy Consultants

The Forum, 74-80 Camden Street, London NW1 0EG
Telephone 071-383 7071 Fax 071-383 7140

20/20 is a commercial consultancy offering both design and strategic advice to retailers, manufacturers and service companies. The founders of 20/20 have worked for major companies in most areas of business for clients such as Next, National Westminster Bank and Grand Metropolitan. This breadth of experience allows us to assess the real potential and viability of a commercial proposition. We are currently undertaking projects for, amongst others, Sears, Virgin Retail, Dolland & Aitchison, Hatchards and Black & Decker in the UK, SOK Group in Finland and Unilever in Belgium.

Contact Ms Joanne Peace
Size 11-20
Affiliations DBA, Mktg Soc

Walker Wright Partnership

Studio 2, Kingsley House, Avonmore Place, London W14 8RY
Telephone 071-603 6674 Fax 071-371 1017

The Partnership was founded in 1966 so has a wide and varied experience of interior and furniture design. Executed work ranges from individual pieces of furniture to private houses, hotels, restaurants, offices and exhibitions. We have worked both directly for clients or as part of a consultative team. Latest projects include hotel renovation for Trusthouse Forte, studios and offices for London Jazz Radio, executive offices for advertising agents Young and Rubicam and the Technical Centre for L'Oréal Salon Coiffure.

Contact Mr John Wright
Size 1-5
Affiliations RCA, RIBA

Whitecroft Designs Ltd

Albany House, Hurst Street, Birmingham, West Midlands B5 4BD
Telephone 021-643 5364 Fax 021-643 3895

Whitecroft Designs specializes in exhibition stand design and management. We design stands, build them and organize practically every aspect of international exhibition participation at home and overseas. We handle varying demands from multi-company group stands to simple displays for shell scheme interiors, proprietary modular systems and hotel-based functions. We are also engaged in product launches, conference sets, showrooms, reception displays, travelling exhibitions and museum and interpretative work, in fact almost every type of activity where the design of three-dimensional displays is required. A complete professional exhibition service.

Contact Mr Alan Cutler
Size 1-5
Affiliations CSD, CIM, DIA, DBA

Witchell Associates

115 Woodville Road, Cardiff, South Glamorgan, Wales CF2 4DY
Telephone (0222) 340962 Fax (0222) 394148

Witchell Associates specializes in furniture, interior and exhibition design, space-planning and complete design and management facilities. Creative energy is channelled into a highly disciplined appraisal of the task, professional design skills and implementation of the solution to provide a total service. The aim is performance, service and design excellence. Clients range from local enterprises to multinationals in Cardiff, Bristol and London: London Commodity Exchange, LEB, National Association of Goldsmiths, Ernst & Young, Bank of Wales, Touche Ross, Mitel Telecom, Principality Building Society, Target Computers, Bank of Scotland, National Rivers Authority, The Design Council, Cad W.

Contact Mr Roger Witchell
Size 1-5

XMPR plc

151 Freston Road, London W10 6TH
Telephone 071-229 1010 Fax 071-792 9462

At XMPR we develop strategy-led design solutions. We view design as a means of achieiving specific commercial objectives. Whilst our approach is business focused, creativity is the essence of XMPR – this is reflected in our work, our people and our approach to projects.
Committed to developing successful long-term relationships, an experienced Project Principal remains the client's key contact throughout – much of his time is provided free of charge.
Our experience across Europe is testimony to our commitment to creativity and the development of outstanding and effective design solutions.

Contact Mr John Greensword
Size 21-50

YRM Interiors

24 Britton Street, London EC1M 5NQ
Telephone 071-253 4311 Fax 071-250 1688

YRM Interiors is concerned with all aspects of the interior environment, from overall spatial concept through refurbishment and fitting-out contract management, to selection of furniture, furnishings, graphics and artwork. Its leading position in the design industry is maintained through a commitment to project management with strong emphasis on CAD and space planning. As part of YRM Partnership, with 500 professional staff, YRM Interiors can draw on the resources of the architectural and engineering divisions to provide a genuine multidisciplinary service to clients. UK and overseas experience includes airports, offices, hotels, hospitals, universities, civic and residential buildings as well as the corporate interiors for the City and the professions for which YRM Interiors is best known.

Contact Mr Garry Griffiths
Size 21-50
Affiliations CSD

INTERIORS & RETAIL

DIRECTORY OF

EXHIBITION DESIGN

All Communications Ltd

PO Box 19, Henley on Thames, Oxfordshire RG9 4GY
Telephone (0734) 402669 Fax (0734) 404585

Newly formed association of Lea Design in Henley on Thames and Lines Design, Forge House, The Green, Bearstead, Kent. Tel: 0622 30068. A multidisciplined practice specializing in exhibitions, interiors and graphics. Main clients: Air Canada, Bell Helicopter, Boeing Helicopter, Cessna Aircraft Geco, IBM, IPE, Lliffe, Mobil Oil, Schlumberger, TWA.

Contact Mr Ian Lea
Size 6-10
Affiliations CSD

The Association of Ideas (AOI Ltd)

9 Paddington Street, London W1M 3LA
Telephone 071-486 9800 Fax 071-935 6945

The Association of Ideas was formed through a close co-operation between architects and graphic designers keen to develop a new quality in exhibition design.
Our clients include: British Telecom, Cumulus Systems, Friends of the Earth, Vidal Sassoon and VSO.

Contact Mr Jonathan Lovett
Size 1-5
Affiliations RIBA

Bowes Darby Design Associates

DESIGN COUNCIL REGISTERED

Magdalen House, 136 Tooley Street, London SE1 2TU
Telephone 071-378 0637 Fax 071-378 0692

Design is a powerful business tool. Used effectively it can achieve significant benefits. We aim to provide the very best creative solution relevant to specific business objectives. We are specialists in the field of exhibition design.
Clients include: British Rail, Merseytravel, British Toy & Hobby Association, Imperial War Museum, Hawker Siddeley, Wiggins Teape, Royal Bank of Scotland, Trafford Park Development Corporation.
A top 30 UK consultancy with offices in London and Manchester. For further information on the proven benefits of effective creative design, contact our marketing department.

Contact Mr P Kelly
Size 21-50

Bowyer Langlands Batchelor — Chartered Architects & Designers

Russell Chambers, The Piazza, Covent Garden, London WC2E 8RH
Telephone 071-836 1452 Fax 071-497 9581

The practice began with the 1951 Exhibition and has since specialized in exhibitions, interior design and restoration. Recent projects include: the new Japanese Gallery and Prints and Drawings Collection at the British Museum, the Barry Rooms at the National Gallery, Cabinet War Rooms Museum, Gloucester Cathedral Treasury, National Portrait Gallery and the East Hall, Science Museum. Current projects include more work at the Science Museum.

Contact Ms Ursula Bowyer
Size 11-20
Affiliations RIBA, CSD, RSA

Cairnes Design Associates Ltd

1 Smiths Yard, Summerley Street, London SW18 4HR
Telephone 081-879 1233 Fax 081-947 1072

We bring both graphic and structural skills to the special needs of exhibition design and our 12 years' experience of working for clients, both in the UK and overseas, ranges from simple modular stands to complex double-deck structures.
In addition to exhibitions we design and produce road shows, conference sets, product launches and mobile exhibition units. We like to maintain a close working relationship with our clients, acquire a thorough knowledge of their products or services, and retain their loyalty by providing a consistently friendly, personal and efficient service.

Contact Mr Denis Cairnes
Size 11-20
Affiliations CSD, DBA

Checkland Kindleysides Design

Fowke Street, Rothley, Leicester, Leicestershire LE7 7PJ
Telephone (0533) 374282 Fax (0533) 374649

Established in 1979, Checkland Kindleysides has a reputation for highly creative work, matched with a mature ability for project management. Our approach puts total emphasis on the understanding of our clients' business aims and ambitions, enabling us to produce authoritative creative solutions that encompass many design disciplines including retail and interiors, graphics, corporate literature, packaging, furniture and product.
Clients include: Levi Strauss (UK), Olympus Sport, Toyota (GB), Dupont, Alfred Dunhill, Ballantyne Cashmere, Alexon and Lexus.

Contact Ms Marie Cooke
Size 21-50

Communication by Design

6 The Courthouse, 38 Kingsland Road, London E2 8DD
Telephone 071-729 4000 Fax 071-739 5728

Communication by Design was established in 1978. As a multidiscipline consultancy the company specializes in exhibitions, museums, roadshows, multimedia events, interiors and conferences. Our design teams have worldwide experience working on projects throughout Europe, the Far East and America on large and small projects alike. Our clients include individual entrepreneurs and multinational organizations as well as government departments, working on a diverse range of projects for: Lloyd's Register, British Aerospace, Mobil Shipping, British Gas, BBC, BP Chemicals, Metropolitan Police and Hampton Court Palace amongst others.

Contact Mr David Angus
Size 11-20
Affiliations CSD, DBA

Design Contracts

Hayhill Industrial Estate, Sileby Road, Barrow Upon Soar, Leicestershire LE12 8LD
Telephone (0509) 814720 Fax (0509) 816098

Design Contracts, a division of John Kirk Design, a leading design consultancy based in the Midlands, specializes in the manufacture and production of exhibitions and point-of-sale.
Our talents and expertise guarantee a high degree of commitment to detail from concept proposals through manufacture and final installation, all of which is led by a project management team.
Design Contracts' key to success lies in having extensive in-house production facilities, which enables us to offer these services to other design consultancies on a cost-effective contract base.
Principal clients: Stiebel, Dixons, Quicksilver.

Contact Mr Gerard Quinn
Size 11-20
Affiliations BECA, GDIM, DBA

EXHIBITION DESIGN

Event Communications Ltd

The Loft, Lloyds Wharf, Mill Street, London SE1 2BQ
Telephone 071-232 1365 Fax 071-252 0287

Event is a creative group specializing in the design of public exhibitions and corporate events. Our aim is to communicate information in a dramatic and enjoyable fashion.
For museums, heritage sites and leisure attractions we have an excellent record of achievement. Over the past six months we have completed The Living Thread, Royal Botanic Gardens, Kew, the Gurkha Museum, Winchester and Cadbury World, Bournville and are currently finalizing work for the Historic Royal Palaces Agency, The Royal Scots and Whitbreads. For corporate events, clients include Glaxo and Arthur Andersen.

Contact Ms Celestine Phelan
Size 21-50
Affiliations CSD

The Four Hundred Ltd

6a New Concordia Wharf, St Saviours Dock, Mill Street, London SE1 2BA
Telephone 071-237 0587 Fax 071-231 6064

The Four Hundred is a well established design practice which until this year was known as H & P Design. Our new name has not changed our philosophy; we believe a company makes a statement about itself with everything it produces. Our combination of talents in both 2 and 3D enables us to develop an image and effectively apply it to all aspects of a project from corporate identity and printed matter through to exhibitions and interiors.

Contact Ms Win Rogers
Size 6-10
Affiliations CSD

Furneaux Stewart

DESIGN
COUNCIL
REGISTERED

24 Beaumont Mews, London W1N 3LN
Telephone 071-935 5724 Fax 071-486 0304

Our special quality as a company is the fertile combination of pure graphics and three-dimensional design to create realistic but lateral-view interpretations of client needs. Our field of activity includes exhibitions and special events, product launches and conferences, corporate communications, museum, leisure and heritage sites and commercial interiors. The wide range of our client list reflects the diversity of our projects: BET, British Marine Industries Federation, British Telecom, City of Westminster, English Heritage, Hewlett-Packard, ICL, Natural History Museum, Nuclear Electric, Porsche Cars, STC, Sultanate of Oman.

Contact Mr John Furneaux
Size 6-10
Affiliations CSD, IOD, DBA

James Gardner (3D Concepts) Ltd

Studio, 144 Haverstock Hill, London NW3 2AY
Telephone 071-586 1151 Fax 071-722 1945

Our group is renowned internationally for producing successful and imaginative museum and exhibition projects – on time and within budget. Transforming our clients' requirements into visually exciting and informative displays is our forte, and we have many years' experience in handling complete projects, from initial concept to final installation. Our design treatments, whilst authoritative, are refreshing and popular. Getting the balance right is the criterion we use in our museum and exhibition designs. Brochure and company profile available on request.

Contact Mrs Eve Harrison
Size 11-20
Affiliations RDI, RCA, CSD

Graphik Fifteen Associates

Unit 36, Limehouse Cut, Morris Road, London E14 6NT
Telephone 071-987 0382 Fax 071-537 4001

Established over 20 years, the organization has enjoyed a reputation for producing creative yet appropriate design solutions, in graphics, conferences and exhibitions. Designers working with modular systems as well as creating purpose-built structures, and backed by efficient budget control and project management, have established a long-standing client list with projects ranging from a few metres to international corporate presentations: British Petroleum, British Sugar, Ciba Corning Diagnostics, Heuga UK, Institute of Housing, John Brown Engineers & Constructors, Seismograph Service, Taylor Woodrow Group.

Contact Mr Roger Hartwell
Size 1-5
Affiliations CSD

Haley Sharpe Associates

DESIGN COUNCIL REGISTERED

11-15 Guildhall Lane, Leicester, Leicestershire LE1 5FQ
Telephone (0533) 518555 Fax (0533) 519119

Haley Sharpe Associates is an interior, graphics and interpretive design consultancy specializing in three main areas: exhibitions, retail and museums. Exhibition expertise is in the design and project management of projects varying in size from 25 sq metres to 25,000 sq metres for clients in the UK as well as Europe where we have designed exhibitions in Frankfurt and Berlin in 1990.
Our exhibition clients include Mars Inc UK, BP, Mattel, Sony, Pedigree Petfoods and Heuga.

Contact Mr Graham Brock
Size 21-50

Jarvis White Design

DESIGN COUNCIL REGISTERED

The Old Mill, Mill Lane, Avening, Near Tetbury, Gloucestershire GL8 8PD
Telephone 045-383 5516 Fax 045-383 5561

Jarvis White were judged to be producing some of the most successful exhibitions in 1989 through the Design Effectiveness scheme. This exemplifies the Jarvis White approach: to find the right solution – on brief, on schedule and on budget.
Our experience in corporate and brand identity design will enable us to retain your corporate image sensitively, but yet provide that vital spark of differentiation.
We have produced stands from 20 to 900 sq metres, purpose-built or reusable modular systems design. Product or launch presentations and markets as diverse as garden products and international finance.

Contact Mr Terry White
Size 11-20

Iain S Martin

DESIGN COUNCIL REGISTERED

Tudor House, Maidenhatch, Pangbourne, Reading, Berkshire RG8 8HP
Telephone (0734) 744482

Iain S Martin provides an exhibition design service to manage the project right through all its stages, from concept to debriefing after the show. Personal individual attention by Iain Martin to each client's specific needs and requirements. Specializing in exhibition design of all types and sizes, throughout the UK and overseas. Established for over 20 years and still servicing original clients: a proven track record for reliability. Client list includes Alumasc, Cross Paperware, Remploy, Speedo (Europe), Group Sales and VBG Produkter.

Contact Mr Iain Martin
Size 1-5
Affiliations CSD

Media Projects International Ltd

7 Cameron House, 12 Castlehaven Road, London NW1 8QW
Telephone 071-485 5657 Fax 071-482 4995

Media Projects specializes in the design and production of interactive media and sophisticated multimedia presentations. Media Projects' work is known for high-quality visual design. The Directors have a depth of background experience in an unusual range of production skills – A/V, high-quality films, video, broadcast television and print. Media Projects successfully combines the use of leading edge technology with skilled and imaginative design and production. Clients include governments, museums, leisure developments and large and small corporations around the world, with numerous awards for all types of design and production.

Contact Ms Rosalie Vicars-Harris
Size 6-10
Affiliations IVCA, AVA, BIM, ICOM

Smith Browne Partnership

No 1 Lammas Gate, 84a Meadrow, Godalming, Surrey GU7 3HT
Telephone (0483) 861116 Fax (0483) 860112

We are a small established group with a successful track record that specializes in the design of exhibition, heritage and interior projects for leading UK and international companies. Our proven skills enable us to manage small through to large projects from the initial idea to completion, providing our clients with creative solutions backed up with expertise and attention to detail in presentation and drawings.

Contact Mr Roger Smith
Size 1-5
Affiliations CSD

Tayburn Design Ltd

DESIGN
COUNCIL
REGISTERED

15 Kittle Yards, Causewayside, Edinburgh, Scotland EH9 1PG
Telephone 031-662 0662

Graphic, exhibition and interior design group rated in the UK top 20.
Projects include corporate identity, packaging, corporate literature and annual reports, as well as bank, retail and leisure interiors, exhibition stands and museums. Staff number 60. Turnover around £5 million. Clients include: Bank of Scotland, Gleneagles, United Distillers, Standard Life, Coopers & Lybrand Deloitte, Wm Low, Ericsson, Scottish Enterprise.

Contact Mr Erick Davidson
Size 51-100
Affiliations CSD, INSTM

Timewise Design Ltd

Home Park House, Hampton Court Road, Hampton Wick, Kingston-upon-Thames, Surrey KT1 4AE
Telephone 081-943 4933 Fax 081-943 0066

Timewise Design specializes in exhibition and interior design and has won a number of international awards during its 18-year history. Operating from a seventeenth-century listed building is a versatile team of designers, headed by founders Peter Askew and John Bird. Other areas of expertise include corporate identity, graphic and product design.
Personal service, creativity and efficiency have won the company blue-chip clients including Armitage Shanks, Bass Leisure, Cummins Engine Co, Department of Energy, The Electricity Association, Hitachi, Redland, Singer, Solaglas, Thorn-EMI and Westland.

Contact Mr John Bird
Size 11-20
Affiliations CSD

DIRECTORY OF

DES
ign
ERS
1991

Childrenswear
Fashion Accessories
Fashion Forecasting
Fashion Illustration
Fashion Textiles
Floorcovering/Carpets
Footwear
Furnishing Textiles
Jewellery
Knitted Textiles
Knitwear
Leisure/Sportswear
Lingerie
Menswear
Millinery
Pattern Cutting
Printed Textiles
Surface Pattern
Uniforms
Womenswear
Woven Textiles

Linda Bee

Ivy Cottage, 6 Belvoir Road, East Dulwich, London SE22 0QY
Telephone 081-693 8012

Freelance design service to knitwear manufacturers with 17 years' experience in mens, ladies and childrenswear, cut and sewn and fully fashioned. Overseas experience in Eire, Hong Kong, Portugal, Holland and Italy. Service includes market research, design portfolio, accurate jacquard and intarsia graphs, specifications, pattern cutting, supervision of sample production and trouble-shooting. Wide experience of all yarns from acrylics through to silk and cashmere, and latest machines and production methods. Market experience from mail order and chain store to luxury designer ranges for export.

Contact Ms Linda Bee
Size 1-5

Janet Bevan Designs

Suite 10, 57 Victoria Street, Wolverhampton, West Midlands WV1 3NX
Telephone (0902) 20170 Fax (0902) 714837

Janet Bevan Design Studio has been established over 15 years and specializes in dobby and jacquard woven designs. The dedication to quality and design is evident from the proven track record in international markets. Using advanced CAD systems, the experienced design team prepares concepts and develops samples and colourways on 24-shaft handlooms producing innovative designs for automotive fabrics, wallcoverings, curtains, upholstery, vertical blinds and yarns.
Recognized as a leading authority on colour and design trends, the studio is a member of the Color Marketing Group in the USA and the UK Colour Group.

Contact Ms Janet Bevan
Size 1-5
Affiliations CSD

Tony Cunliffe Shudesign

45 The Chase, Shann Park, Keighley, Yorkshire BD20 6HU
Telephone (0535) 665927 Fax (0535) 690289

A footwear design consultancy with broad industrial experience in most areas of manufacture including sports, cemented and moulded constructions, slippers and leisure areas, in men's, ladies' and children's footwear.
Our services extend from concept and development sketches to prototype models, range-building, mould design and specification drawings. Also selected services for ancillary suppliers, ie components and materials etc.

Contact Mr Tony Cunliffe
Size 1-5

Jane Eastwood

The Old Power House, Kew Gardens Station, Kew, Surrey TW9 3PS
Telephone 081-940 2642 Fax 081-940 3698

Jane Eastwood's weave studio offers a complete design/colour service from yarn development, woven fabric with colourways, mill liaison through to final product.
Market areas: residential and contract interior woven fabrics for UK, European and US markets.
Areas of expertise: woven fabrics (jacquard and dobby with CAD facilities) – upholstery, drapes, wallcovering, yarn design, flooring, market research, storyboards and colour direction.
Listed as a consultant under the Department of Trade and Industry Design Initiative. Leading member of the Colour Group.

Contact Ms Jane Eastwood
Size 1-5
Affiliations RCA

Escort Menswear Services

Chesney Park Industrial Estate, Hillidge Road, Hunslet, Leeds, West Yorkshire LS10 1DG
Telephone (0532) 777176 Fax (0532) 718603 Telex 557834

Specialist in tailored menswear. We offer a complete service; once briefed we can undertake the styling, technical design, grade rules, product development, fabric and trimming sourcing, production techniques, quality control and customer liaison.
Quality hand or engineered garments, lightweight cloths a speciality. We have worked closely with a leading French/International label, manufacturers who supply leading department stores and independent retailers. Fully experienced regarding America, Japan and France.

Contact Mr Dennis Weathers
Size 1-5

Furphy Simpson

234 Rye Lane, Peckham, London SE15 4NL
Telephone 071-635 8344 Fax 071-252 8037

Furphy Simpson is a small specialized partnership which has been established since 1976. We produce textile print designs, mainly for the fashion market. We work with ladies and menswear, childrenswear, and increasingly with sportswear and beachwear. Our clients range from couture to the larger department stores. In our showroom we always keep at least two collections of print design, showing Spring/Summer and Autumn/Winter seasons, but we also work on a consultancy basis, usually developing design stories from an initial design in our collection.

Contact Ms Val Furphy
Size 1-5

Grant Walker Ltd

4-5 Broadbent Close, Highgate, London N6 5JP
Telephone 081-341 9119 Fax 081-348 0078

A team of highly qualified and innovative designers (all first-class honours graduates), who understand the jewellery trade and allied areas in great depth from production to marketing. Time is taken to learn clients' manufacturing strengths, weaknesses, price breaks etc. We are entirely flexible – working on gradual range-building, entire collections, fresh images or branding. Practical expertise runs from costume jewellery to 18 carat and diamond work, watches to objets d'art and silverware to cutlery.
Clients range from smaller workshops to public companies. Advisers to the UN and EEC on jewellery design, production and marketing.

Contact Mr Norman Grant
Size 1-5

Haydon Williams International Ltd

121 Mortlake High Street, Mortlake, London SW14 8SN
Telephone 081-392 1444/5/6/7 Fax 081-876 9661 Telex 936268 COLOUR G

Consultants in design, colour and style: embracing automotive industry, textiles, carpets, plastics, consumer products, white goods. Specialists in product development opposite the volume market. Involvement also in sporting goods market and luggage.
International involvements in Japan/Austalia/New Zealand/USA/Europe/UK. Expertise in market development and presentation, and colour for the consumer and contract markets.

Contact Mr Haydon Williams
Size 6-10
Affiliations DBA

Jill Lawrence Design

236a Cricklewood Lane, London NW2 2PU
Telephone 081-452 5190 Fax 081-208 4558

Jill Lawrence Design is a long-established design studio specializing in personalized consultancy for the women's and children's and sports industries. Particular areas of expertise include: developing fashion colour ranges; fabric design development presentation; garment design; marketing concepts and sales aids design. Special emphasis on the design, development and marketing of denim fabric and jeanswear.
Bespoke projects include hosiery, swimwear, body fashion, tennis wear, skiwear.
Jill Lawrence design has many years of experience working with clients such as: DuPont, Courtaulds, Burlington Industries, Atlantic Mills, Klopman, Littlewoods, Marks & Spencer, Coats Viyella, Guilford Mills and Reebok.

Contact Ms Jill Lawrence
Size 1-5
Affiliations RSA

Colin Leighton Associates

19 Allerton Grange Vale, Leeds, West Yorkshire LS17 6LS
Telephone (0532) 685942

Colin Leighton Associates offer a complete design package for the clothing industry. This package includes the creation of an original engineered pattern, computerized grading, providing size charts, providing lay plans, and ensuring that the resulting garments will go smoothly through the factory.
Colin Leighton Associates is a division of Bracken Enterprises Ltd.

Contact Mr Colin Leighton
Size 1-5

Yvonne Le Rolland

The Studio, Porch House Farm, Pateley Bridge, Harrogate, North Yorkshire HG3 5PJ
Telephone (0423) 712516

After working in the clothing industry for several years at a senior level, dealing with the major high street chains, Yvonne Le Rolland set up a specialist design service from her well-equipped studio/workroom. Her client list varies from companies at the start-up point·to large international groups. Assignments range from style, trend and colour guidance to complete design collections. The practical realization of design work is subject to each individual client's specific requirements: initial concept sketches may be taken through to full working drawings and/or artwork, or presented as prototype sample garments.

Contact Ms Yvonne Le Rolland
Size 1-5
Affiliations CFI

Nightingale Marbled Designs

Units 3 & 4, Abbey Farm Enterprises, North Creake, Fakenham, Norfolk NR21 9LF
Telephone (0328) 730155

Hand-marbled designs on silk, leather and paper, using the finest quality natural materials.
Marianne Nightingale is in the forefront of the revival of this ephemeral art and by innovative use has opened up infinite design possibilities. It is the ideal medium for creative interpretation of clients' ideas in product and packaging design for marketing, interiors (wall coverings, curtains, upholstery), gift and fashion accessories, and incentive and corporate gifts. Each marbled piece is unique; the techniques dictate that each design can never repeated exactly, creating an exclusive product.

Contact Ms Marianne Nightingale
Size 1-5

Nottingham Consultants Ltd

Burton Street, Nottingham, Nottinghamshire NG1 4BU
Telephone (0602) 418418 ext 2565 Fax (0602) 486403 Telex 377534 Polnot G

Design consultancy covering the general areas of men's, women's and children's fashion and clothing, knitwear and knitted fabric design. Specialist knowledge of computer aided design in all of the areas stated. The expertise is available to ensure that designs can be produced from prototype first sample stage to final approval of production samples with appropriate production patterns. In knitwear, control discs and tapes can be produced for a wide range of machinery. Design and development work undertaken in the specialist areas of outdoor and survival clothing, workwear and protective clothing, career apparel and corporate identity clothing.
Services include: Design Management, CAD.

Contact Prof Edward Newton
Size 11-20
Affiliations CSD, CFI, TI

Helen M Rees

73 Fotheringay Road, Pollokshields, Glasgow, Scotland G41 4LQ
Telephone 041-423 2426 Fax 041-424 0646

Knitwear designer. Broad industrial-based experience supports the design of ranges which vary from cut-and-sew mass production to fully fashioned cashmere and intarsia garments.
Knowledge of home and international manufacturing for diverse markets in UK, Europe, USA and Japan. Total design service offered. Ideas followed through from customer liaison, sketches and swatches to prototype garments.

Contact Ms Helen Rees
Size 1-5

Jane Spencer Associates

5 New Broadway, Ealing, London W5 5AW
Telephone 081-840 7737 Fax 081-567 4655

JSA is a London-based household textile design studio. An extensive portfolio of both traditional and contemporary design for furnishing fabrics, bed linen, mattress ticking, wallcovering, tea towels, kitchen co-ordinates, beach towels, and related products is always available.
JSA design management provides a full professional consultancy service including market and colour forecasting, individual design commissions and the design and styling of complete collections. The client list covers a wide market sector in the UK and overseas, and includes leading manufacturers, specialist companies, major multiples and chain store groups.

Contact Mr Maurice Spencer
Size 6-10
Affiliations CSD, IMechE

Antonia Spowers Designs

Unit 3, Ransome's Dock, 35/37 Parkgate Road, London SW11 4NP
Telephone 071-622 3630 Fax 071-228 2118

Antonia Spowers Designs specializes in surface design for furnishings and gift products. Services include concept origination and product development.
Clients include Museums and Galleries Marketing, the National Trust for Scotland, the Ashmolean Museum and the British Library. Services include design management.

Contact Ms Antonia Spowers
Size 1-5

Studio M

7 Tyers Gate, London SE1 3HX
Telephone 071-403 8090 Fax 071-403 5424

The Studio has expanded and changed its original name from Stephen Morris. The studio now has three divisions: Menswear Product, Womenswear Product and Marketing Services (see Graphics section). We specialize in the middle-to-upper market sector and as always we pride ourselves on quality of design rather than quantity.
Clients: UK – Aquascutum, Henri Lloyd, International Wool Secretariat, Laurence J Smith, L'Uomo Menswear, Next Directory, Next Retail; Brazil – Jack SA; Japan – Kakiuchi, Ogorishoji.

Contact Miss Kenya Chapman
Size 6-10

Surface Design Consultants

186c London Road, Leicester, Leicestershire LE2 1ND
Telephone (0533) 543066 Fax (0533) 550624

Surface Design Consultants has become well established in the field of printed surface design. Our work is predominantly involved with producing design commissions for the fashion industry, although our expertise has been realized in other related areas such as greetings cards and stationery, giftwrap, packaging and ceramics. The consultancy prides itself on providing a versatile design capability, enabling us to offer a comprehensive service from initial generation of ideas to final tailoring and refinement to meet our clients' requirements.
Clients include: Boots, Children's World, BHS, Next, Marks & Spencer, Woolworths, Burtons, Umbro International and Donnay UK.

Contact Ms Angela Setterfield
Size 1-5

Robert Weldon Studios

2 Broadway, Lace Market, Nottingham, Nottinghamshire NG1 1PS
Telephone (0602) 584331 Fax (0602) 504074

Our design consultancy specializes in the development of men's knitwear and hosiery ranges. The studio offers design, prediction and product development considerate of clients' brief and market position, effectively utilizing a broad basis of knitting machinery and providing total technical back-up.
Clients: Bonner of Ireland, Next Menswear, Robert Weldon (own label), Whyte & Smith.

Contact Mr Robert Weldon
Size 1-5

ROBERT WELDON

West Midlands Clothing Resource Centre

First Floor, Smethwick Enterprise Centre, Rolfe Street, Smethwick, West Midlands B66 2AR
Telephone 021-558 0474 Fax 021-555 5748

Provides computer-based (microdynamics) design, pattern cutting, grading and lay planning including creation of (and working from sketches, illustrations, first patterns and size charts) first patterns. Fabric and trimming sourcing, advice on business start up to full design and marketing projects. Technical advice on production methods and machinery, management and marketing. Training courses for designers, owners, managers and supervisors in all business activities. Quality standard and control advice and training.

Contact Mr Christopher Hardwicke-Garner
Size 6-10
Affiliations SMM, CDE, CIM, CFI

Linda Wood Designs Ltd

Rutland House, 33 Rutland Street, Leicester, Leicestershire LE1 1RE
Telephone (0533) 536226 Fax (0533) 539827

Linda Wood Designs is a surface pattern design consultancy. Our work in fabrics, bed linen, wallpapers, kitchen products, electrical goods and stationery is renowned, while our design policy on range co-ordination has benefited a growing list of national and international clients. We know how important it is to offer a comprehensive service, and our close links with Renfrew Associates enable us to carry a project right through from concept to colour specification, models and prototypes, packaging and point-of-sale. Full screen printing facilities are available in-house.
Clients: Boots, BHS, Swan, Sundour, Coloroll, J P Stevens, Croydex, W H Smith.

Contact Ms Linda Wood
Size 6-10
Affiliations CSD, RSA

DIRECTORY OF **DES**_ign_ERS 1991

Landscape Architecture
Leisure
Residential
Street Furniture
Town Planning

Celyn

Archway House, Centre Court, Main Avenue, Treforest Estate, Treforest, Cardiff,
Mid Glamorgan, Wales CF37 5YL
Telephone (0443) 841497 Fax (0443) 841288

Celyn is a multidisciplinary design practice specializing in landscape planning and design. We provide a
range of town planning services and work extensively in the leisure industry. Celyn operates throughout
the UK and Europe and has developed a reputation as the fastest growing golf course design practice in
the UK. We are particularly noted for our graphics and presentation skills and are able to mount
exhibitions for clients. Celyn can produce results quickly.

Contact Mr Iwan Richards
Size 1-5
Affiliations RTPI, LI, IHort, BIM

IMA Design Consultants

346 Old Street, London EC1V 9NQ
Telephone 071-729 4473 Fax 071-729 6214

Established in 1987, four years have produced many exciting and successful projects within diverse
business arenas for clients such as: Association for the Monetary Union of Europe, Avatar, Bovis
Construction Group, Digital, the Enterprise International Development Company, Euro Disneyland,
Kumagai Gumi, Le Manoir aux Quat' Saisons, Letraset International, Marlin Lighting, MEPC, Merlin
International Properties, Midland Bank Group Treasury, Midland Bank Trust Corporation (Jersey), Midland
Montagu, Olympia & York, Open-Plan, Reed Business Publishing Group, Regalian Properties, Shimizu
Corporation, TSB (South Wales), Young & Co.
IMA is presently working with a variety of UK based clients and is involved with projects within Europe
and Japan.

Contact Mr Ian Hatton
Size 11-20
Affiliations DBA, CSD, STD

Adrian Lisney & Partners

1 Colliton Walk, Dorchester, Dorset DT1 1TZ
Telephone (0305) 266501 Fax (0305) 269217

Landscape architects, offering services including landscape design and planning, environmental impact
assessment and landscape management. We have a wide range of experience in commercial, residential
and leisure developments, infrastructure and the power industry. In addition, restoration and ecology are
forming an increasingly important area of our work. The majority of projects involve the practice working
as part of a multidisciplinary design team. Many involve public inquiries or planning appeals. We currently
cover the south of England, the Midlands and Wales, but are looking towards Europe and further afield.

Contact Mrs Ann Lisney
Size 21-50
Affiliations FLI, RIBA

McGown Snowden Designers

Broad Court, 43 Drury Lane, London WC2B 5RT
Telephone 071-240 0337 Fax 071-240 1157

McGown Snowden Designers was established in 1976, with the view to develop and express design
attitude and solutions – tuned to clients' specific problems and design needs.
The practice has developed a range of skills and expertise which encompass environmental/office design,
from analysis of clients' problems through to completion. Exhibition/graphic design work includes a number
of marketing suites incorporating AV facilities. Retail design has been maintained with a number of our
franchise sector clients.
Recent clients include: Cowen, Holmen, International Clearing Services, Legal & General, J P Morgan,
Nomews UK, Pierson Heldring & Pierson, Prontaprint, Prudential, Skipton Building Society, Speyhawk.

Contact Mr Robert McGown
Size 1-5
Affiliations CSD

Patterson, Fenton-Jones Ltd

28-32 Shelton Street, London WC2H 9HP
Telephone 071-836 8890 Fax 071-240 3762

Patterson, Fenton-Jones is a creative design consultancy providing a full range of services in all areas of three-dimensional design. Our specialities lie in the fields of leisure, retail, commercial and exhibition design. The company's client base includes established commercial operators, many of which are household names. Patterson, Fenton-Jones is a member of Group Three, a company of parallel partnerships whose combined services cover the disciplines of architecture, interior and graphic design. Individually or together, the combined expertise provides creative, efficient and intelligent solutions to our clients' needs.

Contact Mr Doug Patterson
Size 11-20
Affiliations RCA, AA

P S D Associates Ltd

The Studio Workshops, 5 Swan Street, Old Isleworth, Middlesex TW7 6RJ
Telephone 081-569 9333 Fax 081-569 9100

PSD Associates is a rapidly developing, broadly based design practice, specializing in three-dimensional design – product, furniture and environmental.
We are working with a growing body of international clients across a wide range of industries. Current projects include office furniture systems, environmental furniture, seating, airport interiors, service environments, signage systems, telecommunications equipment and domestic appliances.
PSD believes in design that provides tangible commercial results that contribute effectively to our clients' overall business performance. At the same time, we consistently produce work that meets the highest design standards.
Creative design for successful, profitable companies.

Contact Mr Paul Stead
Size 11-20
Affiliations CSD, FIRA

Randall Thorp, Landscape Architects

105 Princess Street, Manchester M1 6DD
Telephone 061-228 7721 Fax 061-236 9839

The Randall Thorp Landscape consultancy is a small practice, established in 1986, dedicated to providing the highest quality professional and design services for all clients. We believe that the design of the outdoor environment must satisfy three criteria: function, durability and aesthetic delight, and that within this philosophy we can create a wealth of rich and varied landscapes to suit individual client needs. Current work includes planning and design of landscape settings for business, housing and recreation; environmental assessment and public inquiries for a range of public, commercial and private clients.

Contact Mr Edward Thorp
Size 1-5
Affiliations LI

AA	Architectural Association
ABTT	Association of British Theatre Technicians
ACA	Association of Consulting Architects
ACD	American Centre for Design
ACE	Association of Consulting Engineers
ACS	Association of Consulting Scientists
ACTT	Association of Cinematograph TV Technicians
ADI	Associazione per il Disegno Industriale
Adv Tech Advy Consrtm	Advanced Technology Advisory Consortium
AFAEP	Association of Fashion, Advertising and Editorial Photographers
AFMP	Association of Free Magazine Publishers
AGI	Alliance Graphique Internationale
Agric & Food Res Cncl	Agriculture and Food Research Council
AIA	American Institute of Architects
AICRO	Association of Independent Contract Research Organisations
AICS	Association of Independent Computer Specialists
AID	Association of Industrial Development
AIGA	American Institute of Graphic Arts
AIRTO	Association of Independent Research and Technology Organisations
AMS	Association of Metal Sprayers
AMSRA	American Society of Refrigeration and Air Conditioning
ANC	Association of Noise Consultants
APDF	Association of Professional Design Firms
APM	Association of Project Managers
APSA	Association of Point-of-Sale Advertising
AQMC	Association of Quality Management Consultants
ARCUK	Architects' Registration Council of the United Kingdom
ASAE	American Society of Automotive Engineers
ASBOF	Advertising Standards Board of Finance
ASFD	American Society of Furniture Designers
ASHRAE	American Society of Heating, Refrigeration and Air Conditioning Engineers
ASME	American Society of Mechanical Engineers
ASP	Alliance of Small Firms and Self-Employed People
Assoc Illrs	Association of Illustrators
Assoc Noise Cnslts	Association of Noise Consultants
ATypl	Association Typographique Internationale
AVA	Audiovisual Association
BAIE	British Association of Industrial Editors
BARSC	British Association of Remote Sensing Companies
BCB	British Consultants Bureau
BCS	British Ceramics Society; British Computer Society
BCSC	British Council of Shopping Centres
BDMA	British Direct Marketing Association
BDS	British Display Society
BECA	British Exhibition Contractors Association
BEDA	Bureau of European Designers' Association
BES	Biological Engineering Society
BGA	British Graduates Association; British Gear Association
BHRA	British Hydromechanics Research Association
BIAT	British Institute of Architectural Technicians
BIM	British Institute of Management
Bio Eng Inst	The Bio-Engineering Institute
BIPP	British Institute of Professional Photography
BIVA	British Interactive Video Association
BKST	British Kinematograph, Sound and Television Society
BNCE	British National Committee on Electroheat
BNES	British Nuclear Engineering Society
BPF	British Plastics Federation
BPICS	British Productivity Inventory Control Society
BPsS	British Psychological Society
BQA	British Quality Association
BRA	British Robot Association
Br Cncl Shp Ctrs	British Council of Shopping Centres
Br Nuc Forum	British Nuclear Forum
Br Tex Col Gp	British Textile Colour Group
BSI	British Standards Institution
BSSM	British Society of Strain Measurement
BTAS	British Technology Advisory Services
BTEC	Business and Technician Education Council
CA	Chartered Accountant
CAA	Civil Aviation Authority
CAM	Communication, Advertising and Marketing Education Foundation
CAUS	Color Association of the United States
CBI	Confederation of British Industry
CChem	Chartered Chemist
CERP	Confédération Européenne des Relations Publiques
CF	Sveriges Civilingenjors Forbund (Sweden's Engineers Association)
CFI	Clothing and Footwear Institute
CGI	City and Guilds of London Institute

CIArb	Chartered Institute of Arbitrators
CIBSE	Chartered Institute of Building Services Engineers
CII	Chartered Insurance Institute
CIM	Chartered Institute of Marketing
CIMA	Chartered Institute of Management Accountants
CIOB	Chartered Institute of Building
CMG	Color Marketing Group
CPhys	Chartered Physicist
CREA	Conselho Regional de Engenheiros e Arquitetos (Engineers and Architects Regional Council)
CSD	The Chartered Society of Designers
D&AD	Designers' and Art Directors' Association
DBA	Design Business Association
DIA	Design and Industries' Association
DMA	Design Maunfacturers' Association
DMI	Design Management Institute
DMSSB	Direct Mail Services Standards Board
EEA	Electrical Engineers Association
EEF	Engineering Employers Federation
EIA	Engineering Industries' Association
EMDC	English Menswear Designer Collection
EMUG	European MAP (Manufacturers Automation Protocol) User Group
ES	Ergonomics Society
ESB	European Society of Biometals
ESOMAR	European Society for Opinion Surveys and Market Research
FAS	Faculty of Architects and Surveyors
Fashn Gp	The Fashion Group
FB	Faculty of Building
FCDE	Federation of Clothing Designers and Executives
FCS	Federation of Communication Services
FEDC	Federation of Engineering Design Companies
FIRA	Furniture Industry Research Association
FS	Faculty of Surveyors
GDIM	Group of Designers Interpretations of Museums
GMF	Glass Manufacturers' Federation
GS	Geological Society
HEVAC	Heating, Ventilating and Air Conditioning Manufacturers Association
HFS	Human Factors Society
Human Fac Soc	Human Factors Society
IAA	International Advertising Association
IAM	Institute of Administrative Management
IAgrE	Institution of Agriculture Engineers
IABC	International Association of Business Communicators
IALD	International Association of Lighting Designers
IAS	Institute of Architects and Surveyors
IBCAM	Institute of British Carriage and Automobile Manufacturers
IBF	Institute of British Foundrymen
ICE	Institute of Civil Engineers
IChem	Institute of Chemical Engineers
ICMA	Institute of Cost and Management Accountants
ICOM	International Council of Museums
ICorrE	Institute of Corrosion Engineers
ICorr ST	Institution of Corrosion Science and Technology
ICSID	International Council of Societies of Industrial Design
IDDA	Interior Designers' and Decorators' Association
IDM	Institute of Data Processing Management
IDSA	Industrial Design Society of America
IED	Institution of Engineering Designers
IEE	Institution of Electrical Engineers
IEEE	Institute of Electrical and Electronics Engineers
IERE	Institution of Electronic and Radio Engineers
IES	Illuminating Engineering Society
IEx	Institute of Export
IF	Institute of Fuel
IGE	Institution of Gas Engineers
IHort	Institute of Horticulture
IIM	Institute of Industrial Managers
ILA	Institute of Landscape Architects
IMA	Institute of Mathematics and its Applications
IMarE	Institute of Marine Engineers
IMatM	Institute of Materials Management
IMC	Institute of Management Consultants; Institute of Measurement Control
IMechE	Institution of Mechanical Engineers
IMet	Institute of Metals
IMinE	Institution of Mining Engineers
IMM	Institute of Mining and Metallurgy
IMPI	International Microwave Power Institute
IMRA	Industrial Market Research Association
IMS	Institute of Management Services

Incpen	Industry Council for Packaging and the Environment
InstBE	Institute of British Engineers
InstDesE	Institution of Design Engineers
Inst Dsl Eng Users	Institute of Diesel Engine Users
InstE	Institution of Electronics, Institute of Energy
Inst Eng (Aust)	Institute of Engineers (Australia)
Inst Groc Distrib	Institute of Grocery Distributors
InstInfSci	Institute of Information Scientists
InstLEng	Institute of Lighting Engineers
Inst Occptnl & Health	Institution of Occupational Safety and Health
InstP	Institute of Physics
InstPI	Institute of Patentees and Inventors
InstR	Institute of Refrigeration
InstSEM	Institute of Sales Engineering Management
INucE	Institute of Nuclear Engineers
IOA	Institute of Acoustics
IOD	Institute of Directors
IoEX	Institute of Export
IOJ	Institute of Journalists
ION	Industrieel Ontwerpen Nederland (Industrial Design Holland)
IOP	Institute of Packaging
IoP	Institute of Printing
IOS	Institute of Oceanographic Studies
IoS	Institute of Statisticians
IP	Institute of Petroleum
IPA	Institute of Practitioners in Advertising
IPG	Institute of Professional Goldsmiths
IPlantE	Institution of Plant Engineers
IPR	Institute of Public Relations
IProdE	Institution of Production Engineers
IQA	Institute of Quality Assurance
IQS	Institute of Quantity Surveyors
IRTE	Institute of Road Transport Engineers
ISCE	Institute of Sound and Communication Engineers
ISEM	Institute of Sales Engineering Management
ISMM	Institute of Sales and Marketing Management
ISP	Institute of Sales Promotion
ISTC	Institute of Scientific and Technical Communications
IStructE	Institution of Structural Engineers
ITD	Institute of Training and Development
ITVA	Independent Television Association
IVCA	International Visual Communications Association
IWEM	Institute of Water Environmental Management
JIDA	Japanese Industrial Design Association
KIO	Kring Industriale Ontwerpers (Circle of Industrial Designers)
LA	Library Association
LES	Licensing Executives' Society
LI	Landscape Institute
LIF	Lighting Institute Federation
LMS	London Mathematical Society
MA	Microwave Association
MAPCON	Microprocessor Application Project Consultancy
MCA	Management Consultancies Association
MCT	Manchester College of Technology
MIRA	Motor Industry Research Association
Mktg Soc	Marketing Society
Modmkrs Assoc	Modelmakers' Association
MRS	Market Research Society
MTIRA	Machine Tool Industry Research Association
NAG	National Association of Goldsmiths
NCC	National Computing Centre
NGA	National Graphical Association
NPA	Newspaper Publishers Association
NRS	National Readership Survey
NS	Newspaper Society
NUJ	National Union of Journalists
PE	Professional Engineer (State of California)
PERA	Production Engineering Research Association
PPA	Periodical Publishers Association
PRCA	Public Relations Consultancy Association
PRI	Plastics and Rubber Institute
RA	Royal Academy
RAeS	Royal Aeronautical Society
RAIA	Royal Australian Institute of Architects
RAPRA	Rubber and Plastics Research Association
RBSA	Royal Birmingham Society of Artists
RCA	Royal College of Art
RDI	Royal Designer for Industry
REngDes	Register of Engineering Designers

RIA	Royal Irish Academy
RIAI	Royal Institute of the Architects of Ireland
RIAS	Royal Incorporation of Architects, Scotland
RIBA	Royal Institute of British Architects
RICS	Royal Institution of Chartered Surveyors
RINA	Royal Institution of Naval Architects
RS	Royal Society
RSA	Royal Society for the encouragement of Arts, Manufactures and Commerce
RSC	Royal Society of Chemistry
RSM	Royal Society of Medicine
RSS	Royal Statistical Society
RTPI	Royal Town Planning Institute
RTS	Royal Television Society
SAAT	Society of Architectural and Associated Technicians
SAE	Society of Aeronautical Engineers; Society of Automotive Engineers
SBAC	Society of British Aerospace Companies
SCA	Society of Company and Commercial Accountants
SD-C	Society of Designer-Craftsmen
SDC	Society of Dyers and Colourists
SEE	Society of Environmental Engineers
SEM	Society of Experimental Mechanics
SEng	Sales Engineer
SF	Svensk Form Forening (The Swedish Industrial Designers Association)
SGT	Society of Glass Technology
SI	Society of Indexers
SIF	Svenska Industritjanstemanna Forbundet (Swedish Union of Clerical and Technical Employees in Industry)
SMBA	Scottish Marine Biological Association
SME	Society of Mechanical Engineers (USA)
SMF	Sveriges Mekanistersriksforening (The Swedish Mechanical Engineers Association)
SMMT	Society of Motor Manufacturers and Traders
SNAME	Society of Naval Architects and Marine Engineers (US)
SPE	Society of Petroleum Engineers
SPIE	Society for Photo-Optical Instrumentation Engineers
SRS	Safety and Reliability Society; Systems Reliabilty Services
STD	Society of Typographic Designers
SUT	Society for Underwater Technology
TEng	Technician Engineer
TI	Textile Institute
UEG	Underwater Engineering Group
UILI	L'Union Internationale de Laboratoires Indépendants
UKISC	United Kingdom Industrial Space Committee
VDID	Verband Deutscher Industrie Designers
WeldI	Welding Institute

DIRECTORY OF

DES *ign* ERS 1991

INDEXES

LOCATION

INTERNATIONAL EXPERTISE

CONSULTANCIES A to Z

Avon

Chameleon Group Two GRA 91
Dowry Design Associates GRA 97
Elgood & Dye Services Ltd ENG 55
Fox + Partners GRA 101
The Idea Works GRA 109
Kinneir Dufort Design Ltd PRO 25
Patrick H Lynch PRO 27
The Picador Group GRA 124
Proctor & Stevenson GRA 126
Robelen Products Ltd ENG 66
Springboard Design Group PRO 41
Steel Designs GRA 130
TST Associates PRO 43

Bedfordshire

Cranfield Engineering and Technology Enterprise
　　Ltd (CREATE Ltd) ENG 52
Form Factor PRO 17
MATRIX Systems ENG 60

Berkshire

Fulmer Systems Ltd ENG 56
Gardiner and Torne Ltd INT 147
Industrial Design Consultancy Ltd PRO 23
Jekyll Electronic Technology Ltd ENG 59
Langley Design Associates PRO 26
Iain S Martin EXH 164
Mark Plumtree Design Associates INT 153
Splash of Paint Ltd GRA 130

Buckinghamshire

Bentley Woolston Ltd GRA 88
Birt Electronic Systems Ltd ENG 50
Fir Tree Design Company Ltd GRA 99
Freestone Design Consultants Ltd GRA 101
Malcolm Hastings Design PRO 20
Interdec Design Group Ltd INT 148
David Muston Design Ltd PRO 30
Benjamin Nazroo Associates GRA 120
Watermark Communications Group Ltd
　　GRA 136

Cambridgeshire

Baddeley Associates GRA 87
CAMBIT, The User Interface HUM 75
Cambridge Consultants Ltd PRO 8, ENG 51
Cambridge Engineering Design Ltd ENG 51
Cambridge Industrial Design PRO 8
Cambridge Product Design Ltd PRO 8
Camtech Systems Ltd ENG 51
Carrods Design and Communication GRA 90
Warwick Evans Design PRO 15
Huxley Bertram Engineering ENG 58
Ingenion Design Ltd ENG 58
Omega GRA 121
Pinkney Byatt Associates ENG 64
Precept Design Communications Consultants
　　Ltd GRA 125
Peter Ralph Design Unit PRO 36
Marcus Smith – Industrial Design PRO 40
TDC Ltd ENG 69
Walkbury Ltd ENG 71

Cheshire

AMTRI ENG 49
Broadoak Design Partnership PRO 7
Cheshire Engineering and Design Consultants
　　Ltd ENG 52
Philip Dunbavin Acoustics Ltd ENG 55
Forman Peacock Advertising Ltd GRA 100
Mustard Design Ltd GRA 109
NNC Ltd ENG 63
Northwest Design Associates Ltd INT 152
Raffo Design Associates PRO 35
Systems Technology Consultants PRO 42

Cleveland

The New Product Unit PRO 30

Stable Block Design Consultants Ltd PRO 42

Co Durham

Dow Design Group Ltd PRO 14

Cornwall

Direct Data Design & Development PRO 14
Timothy Guy Design GRA 104

Derbyshire

Brian Asquith Design Partnership PRO 4
Marvell Consultants Ltd ENG 60
Roland S Wagstaff BSc, CEng ENG 71

Devon

ACP Design　PRO 3
Anthony Manners & Associates, Consulting
　　Mechanical Engineers ENG 60

Dorset

Adrian Lisney & Partners ENV 177
Michael Stewart Design Ltd GRA 131
Elaine Williamson Design Consultancy PRO 45

Essex

Alpha Thames Engineering Ltd ENG 49
Bottom Line Design GRA 88
Destech (UK) Ltd ENG 54
MRDC Ltd PRO 29
Pemberton Dear PRO 32
John Reynolds and Associates ENG 66
Silk Pearce GRA 129
The Tooley & Foster Partership INT 155
Wiggins Electronics PRO 45

Gloucestershire

Nick Allen Design GRA 86
Anthony R Brookes PRO 7
L N Burgess ENG 51
Cooper Design Associates PRO 9
Designex ENG 53
DHA Industrial Design PRO 13
Earl & Thompson Marketing GRA 97
David Hayward Product Design PRO 21
Jarvis White Design GRA 110, EXH 164
Helen Morris Graphics GRA 119
Robinson Associates HUM 77
Set Square Design Ltd GRA 128
Ed Turnbull Design Associates GRA 135

Hampshire

Associated & Marine Technology Ltd (A.MTEC)
　　ENG 49
Diametric Design Associates PRO 14
Engineering Innovations ENG 56
Gill Electronic & Research Development
　　ENG 57
The Paul Martin Design Company Ltd GRA 116
MFD Design PRO 28, ENG 61
Reliability Consultants Ltd ENG 65
Rodd Industrial Design POR 37
Siemens Plessey Assessment Services Ltd
　　ENG 67
Wolfson Unit M I T A ENG 72

Hertfordshire

Colin Cheetham Design Partnership PRO 9,
　　GRA 92
Daglish Hurst Ltd GRA 94
Davis Associates HUM 76
Durbin Associates PRO 15
FIRA (Furniture Industry Research Association)
　　PRO 16
Grove Design ENG 57
Level Six Design Consultants Ltd PRO 26
London Associates PRO 27
Clyde Millard Design PRO 28
MJL Ltd GRA 118
Pape Woodward Partnership PRO 31

Pathway Systems ENG 64
Ricardo – AS&A Ltd PRO 37, ENG 66
Rubber Consultants ENG 66, MAT 82
Team Consulting Ltd ENG 69
The Technology Partnership Ltd ENG 70
Alan Tye Design RDI Ltd PRO 44
Paul Usher Design PRO 44

Humberside
J M Dickenson ENG 54
University of Hull ENG 58

Kent
Bartingale Design Associates PRO 5
Matthew Finch Design Consultants Ltd
Sira Ltd ENG 68
Tristram Kent Associates GRA 134

Lancashire
Design Marketing PRO 12
Lawton Hawthorne Advertising Ltd GRA 113
Roberts Design Associates PRO 37
Howard Davidson Ryles Design Associates
    PRO 38
Studio 74 Ltd GRA 131

Leicestershire
Atkinson Design Associates Ltd PRO 4
Brick Studio & Manufacturing Ltd INT 142
Checkland Kindleysides Design GRA 101,INT
    143, EXH 162
Design Contracts EXH 162
Engineering Research Centre ENG 56
Haley Sharpe Associates INT 157, EXH 164
The HCI Service HUM 76
Hodges & Drake Design PRO 22
ICE Ergonomics HUM 77
Jones Garrard Ltd PRO 24, ENG 59
John Kirk Design Ltd GRA 112, INT 149
Loughborough Consultants Ltd ENG 59, HUM
    77, MAT 81
PERA PRO 33, ENG 64, MAT 81
Renfrew Associates PRO 36
Surface Design Consultants FAS 173
Linda Wood Designs Ltd FAS 174

Lincolnshire
Geoffrey Duff Associates Ltd ENG 54

London
ACL & Partners INT 141
AD Creative Consultants Ltd GRA 85
Addison PRO 3, HUM 75, GRA 85, INT 141
Diana Allen Associates GRA 86
The Anderlyn Consultancy plc INT 141
Applied Products Ltd PRO 3
ASA Designers Ltd PRO 3
Associated Design Consultants Ltd GRA 86
Associated Design Managers Ltd (ADM)
    INT 141
The Association of Ideas (AOI Ltd) EXH 161
Atlantic Design PRO 4
Axis Design Europe PRO 5, INT 142
Banks & Miles GRA 87
Barrow Parkhill Associates Ltd GRA 88
Linda Bee FAS 169
BIB Design Consultants Ltd PRO 6
Bowes Darby Design Associates GRA 89,
    EXH 161
Bowyer Langlands Batchelor INT 142, EXH 161
Brauer Associates PRO 6, GRA 89
Brend Thomsen Shepherd GRA 89
Maurice Broughton Associates INT 142
Julian Brown Associates PRO 7
Jennie Burns Design GRA 89
Business Design Group GRA 90, INT 143
Cairnes Design Associates Ltd GRA 90,
    INT 143
Carroll Dempsey & Thirkell Ltd GRA 91

The Chadwick Group INT 143
Chrissie Charlton and Company GRA 91
Kim Church Associates GRA 92
Citigate Design Ltd GRA 92
David Clarke Associates INT 143
Roger Clinton-Smith Ltd GRA 92
Coley Porter Bell GRA 93
Communication Design Partnership GRA 93
Communication by Design GRA 93, EXH 152
Simon Conder Associates INT 144
Control Room Projects HUM 75
John Cox Associates PRO 9, ENG 52
Czarska Designs Ltd INT 144
Dalziel & Pow INT 144
Davies Design Ltd INT 144
Davies Hall Ltd GRA 94
Brian Delaney Design Associates GRA 95
Design Acumen PRO 11
Design + Development PRO 11
The Design Bridge UK Ltd GRA 95
The Design Department Ltd GRA 95
Design For Change Ltd HUM 76
Design House Consultants Ltd PRO 12,
    GRA 96, INT 145
Design Research Unit (DRU) GRA 94, INT 145
Dimension Design Consultants PRO 14
'Eleventh Hour' WZM Ltd GRA 98
Epps Ransom Associates GRA 98
Event Communications Ltd EXH 163
John Ewans Design PRO 15
Fielding Rowinski GRA 98
Fitch RS Design Consultants PRO 16, GRA 99,
    INT 146
FM Design Ltd PRO 16
FMO Design Consultants GRA 99
Fosbueary Hamblin Design Associates GRA 100
The Four Hundred Ltd GRA 100, INT 146,
    EXH 163
Frazer Designers PRO 17
Furneaux Stewart GRA 101, EXH 163
The Furniture Consultancy Ltd PRO 18
Furphy Simpson FAS 170
Gannon Design & Advertising GRA 101
James Gardner (3D Concepts) Ltd EXH 163
Genesis Advertising & Design Consultants Ltd
    GRA 102
Grandfield Rork Collins GRA 102
Grant Walker Ltd FAS 170
Graphex Design Consultancy GRA 102
Graphik Fifteen Associates EXH 164
Grey Matter Design Consultants plc PRO
    GRA 103
Martin Grierson PRO 19
Grundy & Northedge Designers GRA 103
GWA Design Consultants Ltd GRA 104
Haley Pearson Design PRO 19
Ivor Hall & Associates Ltd INT 147
HALLRichards PRO 20, GRA 104
Halpen Graphic Communication Ltd GRA 104
John Harris Design Consultants Ltd GRA 105
Harrison/Zulver (Design & Marketing
    Consultants) GRA 105
Haydon Williams International Ltd PRO 20,
    MAT 81, FAS 170
Derek Henden & Co Ltd PRO 21
Henrion, Ludlow & Schmidt GRA 105
John Herbert Partnership GRA 106, INT 148
Heritage Design PRO 22
Barry Hill Design GRA 106
Glenn Hilling GRA 106
Derek Hodgson Associates PRO 22
Sarah Holland GRA 107
Hollington Associates PRO 23
Holmes Linnette Ltd GRA 107
Susan Holton Design Consultancy GRA 108
Hothouse Product Development Partners
    PRO 23
David & Miriam Howitt INT 148
Hutton Staniford GRA 108

Oxfordshire

AIT Ltd HUM 75, GRA 85
All Communications Ltd EXH 161
Marketplace Design Partnership Ltd GRA 116,
INT 150
John Sermon & Associates INT 154

Shropshire

Kubiak & Grange Design Associates GRA 112

Somerset

The Advertising Design Partnership GRA 85
Magus Advertising GRA 116
Robson Design Associates Ltd GRA 127

Staffordshire

Ceramic Modelling Services Ltd PRO 8
John David & Associates PRO 10
Alan Davies Design Projects Ltd PRO 10
J W Hand & Partners PRO 20
Lawton Design Studio GRA 113
Origin Studios (S-o-T) Ltd GRA 121
Regatta Design Consultants GRA 126
Roger Smith Design PRO 40
Staffordshire Polytechnic ENG 68

Suffolk

M A Banham & Company ENG 50
Design Technology PRO 12
Dialog Design PRO 13
Sally Jeffery GRA 111
Ruth Lowe Advertising & Graphic Design
GRA 115
Sound Research Laboratories Ltd ENG 68

Surrey

Ashton & Cordell Associates PRO 4
Design Matters PRO 12
Jane Eastwood FAS 169
Goodwin Emck PRO 18
The Grand Design GRA 102
Isherwood Design Associates PRO 24
Katz Vaughan Meyer & Feltham INT 148
Colin Marsh Design Consultant PRO 28
MEJ Electronics Ltd ENG 61
Michael Neale & Associates Ltd ENG 63
Pira International GRA 125
John Ryan Design PRO 38
Smith Browne Partnership EXH 165
T-Cubed Consultants Ltd ENG 69
Timewise Design Ltd EXH 165
Trog Assoc Ltd ENG 71
Wigram Tivendale Associates PRO 45
Windsor Jennings GRA 137

Sussex

Chris Dawson Associates PRO 10
The Design Revolution GRA 96
Gripgold Ltd PRO 19
Ben Johnson Design Consultancy PRO 24
Maddison Ltd PRO 28
Panel Design GRA 122
Peamore Electronics Ltd ENG 64
Sadler Associates PRO 38, ENG 67
Shearing and Partners GRA 129

Tyne & Wear

Bonas Griffith Ltd ENG 50
Hi-Tech Video GRA 107
Kirk Design Studio Ltd GRA 112
Micro Tech Ltd ENG 62
Northern Electronic Technology Ltd ENG 63
Oliver and Company Ltd GRA 121
Product First PRO 34
Rossetti Interiors Ltd INT 154

Warwickshire

DCA Design Consultants PRO 11
The Drawing Room GRA 97

Herron Oakley Design GRA 106
Marion James Design Consultants GRA 110
Kilvingtons Design Consultants GRA 112
Microsys Consultants Ltd ENG 61
Myatt Design PRO 30, ENG 62
Smallfry PRO 40
3T Ltd PRO 43, ENG 70
John Towersey Design Associates Ltd GRA 134
Warwick Design Consultants Ltd PRO 44

West Midlands

Janet Bevan Designs FAS 169
The Design Board GRA 95
Dudley Designs & Equipment ENG 54
Harland Simon ENG 58
The Harrison Greenwell Partnership Ltd
GRA 105
HRO'C Design Ltd GRA 108
Malcolm Payne Design Group Ltd GRA 13,
INT 152
P-E International PRO 31
Ryland Davis Associates PRO 38
Tibbatts & Co Design Group Ltd INT 155
West Midlands Clothing Resource Centre
FAS 173
Whitecroft Designs Ltd INT 156
Zappia & Zappia Design Partnership GRA 138

Wiltshire

Anthony Best Dynamics Ltd ENG 50
Engineered Design ENG 55
Illsley Wilson Baylis Ltd GRA 109
MPC Data Ltd ENG 62
Alan Tilbury Associates PRO 43
Wessex Designdraft Ltd ENG 71

Worcestershire

Ian Crook, Chartered Designer PRO 10
John Payne Industrial Designers PRO 122
Wulstan Designs & Controls Ltd ENG 72

Yorkshire

Tony Cunliffe Shudesign FAS 169
Design 4 (Plastics) Ltd PRO 11
Escort Menswear Services FAS 170
Glazebrook Interior Architects INT 147
Heights Design PRO 21
Colin Leighton Associates FAS 171
Yvonne Le Rolland FAS 171
Oak Design Consultancy Ltd GRA 120
PFB Designers and Print Consultants Ltd
GRA 124
The Arthur Quarmby Partnership PRO 35
Vivienne Rawnsley Graphic Design GRA 126
Sheffield University ENG 67, MAT 82
System Applied Technology Ltd HUM 78
Gordon Wilson Design PRO 46
York Electronics Centre PRO 46

Northern Ireland

AVB Design GRA 86
The McCadden Design Group GRA 117
The Plastics Development Centre PRO 33
Triplicate Design Ltd GRA 134

Scotland

Baillie Marshall Design GRA 87
Benson Design Ltd GRA 88
Crombie Anderson PRO 9, ENG 53, HUM 76,
GRA 94
Dickson Huggins Associates Ltd GRA 96,
INT 145
Epic Interior Design Ltd INT 145
Eyedea Creative Consultancy Ltd GRA 98
Fleming Thermodynamics Ltd (FTD) PRO 16,
ENG 56
Fletcher Design Ltd INT 146
Forth Product Design GRA 100
Gerrard and Medd PRO 18

Grad Ltd ENG 57
Graphic Partners GRA 103
Innes Design PRO 23
Lackie Newton Ltd GRA 113
MKW Design Partnership INT 151
Jack Notman INT 152
Pointsize Associates GRA 125
Helen M Rees FAS 172
Russell Design Associates Ltd GRA 127
Shaw Design Marketing & Print Consultants Ltd
    GRA 128
Tayburn Design Ltd GRA 132, EXH 165
Teviot Design Ltd GRA 133
Visible Means Ltd GRA 135
West Midlands Clothing Resource Centre
    FAS 173

Wales
Design Workshop PRO 13
Celyn ENV 177
Cosine Ltd ENG 52
CTS Design Ltd ENG 53
E & L Instruments Ltd ENG 55
Folio Graphics GRA 100
Graham Frecknall Architecture and Design
    INT 146
Nick Holland Design Group Ltd PRO 22,
    GRA 107
Martin Hopkins Partnership GRA 108
Sector Design PRO 39, GRA 128
Stills Design Group GRA 131, INT 154
Strata'Matrix Ltd GRA 131
Nicholas Syred, Consultant ENG 68
Technology Concepts Ltd ENG 69
Witchell Associates INT 157

Canada
Dessuro-Dufour Design Inc PRO 13

Germany
Slany Design Team PRO 40

Irish Republic
Blackbox Ltd PRO 6

Netherlands
Landmark Design & Consult bv PRO 25
Ninaber/Peters/Krouwel PRO 30

Sweden
Bernado R&D Ltd PRO 6
Hampf Industridesign AB PRO 20

USA
Henry Dreyfuss Associates PRO 15
GVO, Inc PRO 109, ENG 57

AFRICA

Egypt
Barrow Parkhill Associates Ltd GRA 88
Czarska Designs Ltd INT 144
FIRA (Furniture Industry Research Association)
    PRO 16
Sears Davies Ltd GRA 128
Ethiopia
John Reynolds and Associates ENG 66
Kenya
Jennie Burns Design GRA 99
John Reynolds and Associates ENG 66
Ed Turnbull Design Associates GRA 135
Libya
Cranfield Engineering and Technology
    Enterprise Ltd (CREATE Ltd) ENG 52
Malawi
FIRA (Furniture Industry Research Association)
    PRO 16
John Reynolds and Associates ENG 66
Mauritius
Banks & Miles GRA 87
Robert Weldon Studios FAS 173
Mozambique
FIRA (Furniture Industry Research Association)
    PRO 16
Nigeria
FIRA (Furniture Industry Research Association)
    PRO 16
John Harris Design Consultants Ltd GRA 105
Susan Holton Design Consultancy GRA 108
Tor Pettersen & Partners Ltd GRA 124
Rubber Consultants ENG 66, MAT 82
Smith Browne Partnership EXH 165
South Africa
Alan Davies Design Projects Ltd PRO 10
FIRA (Furniture Industry Research Association)
    PRO 16
Kirkbride Payne Rick Partnership PRO 25
Anthony Manners & Associates,
    Consulting Mechanical Engineers ENG 60
PERA PRO 33, ENG 64, MAT 81
Sudan
John Reynolds and Associates ENG 66
Zambia
Anthony Manners & Associates,-
Consulting Mechanical Engineers ENG 60
Proctor & Stevenson GRA 126

AUSTRALASIA

Australia
Janet Bevan Designs FAS 169
BIB Design Consultants Ltd PRO 6
Cambridge Engineering Design Ltd ENG 51
DCA Design Consultants PRO 11
Jane Eastwood FAS 169
Fleming Thermodynamics Ltd (FTD) PRO 16
    ENG 56
James Gardner (3D Concepts) Ltd EXH 163
GVO, Inc PRO 109, ENG 57
Ivor Hall & Associates Ltd INT 147
J W Hand & Partners PRO 20
Haydon Williams International Ltd PRO 20,
    MAT 91, FAS 170
ICE Ergonomics HUM 77
IMA Design Consultants GRA 109, ENV 177
Jill Lawrence Design FAS 171
Lloyd Northover Ltd GRA 114, INT 150
Minale Tattersfield & Partners Ltd PRO 29,
    GRA 118, INT 151
John Nash & Friends Ltd GRA 119
Michael Neale & Associates Ltd ENG 63
PERA PRO 33, ENG 64, MAT 91
Proctor & Stevenson GRA 126
Robson Design Associates Ltd GRA 127

Satherley Design PRO 39, HUM 78
Nicholas Syred, Consultant ENG 68
Tibbatts & Co Design Group Ltd INT 155
Wolfson Unit for Marine Technology and
    Industrial Aerodynamics ENG 72
New Zealand
Associated & Marine Technology Ltd
    (A.MTEC) ENG 49
J M Dickenson ENG 54
Haydon Williams International Ltd PRO 20,
    MAT 81, FAS 170
Satherley Design PRO 39, HUM 78
Ed Turnbull Design Associates GRA 135
Wolfson Unit for Marine Technology and
    Industrial Aerodynamics ENG 72
Papua New Guinea
N & N Ltd GRA 13
Australasia – General
Barrow Parkhill Associates Ltd GRA 88
FIRA (Furniture Industry Research Association)
    PRO 16

EUROPE

Andorra
Paul Sutton Design Group INT 154
Austria
Haley Sharpe Associates INT 147, EXH 164
University of Hull ENG 58
Lane Design PRO 26, GRA 113
MRDC Ltd PRO 29
Pemberton Dear PRO 32
Belgium
AD Creative Consultants Ltd GRA 85
Associated & Marine Technology Ltd (A.MTEC)
    ENG 49
Associated Design Consultants Ltd GRA 86
Banks & Miles GRA 87
Janet Bevan Designs FAS 169
BIB Design Consultants Ltd PRO 6
Bowyer Langlands Batchelor INT 142, EXH 161
Carroll Dempsey & Thirkell Ltd GRA 91
Cosine Ltd ENG 52
Davis Associates HUM 76
DCA Design Consultants PRO 11
The Design Bridge UK Ltd GRA 95
Design Research Unit (DRU) GRA 94, INT 145
Design Workshop PRO 13
J M Dickenson ENG 54
Geoffrey Duff Associates Ltd ENG 54
Jane Eastwood FAS 169
Matthew Finch Design Consultants Ltd GRA 99
FM Design Ltd PRO 16
The Four Hundred Ltd GRA 100, INT 146,
    EXH 163
James Gardner (3D Concepts) Ltd EXH 163
Genesis Advertising & Design Consultants Ltd
    GRA 102
GVO, Inc PRO 109, ENG 57
HALLRichards PRO 20, GRA 104
The Harrison Greenwell Partnership Ltd
    GRA 105
Derek Henden & Co Ltd PRO 21
University of Hull ENG 58
Imagination Ltd GRA 109
Jones Garrard Ltd PRO 24, ENG 59
Katz Vaughan Meyer & Feltham INT 148
Landmark Design & Consult bv PRO 25
Jill Lawrence Design FAS 171
Yvonne Le Rolland FAS 171
Lloyd Northover Ltd GRA 114, INT 150
Maddison Ltd PRO 28
Minale Tattersfield & Partners Ltd PRO 29,
    GRA 118, INT 151
Moggridge Associates PRO 29, ENG 62,
    HUM 77
Murdoch Associates Ltd INT 152
Oak Design Consultancy Ltd GRA 120

INTERNATIONAL EXPERTISE

Queensberry Hunt PRO 35
Raffo Design Associates PRO 35
Rakar Ltd ENG 65
Peter Ralph Design Unit PRO 36
Random Ltd PRO 36, ENG 65
Recording Architecture Ltd INT 153
Reliability Consultants Ltd ENG 65
Ricardo – AS&A Ltd PRO 37, ENG 66
Robinson Associates HUM 77
Rodd Industrial Design POR 37
Sadler Associates PRO 38, ENG 67
Satherley Design PRO 39, HUM 78
Slany Design Team PRO 40
Smith Browne Partnership EXH 165
Smith & Milton Ltd GRA 129
Somerfield Design PRO 41
Source Product Design PRO 41
Stable Block Design Consultants Ltd PRO 42
Staffordshire Polytechnic ENG 68
Stills Design Group GRA 141, INT 154
Tayburn Design Ltd GRA 142, EXH 165
The Technology Partnership Ltd ENG 70
Tibbatts & Co Design Group Ltd INT 155
Timewise Design Ltd EXH 165
TQC Ltd ENG 70
Trog Assoc Ltd ENG 71
Paul Usher Design PRO 44
Vineyard Design Consultants GRA 135
Visible Means Ltd GRA 135
Alan Wagstaff & Partners GRA 136
Vineyard Design Consultants GRA 135
Visible Means Ltd GRA 135
Alan Wagstaff & Partners GRA 136
XMPR plc INT 157
Andrew Younger & Associates GRA 138

Greece
Associated & Marine Technology Ltd (A.MTEC)
    ENG 49
John David & Associates PRO 10
Fletcher Design Ltd INT 146
J W Hand & Partners PRO 20
ICE Ergonomics HUM 77
Vernon Oakley Design Ltd GRA 120
Paul Sutton Design Group INT 154

Hungary
HALLRichards PRO 20, GRA 104
Sadler Associates PRO 38, ENG 67

Iceland
Design Research Unit (DRU) GRA 94, INT 145
J M Dickenson ENG 54
Fitch RS Design Consultants PRO 16, GRA 99,
    INT 146

Irish Republic
AVB Design GRA 86
Janet Bevan Designs FAS 169
Broadoak Design Partnership PRO 7
Business Design Group GRA 100, INT 143
Carroll Dempsey & Thirkell Ltd GRA 91
DCA Design Consultants PRO 11
Jane Eastwood FAS 169
Event Communications Ltd EXH 163
The Green House GRA 103
Grey Matter Design Consultants plc PRO 18,
    GRA 103
Martin Grierson PRO 19
Ivor Hall & Associates Ltd INT 147
J W Hand & Partners PRO 20
Liz James Design Associates Ltd GRA 110
Lloyd Northover Ltd GRA 114, INT 150
The McCadden Design Group GRA 117
John Michael Design Ltd GRA 118, INT 151
The Pack Design Company GRA 122
Pankhurst Design & Developments Ltd (PDD)
    PRO 31, ENG 63
Mark Plumtree Design Associates INT 153
Pointsize Associates GRA 125
Priestman Associates PRO 34
Queensberry Hunt PRO 35

Shaw Design Marketing & Print Consultants Ltd
    GRA 128
Stills Design Group GRA 131, INT 154
Team Consulting Ltd ENG 69
Vineyard Design Consultants GRA 135
XMPR plc INT 157

Italy
Brian Asquith Design Partnership PRO 4
Associated Design Consultants Ltd GRA 86
Atkinson Design Associates Ltd PRO 4
AVB Design GRA 86
Bell Wickham Associates PRO 5
Janet Bevan Designs FAS 169
BIB Design Consultants Ltd PRO 6
Julian Brown Associates PRO 7
Cairnes Design Associates Ltd GRA 90,
    INT 143
Coley Porter Bell GRA 93
Control Room Projects HUM 75
Davis Associates HUM 76
DCA Design Consultants PRO 11
Design Research Unit (DRU) GRA 94, INT 145
Destech (UK) Ltd ENG 54
Jane Eastwood FAS 169
Epps Ransom Associates GRA 98
Event Communications Ltd EXH 163
The Four Hundred Ltd GRA 100, INT 146,
    EXH 163
The Furniture Consultancy Ltd PRO 18
Furphy Simpson FAS 170
James Gardner (3D Concepts) Ltd EXH 163
Graphic Partners GRA 103
Martin Grierson PRO 19
Timothy Guy Design GRA 104
HALLRichards PRO 20, GRA 104
J W Hand & Partners PRO 20
Heritage Design PRO 22
Imagination Ltd GRA 109
Industrial Design Consultancy Ltd PRO 23
Kirkbride Payne Rick Partnership PRO 25
Lane Design PRO 26, GRA 113
The Ian Logan Design Company GRA 115
Media Projects International Ltd EXH 165
MFD Design PRO 28, ENG 61
John Michael Design Ltd GRA 118, INT 151
Minale Tattersfield & Partners Ltd PRO 29, GRA
    118, INT 151
NNC Ltd ENG 63
Nottingham Consultants Ltd FAS 172
Pape Woodward Partnership PRO 31
Parker Stratton Design PRO 32, GRA 123
Pemberton Dear PRO 32
Pentagram Design Ltd PRO 33, GRA 124,
    INT 153
Priestman Associates PRO 34
Proctor & Stevenson GRA 126
Ricardo – AS&A Ltd PRO 37, ENG 66
Sadler Associates PRO 38, ENG 67
Marcus Smith – Industrial Design PRO 40
Smith & Milton Ltd GRA 129
Staffordshire Polytechnic ENG 68
Steel Designs GRA 130
Paul Sutton Design Group INT 154
Tatham Pearce Ltd GRA 132
Team Consulting Ltd ENG 69
TQC Ltd ENG 70
Paul Usher Design PRO 44
Via Design Ltd GRA 135
Robert Weldon Studios FAS 173
Whitecroft Designs Ltd INT 156
Wings Design Consultants Ltd GRA 137
XMPR plc INT 157

Luxembourg
Pointsize Associates GRA 125
Slany Design Team PRO 40
TQC Ltd ENG 70
Whitecroft Designs Ltd INT 156

Malta
FIRA (Furniture Industry Research Association)
   PRO 16
The David Leon Partnership INT 149
Media Projects International Ltd EXH 165
Portland Design Associates GRA 125
The Netherlands
Atkinson Design Associates Ltd PRO 4
Banks & Miles GRA 87
Barrow Parkhill Associates Ltd GRA 88
Anthony Best Dynamics Ltd ENG 50
Janet Bevan Designs FAS 169
BIB Design Consultants Ltd PRO 6
Cambridge Engineering Design Ltd ENG 51
Cambridge Product Design Ltd PRO 8
Cosine Ltd ENG 52
Alan Davies Design Projects Ltd PRO 10
DCA Design Consultants PRO 11
The Design Bridge UK Ltd GRA 95
Designex ENG 53
Design Research Unit (DRU) GRA 94, INT 145
Dialog Design PRO 13
Jane Eastwood FAS 169
Engineering Research Centre ENG 56
Event Communications Ltd EXH 163
Fitch RS Design Consultants PRO 16, GRA 99,
   INT 146
Forman Peacock Advertising Ltd GRA 100
The Four Hundred Ltd GRA 100, INT 146,
   EXH 163
James Gardner (3D Concepts) Ltd EXH 163
Genesis Advertising & Design Consultants Ltd
   GRA 102
Grey Matter Design Consultants plc PRO 18,
   GRA 103
HALLRichards PRO 20, GRA 104
Malcolm Hastings Design PRO 20
Hollington Associates PRO 23
Isis UK Ltd PRO 24, ENG 59
Liz James Design Associates Ltd GRA 110
Katz Vaughan Meyer & Feltham INT 148
Kirk Design Studio Ltd GRA 112
Lloyd Northover Ltd GRA 114, INT 150
Ruth Lowe Advertising & Graphic Design
   GRA 115
Lyons Ames PRO 27
Maddison Ltd PRO 28
Colin Marsh Design Consultant PRO 28
The Paul Martin Design Company Ltd GRA 116
Millaer Seale GRA 118
Moggridge Associates PRO 29, ENG 62,
   HUM 77
Ninaber/Peters/Krouwel PRO 30
Oak Design Consultancy Ltd GRA 120
Packaging Innovation Ltd PRO 31, GRA 122
The Pack Design Company GRA 122
Parker Stratton Design PRO 32, GRA 123
Pemberton Dear PRO 32
Pentagram Design Ltd PRO 33, GRA 124,
   INT 153
The Picador Group GRA 124
Mark Plumtree Design Associates INT 153
Priestman Associates PRO 34
Proctor & Stevenson GRA 126
Raffo Design Associates PRO 35
Random Ltd PRO 36, ENG 65
Reliability Consultants Ltd ENG 65
Robson Design Associates Ltd GRA 127
Rodd Industrial Design POR 37
Seymour Powell PRO 40
Smith & Milton Ltd GRA 129
Steel Designs GRA 130
Tatham Pearce Ltd GRA 132
Thumb Design Partnership Ltd GRA 133
Timewise Design Ltd EXH 165
Trog Assoc Ltd ENG 71
Ed Turnbull Design Associates GRA 135
Vineyard Design Consultants GRA 135

West Midlands Clothing Resource Centre
   FAS 173
XMPR plc INT 157
Andrew Younger & Associates GRA 138
Norway
Associated & Marine Technology Ltd (A.MTEC)
Janet Bevan Designs FAS 169
BIB Design Consultants Ltd PRO 6
Julian Brown Associates PRO 7
Cambridge Engineering Design Ltd ENG 51
Communication by Design GRA 93, EXH 162
Design Research Unit (DRU) GRA 94, INT 145
Dialog Design PRO 13
Fitch RS Design Consultants PRO 16, GRA 99,
   INT 146
FM Design Ltd PRO 16
James Gardner (3D Concepts) Ltd EXH 163
Grey Matter Design Consultants plc PRO 18,
   GRA 103
Ivor Hall & Associates Ltd INT 147
HALLRichards PRO 20, GRA 104
John Herbert Partnership GRA 106, INT 148
Isis UK Ltd PRO 24, ENG 59
Kirk Design Studio Ltd GRA 112
Lawton Design Studio GRA 113
Patrick H Lynch PRO 27
Ninaber/Peters/Krouwel PRO 30
Oak Design Consultancy Ltd GRA 120
Pemberton Dear PRO 32
Tor Pettersen & Partners Ltd GRA 124
Proctor & Stevenson GRA 126
Satherley Design PRO 39, HUM 78
Stable Block Design Consultants Ltd PRO 42
Tatham Pearce Ltd GRA 132
The Technology Partnership Ltd ENG 70
Timewise Design Ltd EXH 165
Poland
Recording Architecture Ltd INT 153
Portugal
Anthony Best Dynamics Ltd ENG 50
The Design Bridge UK Ltd GRA 95
Design 4 (Plastics) Ltd PRO 11
FM Design Ltd PRO 16
James Gardner (3D Concepts) Ltd EXH 163
J W Hand & Partners PRO 20
Industrial Design Consultancy Ltd PRO 23
Maddison Ltd PRO 28
MRDC Ltd PRO 29
Queensberry Hunt PRO 35
Recording Architecture Ltd INT 153
Rodd Industrial Design POR 37
Staffordshire Polytechnic ENG 68
Spain
APV Baker – Special Projects Division ENG 49
Associated Design Managers Ltd (ADM)
   INT 141
Julian Brown Associates PRO 7
Citigate Design Ltd GRA 92
Coley Porter Bell GRA 93
Communication by Design GRA 103, EXH 162
DCA Design Consultants PRO 11
The Design Bridge UK Ltd GRA 95
Destech (UK) Ltd ENG 54
Jane Eastwood FAS 169
Fitch RS Design Consultants PRO 16, GRA 99,
   INT 146
Fletcher Design Ltd INT 146
The Four Hundred Ltd GRA 110, INT 146,
   EXH 163
James Gardner (3D Concepts) Ltd EXH 163
Timothy Guy Design GRA 104
HALLRichards PRO 20, GRA 104
David Hayward Product Design PRO 21
Derek Henden & Co Ltd PRO 21
Industrial Design Consultancy Ltd PRO 23
Jones Garrard Ltd PRO 24, ENG 59
Lloyd Northover Ltd GRA 124, INT 150
Minale Tattersfield & Partners Ltd PRO 29,
   GRA 128, INT 151

Moggridge Associates PRO 29, ENG 62,
 HUM 77
MRDC Ltd PRO 29
John Nash & Friends Ltd GRA 119
Oak Design Consultancy Ltd GRA 120
Packaging Innovation Ltd PRO 31, GRA 122
Patterson, Fenton-Jones Ltd ENV 178
Pemberton Dear PRO 32
Priestman Associates PRO 34
Proctor & Stevenson GRA 126
Peter Ralph Design Unit PRO 36
Recording Architecture Ltd INT 153
Robinson Associates HUM 77
Rubber Consultants ENG 66, MAT 82
Roger Smith Design PRO 40
Smith & Milton Ltd GRA 129
Staffordshire Polytechnic ENG 68
Paul Sutton Design Group INT 154
Tayburn Design Ltd GRA 142, EXH 165
Visible Means Ltd GRA 135
Linda Wood Designs Ltd FAS 174
XMPR plc INT 177

Sweden
Bartingale Design Associates PRO 5
Bernado R&D Ltd PRO 6
Anthony Best Dynamics Ltd ENG 50
Control Room Projects HUM 75
Design Research Unit (DRU) GRA 94, INT 145
Design Workshop PRO 13
Jane Eastwood FAS 169
Engineering Research Centre ENG 56
Fitch RS Design Consultants PRO 16, GRA 99,
 INT 146
The Four Hundred Ltd GRA 100, INT 146,
 EXH 163
The Furniture Consultancy Ltd PRO 18
James Gardner (3D Concepts) Ltd EXH 163
Timothy Guy Design GRA 104
Ivor Hall & Associates Ltd INT 147
HALLRichards PRO 20, GRA 104
J W Hand & Partners PRO 20
Hodges & Drake Design PRO 22
Hothouse Product Development Partners
 PRO 23
University of Hull ENG 58
Isis UK Ltd PRO 24, ENG 59
Kirkbride Payne Rick Partnership PRO 25
Patrick H Lynch PRO 27
Lyons Ames PRO 27
Alan McCombie ENG 60
Media Projects International Ltd EXH 165
Microsys Consultants Ltd ENG 61
Moggridge Associates PRO 29, ENG 62,
 HUM 77
Oak Design Consultancy Ltd GRA 120
Pemberton Dear PRO 32
Pentagram Design Ltd PRO 33, GRA 124,
 INT 153
Proctor & Stevenson GRA 126
Product First PRO 34
Queensberry Hunt PRO 35
Random Ltd PRO 36, ENG 65
Ricardo – AS&A Ltd PRO 37, ENG 66
Sams Design PRO 39
Tatham Pearce Ltd GRA 132
The Technology Partnership Ltd ENG 70
TQC Ltd ENG 70
Alan Tye Design RDI Ltd PRO 44
Gordon Wilson Design PRO 46

Switzerland
ASA Designers Ltd PRO 3
Associated & Marine Technology Ltd (A.MTEC)
 ENG 49
Banks & Miles GRA 97
Bell Wickham Associates PRO 5
Cairnes Design Associates Ltd GRA 90,
 INT 153
Communication by Design GRA 93, EXH 162
Design Marketing PRO 12

Dialog Design PRO 13
Jane Eastwood FAS 169
Epps Ransom Associates GRA 98
Event Communications Ltd EXH 163
The Four Hundred Ltd GRA 110, INT 146,
 EXH 163
James Gardner (3D Concepts) Ltd EXH 1763
Grant Walker Ltd FAS 170
Graphik Fifteen Associates EXH 164
HALLRichards PRO 20, GRA 104
Jones Garrard Ltd PRO 24, ENG 59
Kinneir Dufort Design Ltd PRO 25
David Lock Design Ltd GRA 115
The Ian Logan Design Company GRA 115
Lyons Ames PRO 27
John Michael Design Ltd GRA 118, INT 151
Minale Tattersfield & Partners Ltd PRO 29,
 GRA 118, INT 151
John Nash & Friends Ltd GRA 119
Ninaber/Peters/Krouwel PRO 30
Oak Design Consultancy Ltd GRA 120
P-E International PRO 31
Pemberton Dear PRO 32
Pentagram Design Ltd PRO 33, GRA 124,
 INT
Tor Pettersen & Partners Ltd GRA 124
Robinson Associates HUM 77
Slany Design Team PRO 40
Technology Concepts Ltd ENG 69
Timewise Design Ltd EXH 165
XMPR plc INT 157

Turkey
Associated & Marine Technology Ltd (A.MTEC)
 ENG 49
Corporate Culture Ltd GRA 93
Philip Dunbavin Acoustics Ltd ENG 55
Fir Tree Design Company Ltd GRA 99
Memotrace Controls Ltd ENG 61
Parker Stratton Design PRO 32, GRA 123
Roundel Design Group GRA 127
Gordon Wilson Design PRO 46

USSR
APV Baker – Special Projects Division ENG 49
Communication by Design GRA 93, EXH 162
The Four Hundred Ltd GRA 100, INT 146,
 EXH 163
Graham Frecknall Architecture and Design
 INT 146
James Gardner (3D Concepts) Ltd EXH 163
HALLRichards PRO 20, GRA 104
Magus Advertising GRA 116
Pentagram Design Ltd PRO 33, GRA 124,
 INT 153
Ricardo – AS&A Ltd PRO 37, ENG 66
Tayburn Design Ltd GRA 132, EXH 165
Timewise Design Ltd EXH 165
Via Design Ltd GRA 135

Europe – General
All Communications Ltd EXH 161
Diana Allen Associates GRA 96
Barron Hatchet Design GRA 97
Cairnes Design Associates Ltd GRA 90,
 INT 143
Cairnes Design Associates Ltd GRA 90,
 INT 143
Philip Dunbavin Acoustics Ltd ENG 55
'Eleventh Hour' WZM Ltd GRA 98
John Ewans Design PRO 15
FIRA (Furniture Industry Research Association)
 PRO 16
Fir Tree Design Company Ltd GRA 99
Gardiner and Torne Ltd INT 147
Graphex Design Consultancy GRA 102
Grundy & Northedge Designers GRA 103
Ivor Hall & Associates Ltd INT 147
Harland Simon ENG 58
Haydon Williams International Ltd PRO 20,
 MAT 91, FAS 170
Imagination Ltd GRA 109

Light & Coley Ltd GRA 114
Patrick H Lynch PRO 27
M & M Design Associates GRA 119
Marketplace Design Partnership Ltd GRA 116,
INT 150
The McCadden Design Group GRA 117
The Partners GRA 123
Product First PRO 34
Vivienne Rawnsley Graphic Design GRA 126
Sira Ltd ENG 68
Systems Technology Consultants PRO 42
Thomson Wright International GRA 133
Wilmot & Partners Ltd GRA 137

FAR EAST

China
All Communications Ltd EXH 161
Gardiner and Torne Ltd INT 147
Ivor Hall & Associates Ltd INT 147
J W Hand & Partners PRO 20
Memotrace Controls Ltd ENG 61
MFD Design PRO 28, ENG 61
John Payne Industrial Designers PRO 122
John Reynolds and Associates ENG 66
Smith Browne Partnership EXH 165
Alan Tye Design RDI Ltd PRO 44
Elaine Williamson Design Consultancy PRO 45

Hong Kong
Bentley Woolston Ltd GRA 88
Broadoak Design Partnership PRO 7
Coley Porter Bell GRA 93
Czarska Designs Ltd INT 144
DCA Design Consultants PRO 11
Design Research Unit (DRU) GRA 94, INT 145
Destech (UK) Ltd ENG 54
Frazer Designers PRO 17
Grant Walker Ltd FAS 170
David Hayward Product Design PRO 21
Hollington Associates PRO 23
Isis UK Ltd PRO 24, ENG 59
Jill Lawrence Design FAS 171
Lees Associates INT 149
Lyons Ames PRO 27
Maddison Ltd PRO 28
Media Projects International Ltd EXH 165
Minale Tattersfield & Partners Ltd PRO 29,
GRA 118, INT 165]
N & N Ltd GRA 120
Nottingham Consultants Ltd FAS 172
Pape Woodward Partnership PRO 31
P-E International PRO 31
Marcus Smith – Industrial Design PRO 40
Studio M GRA 132, FAS 173
Team Consulting Ltd ENG 69
XMPR plc INT 157
YRM Interiors INT 157

Japan
Bernado R&D Ltd PRO 6
BIB Design Consultants Ltd PRO 6
Brauer Associates PRO 6, GRA 89
Julian Brown Associates PRO 7
Chrissie Charlton and Company GRA 91
Simon Conder Associates INT 144
Warwick Evans Design PRO 15
Event Communications Ltd EXH 163
Fleming Thermodynamics Ltd (FTD) PRO 16,
ENG 56
Fletcher Design Ltd INT 146
FM Design Ltd PRO 16
Frazer Designers PRO 17
Furphy Simpson FAS 170
Gannon Design & Advertising GRA 101
James Gardner (3D Concepts) Ltd EXH 163
Graphic Partners GRA 103
Haydon Williams International Ltd PRO 20,
MAT 81, FAS 170
Hollington Associates PRO 23

IMA Design Consultants GRA 109, ENV 177
Imagination Ltd GRA 109
Innes Design PRO 23
Lane Design PRO 26, GRA 113
London Associates PRO 27
Lyons Ames PRO 27
Anthony Manners & Associates,
Consulting Mechanical Engineers ENG 60
Minale Tattersfield & Partners Ltd PRO 29,
GRA 118, INT 151
Moggridge Associates PRO 29, ENG 62,
HUM 77
N & N Ltd GRA 120
NNC Ltd ENG 63
Vernon Oakley Design Ltd GRA 120
Patterson, Fenton-Jones Ltd ENV 178
Pemberton Dear PRO 32
Pentagram Design Ltd PRO 33, GRA 124,
INT 153
Pirate Design Associates PRO 33, ENG 65
Priestman Associates PRO 34
Proctor & Stevenson GRA 126
Ricardo – AS&A Ltd PRO 37, ENG 66
Seymour Powell PRO 40
Slany Design Team PRO 40
Smith Browne Partnership EXH 165
Studio M GRA 132, FAS 173
Technology Concepts Ltd ENG 69
Alan Tye Design RDI Ltd PRO 44
XMPR plc INT 157

Korea
FIRA (Furniture Industry Research Association)
PRO 16
Heights Design PRO 21
Moggridge Associates PRO 29, ENG 62,
HUM 77
NNC Ltd ENG 63
Pirate Design Associates PRO 33, ENG 65
Helen M Rees FAS 172
Ricardo – AS&A Ltd PRO 37, ENG 66
Seymour Powell PRO 40
Roger Smith Design PRO 40

Philippines
FIRA (Furniture Industry Research Association)
PRO 16

Taiwan
Design Research Unit (DRU) GRA 94, INT 145
Design Workshop PRO 13
Destech (UK) Ltd ENG 54
James Gardner (3D Concepts) Ltd EXH 163
Landmark Design & Consult bv PRO 25
Media Projects International Ltd EXH 165
Pirate Design Associates PRO 33, ENG 65
Ricardo – AS&A Ltd PRO 37, ENG 66
Roger Smith Design PRO 40
Stable Block Design Consultants Ltd PRO 42

Thailand
Ceramic Modelling Services Ltd PRO 8
FIRA (Furniture Industry Research Association)
PRO 16
J W Hand & Partners PRO 20
Oak Design Consultancy Ltd GRA 120
Queensberry Hunt PRO 35
Ricardo – AS&A Ltd PRO 37, ENG 66

Far East – General
Cambridge Consultants Ltd PRO 8, ENG 51
Fitch RS Design Consultants PRO 16, GRA 99,
INT 156
Graphex Design Consultancy GRA 102
Ivor Hall & Associates Ltd INT 147
Lloyd Northover Ltd GRA 114, INT 150
Marketplace Design Partnership Ltd GRA 116,
INT 150
Sira Ltd ENG 68

MIDDLE EAST

Bahrain
James Gardner (3D Concepts) Ltd EXH 163

Haydon Williams International Ltd PRO 20,
    MAT 81, FAS 170
Herron Oakley Design GRA 106
Derek Hodgson Associates PRO 22
Hollington Associates PRO 23
Huxley Bertram Engineering ENG 58
IMA Design Consultants GRA 109, ENV 177
Imagination Ltd GRA 109
Industrial Design Consultancy Ltd PRO 23
Innes Design PRO 23
Kinneir Dufort Design Ltd PRO 25
Jill Lawrence Design FAS 171
Lees Associates INT 149
Peter Leonard Associates Ltd INT 149
Level Six Design Consultants Ltd PRO 26
Light & Coley Ltd GRA 114
Lloyd Northover Ltd GRA 114, INT 150
David Lock Design Ltd GRA 115
The Ian Logan Design Company GRA 115
Lyons Ames PRO 27
Maddison Ltd PRO 28
Marketplace Design Partnership Ltd GRA 116,
    INT 150
Colin Marsh Design Consultant PRO 28
Marvell Consultants Ltd ENG 60
The McCadden Design Group GRA 117
Alan McCombie ENG 60
Media Projects International Ltd EXH 165
MFD Design PRO 28, ENG 61
Minale Tattersfield & Partners Ltd PRO 29,
    GRA 118 INT 151
M & M Design Associates GRA 119
Moggridge Associates PRO 29, ENG 62,
    HUM 77
David Morgan Associates PRO 29
Ninaber/Peters/Krouwel PRO 30
N & N Ltd GRA 120
NNC Ltd ENG 63
Nottingham Consultants Ltd FAS 172
P-E International PRO 31
Panel Design GRA 122
Parker Stratton Design PRO 32, GRA 123
The Partners GRA 123
Pemberton Dear PRO 32
Pentagram Design Ltd PRO 33, GRA 124,
    INT 153
Tor Pettersen & Partners Ltd GRA 124
Priestman Associates PRO 34
Proctor & Stevenson GRA 126
Product First PRO 34
P S D Associates Ltd PRO 35, ENV178
Queensberry Hunt PRO 35
Raffo Design Associates PRO 35
Rakar Ltd ENG 65
Peter Ralph Design Unit PRO 36
Random Ltd PRO 36, ENG 65
Recording Architecture Ltd INT 153
Reliability Consultants Ltd ENG 65
Ricardo – AS&A Ltd PRO 37, ENG 66
Rodd Industrial Design POR 37
Rubber Consultants ENG 66, MAT 82
Sadler Associates PRO 38, ENG 67
Sams Design PRO 39
Satherley Design PRO 39, HUM 78
Sira Ltd ENG 68
Slany Design Team PRO 40
Smith Browne Partnership EXH 165
Roger Smith Design PRO 40
Source Product Design PRO 41
Stable Block Design Consultants Ltd PRO 42
Michael Stewart Design Ltd GRA 131
Studio M GRA 132, FAS 173
Paul Sutton Design Group INT 154
Nicholas Syred, Consultant ENG 68
Tatham Pearce Ltd GRA 132
Tayburn Design Ltd GRA 132, EXH 165
The Technology Partnership Ltd ENG 70
Christopher Terrell Associates ENG 70
Thomson Wright International GRA 133

Thumb Design Partnership Ltd GRA 133
TQC Ltd ENG 70
Trog Assoc Ltd ENG 71
TST Associates PRO 43
Ed Turnbull Design Associates GRA 135
Alan Tye Design RDI Ltd PRO 44
Watermark Communications Group Ltd
    GRA 136
Robert Weldon Studios FAS 173
Whitecroft Designs Ltd INT 156
Elaine Williamson Design Consultancy PRO 45
Wolfson Unit M I T A ENG 72
Linda Wood Designs Ltd FAS 174
XMPR plc INT 157
North America – General
BIB Design Consultants Ltd PRO 6
Graphex Design Consultancy GRA 102
Kilvingtons Design Consultants GRA 112

SOUTH & CENTRAL AMERICA

Barbados
FIRA (Furniture Industry Research Association)
    PRO 16
Brazil
Bernado R&D Ltd PRO 6
Minale Tattersfield & Partners Ltd PRO 29,
    GRA 118, INT 151
Colombia
Rubber Consultants ENG 66, MAT 82
Guatemala
Banks & Miles GRA 87
Guyana
FIRA (Furniture Industry Research Association)
    PRO 16
Jamaica
FIRA (Furniture Industry Research Association)
    PRO 16
Mexico
HALLRichards PRO 20, GRA 104
Murdoch Associates Ltd INT 152
South & Central America – General
FIRA (Furniture Industry Research Association)
    PRO 16
Ivor Hall & Associates Ltd INT 147
Minale Tattersfield & Partners Ltd PRO 29,
    GRA 118, INT 151
Patterson, Fenton-Jones Ltd ENV 178
Studio M GRA 132, FAS 173
Timewise Design Ltd EXH 165

SOUTH EAST ASIA

Brunei
James Gardner (3D Concepts) Ltd EXH 163
Indonesia
FIRA (Furniture Industry Research Association)
    PRO 16
J W Hand & Partners PRO 20
David Hayward Product Design PRO 21
London Associates PRO 27
Timewise Design Ltd EXH 165
Malaysia
FIRA (Furniture Industry Research Association)
    PRO 16
Queensberry Hunt PRO 35
Rubber Consultants ENG 66, MAT 82
Gordon Wilson Design PRO 46
Singapore
ASA Designers Ltd PRO 3
Communication by Design GRA 93, EXH 162
FIRA (Furniture Industry Research Association)
    PRO 16
John Harris Design Consultants Ltd GRA 105
IMA Design Consultants GRA 109, ENV 177
Alan Tilbury Associates PRO 43
Gordon Wilson Design PRO 46

SOUTHERN ASIA

Bangladesh

FIRA (Furniture Industry Research Association)
   PRO 16
John Reynolds and Associates ENG 66

India

Jane Eastwood FAS 169
FIRA (Furniture Industry Research Association)
   PRO 16
James Gardner (3D Concepts) Ltd EXH 1763
Grant Walker Ltd FAS 170
Graphic Partners GRA 103
David Hayward Product Design PRO 21
Michael Neale & Associates Ltd ENG 63
NNC Ltd ENG 63
Nottingham Consultants Ltd FAS 172
Pemberton Dear PRO 32
Helen M Rees FAS 172
John Reynolds and Associates ENG 66
Ricardo – AS&A Ltd PRO 37, ENG 66
Smith Browne Partnership EXH 165

Sri Lanka

FIRA (Furniture Industry Research Association)
   PRO 16